The
Indian
Cookbook

The
Indian
Cookbook

Shehzad Husain

LORENZ BOOKS

First published by Lorenz Books in 2002

© Anness Publishing Limited 2002

Lorenz Books is an imprint of Anness Publishing Limited
Hermes House, 88–89 Blackfriars Road, London SE1 8HA

Published in the USA by Lorenz Books, Anness Publishing Inc.
27 West 20th Street, New York, NY 10011

www.lorenzbooks.com

A CIP catalogue record for this book is available from the British Library.

Publisher: Joanna Lorenz
Managing Editor: Linda Fraser
Senior Editor: Susannah Blake
Jacket and Text Design: Chloë Steers
Typesetting: Jonathan Harley
Illustrations: Angela Wood
Recipes: Mridula Baljekar, Kit Chan, Rafi Fernandez, Deh-Ta Hsiung,
Shehzad Husain, Christine Ingram, Manisha Kanani, Sally Mansfield,
Sallie Morris and Jennie Shapter

1 3 5 7 9 10 8 6 4 2

NOTES

Bracketed terms are intended for American readers.

For all recipes, quantities are given in both metric and imperial measures and,
where appropriate, measures are also given in standard cups and spoons. Follow
one set, but not a mixture, because they are not interchangeable.

Standard spoon and cup measures are level.
1 tsp = 5ml, 1 tbsp = 15ml, 1 cup = 250ml/8fl oz

Australian standard tablespoons are 20ml. Australian readers should use 3 tsp in
place of 1 tbsp for measuring small quantities of gelatine, flour, salt, etc.

Medium (US large) eggs are used unless otherwise stated.

CONTENTS

Introduction

India is a vast country, with a total area of around 3.3 million square kilometres (1.3 million square miles) and a population in excess of 859 million. It is a land of striking contrasts, with huge variations in terms of climate, geography, religion, culture and customs. All of these factors have had a great influence on the country's cuisine, which has emerged as one of the most rich and diverse in the world. If there is a common denominator in Indian cuisine, it is the imaginative use of spices.

The country's various climates, which are affected by the geographical conditions, naturally dictate the types of crops that are grown in different regions. In the past, when transport and communications were poor, people had to confine themselves to the ingredients that grew naturally around them. They created a vast array of recipes, with distinct variations between each region.

Religion also played an important role in the development of Indian cuisine. Many religions exist side by side in India, with Hinduism being the indigenous faith. The Sikh and Buddhist religions are both branches of Hinduism. Islam was introduced by foreign traders, and went on to become one of the main religions of the land. Both the Hindu and Muslim religions have certain taboos as far as food is concerned. Hinduism prohibits the eating of beef: the cow is regarded as sacred because Hindu mythology depicts it as the companion of one of the most important Hindu gods, Lord Krishna. The Koran, on the other hand, prohibits the consumption of pork, so beef has become popular among Muslims, and an excellent range of beef-based recipes is found across the country.

Cultures and customs have also had a considerable impact on Indian cuisine. Over the centuries, historical events have imposed many different cultures upon India, and the country has not only absorbed them, but has also encouraged each to flourish individually. The diversity of the food culture across the regions of India may not be as pronounced as it once was, but in a country so vast it is inevitable that long-standing traditions for produce and cooking styles have persisted.

North India

The northern states of India have been subjected to a vast number of foreign invaders, traders and pilgrims throughout history. The north, more than any other region, allows easy access into India, with the Khyber Pass providing a natural link between Afghanistan and present-day Pakistan. Groups of travellers have entered through this long, narrow pass and spread throughout the region. Most notable of these travellers were the Moguls, who invaded India in the 16th century and ruled for almost three hundred years.

During their journey to India, the Moguls came across the much-admired Persian style of cooking, which they adapted and introduced to India. This has become known as Mughlai cuisine, and is now almost as widely eaten in the West as it is in India. Foreign travellers are also credited with introducing exotic fruits and nuts to Kashmir, where they were used to create a variety of sumptuous dishes. Kashmiri cuisine is prized for its unusual richness and varied textures and flavours, and dishes such as kormas, pasandas and biryanis are now firmly established as some of the most popular foods of northern India.

From Kashmir, the Moguls spread south and west into the Punjab, which is renowned for its tandoori cooking. The Punjab is also known as the bread box of India, because of the enormous variety of breads, both leavened and unleavened, it produces. Most breads are made of whole-wheat or wholemeal flour and are freshly cooked for each meal. Naan is the most widely eaten bread among the leavened varieties, while tandoori rotis, which is cooked in a tandoor, or Indian clay oven, is the most common unleavened bread.

Delhi, the capital of India, was once the centre of the Mogul dynasty. The Moguls' love of fine food, along with their exquisite taste in fine art and architecture, are so deeply rooted in Delhi that the city has become a major tourist attraction. As well as the traditional Mughlai food, Punjabi food, which includes a wonderful range of sweets (candies), has made Delhi a true food lover's paradise.

East India

The influence of Mogul cuisine is less pronounced in the eastern region, where local styles of cooking have more of a stronghold. The state of Bengal, for example, has developed in almost total isolation despite its proximity to the northern states. Apart from some minor reminders of the Moguls' brief presence in the region, Bengal has a unique cuisine, which is famous all over India.

Bengalis have always been very proud of their produce and have made full use of home-grown ingredients to create a fascinating style of cooking. Mustard grows extensively in the area, and mustard oil is widely used as a cooking medium. Several vegetarian, meat and poultry dishes also make use of ground mustard. Coconut, another local product, is widely used in both sweet and savoury dishes. Bengalis are immensely proud of the rice grown in their soil, and of the fish found in the waters of the Bay of Bengal. Together, rice and fish curry constitute the everyday diet of the Bengali people, although the state's most significant contribution to Indian cuisine is generally held to be its superb range of sweets.

Calcutta, the capital of West Bengal, has a strong tradition of Anglo-Indian cuisine, which is popular among the city's present-day Anglo-Indian community and in the clubs and sports centres established by the British Raj in the 19th century. These eccentrically outmoded institutions still thrive in the old British manner: cocktails are served by liveried staff and are accompanied by delicious titbits, cooked in the Western style but flavoured with Indian spices.

The streets of Calcutta are bustling with vendors selling all kinds of tempting local and Anglo-Indian sweet and savoury snacks. Ghughni, a spiced chickpea dish served with mouthwatering relishes, is one of the favourite local dishes.

Although the food of Bihar and Orissa, two other eastern states, has not made any significant impact on the cuisine of the subcontinent, Orissa deserves a mention for its excellent fresh fish and shellfish, which it exports worldwide.

South India

The southern states have been greatly influenced by the indigenous Hindu faith. However, on the southern tip of the country, the Malabar Coast provided easy access to the French, Dutch, British and Portuguese, as well as to a small number of Jews from Syria. The French had some influence on the cuisine of this area in the state of Pondicherry, and the Jews contributed meat and poultry dishes to Kerala. As well as making their mark on the eastern region, the British had trading posts in Madras, and an Anglo-Indian community still exists in that area. Otherwise, since the Dutch had no impact on Indian cuisine, and the Portuguese were concentrated in Goa, southern India has remained free of foreign influence seen elsewhere.

South Indian food is quite different from the rich cuisine of the north. It is light and refreshing, and the sauces are enriched with coconut milk, whereas in northern India, dairy cream and nuts are used for the same purpose. The food in the south is generally fiery: the temperature here is hot throughout the year, and chillies are known to have a cooling effect on the body.

Along the coast of southern India, fish curry and rice are eaten on an almost daily basis, but there are two dishes for which the region is famous: dosas, paper-thin pancakes made from ground rice and lentils, are filled with spicy vegetables and served for breakfast with a coconut chutney; idlis, which are steamed rice dumplings, are eaten with spicy lentils and chutneys.

Between Maharashtra in the west and the Bay of Bengal in the east lies the state of Andhra Pradesh, which is famous for its forts and palaces, and for its unique cuisine. Mogul traditions are strong here: even though the state has never been ruled by the Muslim rulers, the last Mogul emperor retired to the capital city Hyderabad, causing a culinary revolution that influenced the whole region. Kababs, biryanis and kormas exist side by side with hot, fiery local foods and a wide variety of rice.

West India

In western India lies the state of Gujarat. Most Gujaratis are strictly vegetarian and, unlike the many non-meat eaters in India who eat fish, they eat neither fish nor eggs. Their religion emphasizes the respect that must be shown to all living beings, and prohibits the taking of any life for reasons of personal enjoyment. As a result, the Gujaratis have truly perfected the art of vegetarian cooking. Fresh vegetables, lentils, beans, peas and dairy products have taken centre stage, and dairy products are abundant. People consume yogurt and buttermilk on a daily basis, and use them in cooking. Breads are made using both millet flour and maize flour (cornmeal).

The most famous culinary export of Gujarat is the vegetable- and lentil-based dhansak. About 13 centuries ago, a group of Persians fled their country to avoid religious persecution. Gujarat, being open to the sea, was the most convenient point at which to enter India. The Persians were made to feel at home here and became known as the Parsis. They adapted the rich and varied culture of Gujarat and over time spread further west to Bombay.

Bombay is situated on the edge of the Arabian Sea, and it is here that the Gateway of India was built during the British Raj, to commemorate a visit by the Prince of Wales. Bombay is the capital of Maharashtra, a mainly vegetarian state with a cosmopolitan population that has given rise to a rich and varied cuisine. Bombay is probably the only city in India where food from almost any part of the country can be sampled. As well as Indian food, Chinese dishes with an Indian twist can be found in numerous restaurants throughout this vibrant city. Fresh fish and shellfish are also plentiful in the area.

To the south of Bombay is Goa, where the lure of Indian spices brought Portuguese traders, who colonized the area. Goa remained under Portuguese rule until 1962, and this has created a happy marriage between East and West. Goa's most famous export is vindaloo, which has Portuguese origins.

THE INDIAN KITCHEN

In a country as large as India, it is no great surprise to find a distinctive range of cooking styles and a preference for using local produce. History and religion have both played an important role in the development of cultural and culinary traditions and the shaping of eating habits. So, too, have the different climates and geographical conditions, which have affected what types of crops grow in different areas. As a result of all these differences, India now has one of the richest and most exciting cuisines in the world. In the north, Kashmir is known for its kormas, pasandas and biryanis, while the Punjab is renowned for its tandoori cooking. The food in the south is hot and fiery to match the climate. Gujarat is famous for its vegetarian dishes and Bengal for its fish.

INDIAN COOKING

U ntil recently, no written record of Indian recipes has existed in India itself. Recipes have traditionally been handed down by word of mouth from one generation to another. Far from being a disadvantage, this has actually helped to fire the imagination of the creative cook, and many dishes that first started out as experiments with spice blends and flavours have now become world classics.

SPICES AND AROMATICS

The key to successful Indian cooking lies in the art of blending spices and herbs, rather than in sophisticated cooking techniques. The traditional Indian cook relies on instinct and experience rather than written recipes when measuring and combining spices, and in this way unique and very personal tastes can be created. This is why two similar dishes from the same region can look and taste quite different: it depends on who has cooked them.

Herbs are added to a dish during the cooking time to add flavour and aroma, but spices, including those used mainly for taste or for aroma, perform a more complex role.

Spices can be divided into two main groups: those that are integrated into a dish by the end of the cooking process, and those that are removed after cooking. The spices in the first group add taste, texture and colour. Different combinations are used, and no single spice is allowed to dominate the final flavour. Useful spices in this group include coriander, cumin, turmeric and garam masala, all in ground form.

The second group of spices add aroma to a dish. They remain identifiable at the end of cooking, as most of them are used whole. Once these spices have released their aroma, their function is complete. They are not eaten, but removed from the dish before serving or simply left on one side of the plate. Examples of this type of spice are whole cloves, cardamom pods, cinnamon sticks and bay leaves. These spices can also be ground, in which case they will blend into the sauce during cooking and will be eaten in the dish in the same way as any other ground spice.

PREPARING SPICES

Spices can be prepared in many different ways, depending on the form of the spice and the dish to which it is to be added. However, the object is always the same – to release the optimum amount of flavour and aroma into a dish.

To dry-fry spices, *heat a small, heavy-based pan over a medium heat for about 1 minute. Add the spices to the pan and cook for 2–3 minutes, shaking the pan frequently to prevent the spices burning. Remove the pan from the heat, tip the toasted spices into a mortar and grind with a pestle.*

To fry spices, *heat a little oil or ghee in a pan, add the spices and cook for about 2 minutes. Whole spices are sometimes fried in oil, either at the beginning of a recipe, before other ingredients are added, or simply to flavour the oil.*

To grind spices, *put the whole seeds in a pestle and crush them with a mortar. Harder spices can be ground in a pepper-mill or an electric coffee grinder.*

CHOOSING SPICES

When buying spices, select whole seeds, berries, buds and bark, such as cumin seeds, cardamoms, peppercorns, allspice, cloves and cinnamon sticks. These will keep their flavour and pungency far longer than the powdered spices and can easily be ground as needed. Fresh roots have an entirely different flavour from the dried version.

ADDING FLAVOUR

Having chosen which spices to use, you can then decide what kind of flavours you would like to create. For instance, dry-frying and grinding flavouring ingredients before adding them to a dish creates a completely different taste and aroma from frying the raw ground spices in hot fat before adding the main ingredients. The flavour of a dish will also vary according to the sequence in which the spices are added, and the length of time each spice is fried and allowed to release its flavour.

The joy of Indian cooking is that it can be personalized by different cooks, and with just two or three spices you can create distinctly varied dishes.

WHAT IS A CURRY?

In India, the word curry refers to a sauce or gravy that is used as an accompaniment to moisten grains of chawal (rice) or to make rotis (bread) more enjoyable. The bread or rice is considered the main dish of the meal.

The word curry is generally believed to be an anglicized version of the south Indian *kaari*. It comes from the Tamil language, which is spoken in the state of Tamil Nadu, of which Madras is the capital. In Tamil, the word means sauce, and it is thought that when the British were active in this area, the spelling was somehow changed to *curry*. Other theories suggest that the word *cury* has existed in English in the context of cooking since the 14th century and that it was originally derived from the French verb *cuire* (meaning 'to cook').

The main ingredients of a curry can vary enormously, and two very dissimilar dishes can be equally deserving of the name. Even the lentil dish known as dhal, which bears no resemblance to a sauce, falls under the definition of a curry; in India, dhal-chawal and dhal-roti are eaten on a daily basis.

A vegetable curry usually consists of a selection of fresh vegetables cooked in a sauce, which can have a thick or a thin consistency, depending on the style of cooking in the region. The sauces for meat, poultry and fish curries can also vary in consistency, and they are all designed to be served with rice or bread. Gujarat in the west and Punjab in the north also make spiced curries using just yogurt mixed with a little besan (gram flour). Made without meat, poultry or vegetables, these dishes are known as *khadis*.

WHAT TO EAT WITH A CURRY

In southern and eastern India, curries are always served with rice, which is the region's main crop and the staple food. Wheat grows abundantly in north India, and in most northern regions breads such as naan, chapatis and parathas are eaten with curries and with dry, spiced vegetable and lentil dishes. In the Punjab, however, breads made from *besan* (chickpea flour) and *makki* (cornmeal) are more usually served with curries. In western India, curries are eaten with breads made with flour prepared from *jowar* (millet) and *bajra* (milo).

PREPARING AN INDIAN MEAL

While there may be no such thing as a definitive curry recipe, there certainly is an established procedure to follow when preparing a curry. Choose the main ingredient and select the cooking pan accordingly. Use a deep-sided pan if the curry is to contain lots of liquid. For fish, a wide, flat pan is needed to allow the pieces of fish to be laid in a single layer.

COOKING FATS

Traditionally, the Indian housewife would use ghee (clarified butter), not just for its rich flavour, but also because dairy products are believed to be highly nutritious. Modern Indian families are now deviating from this practice, however, because of a growing awareness of the dangers of eating too much saturated fat. Sunflower, vegetable and corn oils all make suitable alternatives. Olive oil is not normally used, although a basic cooking version (not virgin or extra virgin) will work well. Ghee can be reserved for special occasion dishes, if you prefer.

COOKING LIQUIDS

Most curries are water-based. Stock is sometimes used in Indian cooking, but this is not a common practice as meat is always cooked on the bone and this creates a sufficiently robust flavour. Whether you use stock or water as your cooking liquid, it is important to make sure the liquid is at least lukewarm. Adding cold liquid to carefully blended spices will impair the flavours.

ADDING SALT

Pay careful attention when using salt in an Indian dish. Do not be afraid to use the amount specified in a recipe. Even if it seems to be a lot, the amount will have been worked out to achieve an overall balance of flavours. There are now several brands of low-sodium salt available.

THICKENING AGENTS

Indian cooking does not rely on flour to thicken sauces. Instead, the consistency is usually achieved by adding ingredients such as dairy cream or coconut cream, nut pastes, onion purée, tomatoes and ground seeds such as poppy, sesame and sunflower.

ADDING COLOUR

Some of the ingredients added to curries not only determine the texture and consistency of the curry, but also its colour. In Mughlai sauces and curries, the onions are softened but not browned, which gives them their distinctive pale colour. Bhuna (stir-fried) curries, on the other hand, use browned onions, making the final dishes reddish-brown in colour.

COLOURING INGREDIENTS

The depth of colour achieved in a curry depends on the amount of colorant used in relation to the other ingredients.
fresh coriander (cilantro) leaves: *green*
garam masala: *deep brown if fried for about 1 minute*
ground coriander: *deep brown if fried for about 5 minutes*
red chillies: *reddish-brown*
saffron: *pale apricot*
tomatoes: *reddish if used alone; pinkish if combined with yogurt*
turmeric: *bright yellow*

SOURING AGENTS

These are widely used and may affect the colour and consistency of the curry as well as its flavour. Tamarind, for instance, both darkens and thickens a sauce, while lime, lemon and white vinegar neither alter the colour of a curry nor thicken it. Ingredients such as dry mango powder (*amchur*) and dried pomegranate seeds (*anardana*), as well as tomatoes and yogurts, are all used to lend a distinctive tangy flavour.

ADDING HEAT

The main ingredient needed to create a fiery flavour and appearance is chilli. Although chillies were unknown in India before the Portuguese settlers introduced them in the 15th century, it is difficult to imagine Indian food without them. Chilli in its powdered form contributes to the colour of a curry, and chilli powder is readily available in a range of heat levels. Always be sure to check the label carefully.

If you want the curry to be appealing to the eye without scorching the taste buds, choose a chilli powder made from either Kashmiri or Byadigi chillies. This will lend a rich colour to the dish, but the flavour will be fairly mild. You can always use it in conjunction with a hot chilli powder if you prefer to give the curry some kick. Another way to achieve both colour and heat in the same dish is to combine chilli powder with fresh chillies: fresh chillies are always hotter than the dried ones.

When buying fresh chillies, look out for the long, slim ones used in Indian cooking, rather than Mexican varieties. They are sometimes labelled "finger chillies". Thai chillies make a good substitute, and are available from Asian food stores.

Paste made from dried red chillies also gives a good colour and quite a different flavour from chilli powder. To make it, all you need to do is soak the chillies for 15–20 minutes in hot water and then purée them. The paste will keep well in an airtight jar in the refrigerator for 4–5 days.

COOKING A CURRY

Several factors will influence the making of a good curry. One of the most important of these is the cooking temperature. The fat should be heated to the right temperature and maintained at a steady heat until the spices have released their flavour. A heavy pan, such as a wok, karahi or large pan, will help to maintain the temperature so that the spices can cook without burning. While recipes may vary, the usual procedure is to start off by frying the onions over a medium heat then, once softened, adding the ground spices and lowering the temperature.

The more finely the onion is chopped, the better it will blend into the sauce. In many recipes, onion, ginger and garlic are puréed to make a wet spice paste, which is fried until all the moisture has evaporated before the ground spices are added. It is crucial to follow the timings specified in a recipe for each of these stages.

Adding spices in the correct sequence is also vital. While some spices take only a few seconds to release their flavour, others need a few minutes. If you add spices that require less cooking time together with those that need more, some will burn and others will remain raw. The simplest way to avoid this is to keep to the order in which the spices are listed in the recipe, and to be very exact about following the specified cooking time for each ingredient.

PLANNING AN INDIAN MEAL

When planning your menu, always bear in mind that an everyday Indian meal features only three items: the main dish, a side dish and a staple, which would be rice or bread. Chutneys, salads and raitas can also be served to add a fresh or tangy flavour to a meal. When entertaining guests, pulaos or fried rice are usually served rather than plain rice.

PLANNING THE MENU

When deciding which foods to serve, consider the main dish. Is it going to be highly spiced, such as a vindaloo or a bhuna? Or will it have subtle flavours, such as a korma or a pasanda? Opt for dishes with flavours that complement, rather than compete with, each other. Choose the side dish according to the strength of the main one. A lightly spiced side dish is more enjoyable when the main dish is spicier. This does not apply in reverse, however, and a side dish with complex spicing is not the ideal accompaniment to a mild main dish.

Drier dishes are usually accompanied by a vegetable curry or a lentil dish. Biryanis are traditionally served with raita, although they are often served with a vegetable curry in Indian restaurants in the West.

HOW TO SERVE AN INDIAN MEAL

An Indian meal is not served in separate courses, with an appetizer followed by a main dish and one or two side dishes. Although the meal will usually consist of several dishes, they are brought to the table at the same time and diners help themselves.

For more lavish occasions, you can add other dishes to the standard three-dish Indian menu. One or two dry meat dishes, such as a kabab or tandoori chicken, in addition to some chutneys, pickles, raitas and poppadums, with a dessert to follow, can turn an ordinary meal into a feast.

INDIAN DESSERTS

In India, a meal will usually end with fresh fruit rather than a dessert. Fruits are often combined with other ingredients to create imaginative and exciting flavours. Choose one or two exotic fruits, such as papaya, pomegranate or star fruit, and combine them with everyday fruits in a fruit salad. Serve the salad with Greek (US strained plain) yogurt flavoured with rosewater and a little ground cardamom. Indian sweets (candies) are quite heavy and are served as a snack with tea and coffee.

REHEATING LEFTOVERS

This method will make leftover food that has been frozen taste really fresh. The method can also be used to reheat food that has been stored in the refrigerator.

1 Heat about 10ml/2 tsp vegetable oil in a wok, karahi or large pan over a medium heat. Add up to 1.5ml/¼ tsp garam masala and allow to bubble gently for 10–15 seconds.

2 Add the thawed food to the pan and increase the heat to high. Let the food bubble or sizzle in the pan until it is heated through, stirring from time to time.

3 Add a little water if the food looks dry. Stir in 15ml/1 tbsp chopped coriander (cilantro). Remove from the heat, transfer to a warmed platter and serve.

Freezing Curries

In today's busy world it is not always possible to serve a meal while it is still sizzling in the pan. If you are entertaining, you may prefer to cook the curry in advance to save yourself time on the day. Or you may like to cook a larger quantity than you will need and freeze some for another meal. You may even have some leftovers, and these can also be frozen.

Spicy food is ideal for freezing because the flavours improve when the food is thawed and reheated. Most of the spices used in Indian cooking have natural preservative qualities, as does the acid in souring agents. However, you should always bear in mind the following factors if you are cooking specifically for the freezer:
• Leave the food slightly underdone.
• Cool the cooked food rapidly. The best way of doing this is to spread it out on to a large tray (a large roasting pan is ideal) and leave it in a cool place.
• Once the food has cooled completely, spoon it into plastic containers. Label the containers and chill them in the refrigerator for a couple of hours before transferring them to the freezer. The frozen food will keep for 6–8 months, depending on the star rating of your freezer.

Food that you did not plan to freeze, such as leftovers, should not be kept in the freezer for longer than 2–3 months, again, depending on the efficiency of your freezer. Meat and poultry curries freeze very successfully, as do curries made from vegetables, lentils and pulses. Fish curries can also be frozen, but they are generally less successful as changes in the water balance may damage the more delicate texture of cooked fish.

Thawing and Reheating

Frozen food should be thawed thoroughly and slowly. Place it in the refrigerator for 18–24 hours before reheating, then heat the food until piping hot before serving. These steps will ensure that any harmful bacteria are destroyed. If you have a temperature probe, check that the food is heated to at least 85°C/185°F right the way through.

Thawed food can be reheated in the microwave or in a covered casserole on the stove top. If using a microwave, cover the food with microwave clear film (plastic wrap). Stir the food from time to time to ensure that the heat passes right the way through. You may need to add a small amount of water to ensure that the dish does not dry out. A certain amount of water separation is to be expected as a defrosted dish thaws. It will return to its normal consistency when it is reheated.

Cooking for a Party

Prepare and cook the curry dishes the day before and store them in the refrigerator until you are ready to reheat them. Dhals can be prepared 24 hours in advance, although the seasonings should not be added until just before serving. Vegetables can be prepared in advance, but do not cook them more than a few hours ahead. Ingredients for raitas can be prepared the day before, but should only be assembled at the last minute. Pickles and chutneys will benefit from advance preparation. The dough for rotis can be made the day before, and rotis can be made about 2 hours before serving. Spread them with butter and wrap in foil to keep warm. Reheat in the oven before serving.

EQUIPMENT

While a reasonably stocked kitchen will provide most of the equipment needed for cooking Indian curries, it may still be necessary to invest in one or two specialist items. If you frequently cook large quantities of rice, an electric rice cooker can be a good investment. When the water has been fully absorbed by the rice, it switches itself off and will keep the rice warm for several hours.

GRINDING STONE AND PIN
The traditional oblong grinding stone is the Indian equivalent of the Western food processor. Fresh and dry ingredients are placed on a heavy slate stone, which is marked with notches to hold the ingredients in place. The ingredients are then pulverized against the stone using a heavy rolling pin.

STONE MORTAR AND PESTLE
A heavy granite mortar and pestle is traditionally used to grind small amounts of ingredients, both wet and dry.

SPICE MILL
An electric spice mill is useful for grinding small quantities of ingredients such as spices. A coffee grinder – used solely for this purpose, as it will retain the strong smell of the spices – would make a good substitute.

STAINLESS STEEL MORTAR AND PESTLE
This is ideal for grinding small amounts of wet ingredients, such as ginger and garlic. Stainless steel is everlasting and will not retain the strong flavours of the spices.

FOOD PROCESSOR
This is essential for blending the ingredients. Smaller quantities can be ground with a mortar and pestle.

KARAHI
Basically an Indian frying pan, the karahi is similar to a wok but is more rounded in shape. Originally, the karahi would be made of cast iron, although a variety of metals are now used. Karahis are available in various sizes, including small ones for cooking individual portions. Serving food from the karahi at the table will add an authentic touch to an Indian meal.

WOK
This is a good substitute for a karahi for cooking most types of Indian dish. Buy the appropriate wok for your stove. Woks with a rounded bottom are for gas hobs only; flat-bottomed woks are for electric hobs.

NON-STICK FRYING PAN
This can be used in place of a karahi or wok. Metal spoons will ruin the non-stick surface, so it is best to have a set of wooden or plastic ones.

Stainless Steel Pans

Quality kitchen pans in various sizes are essential for cooking rice and other foods.

Chapati Griddle

Known in India as a *tava*, the chapati griddle allows chapatis and other breads to be cooked without burning. It can also be used to dry roast spices. Traditionally, the griddle would be set over an open fire, but it will work equally well on a gas flame or electric hob.

Heat Diffuser

Many curries are left to simmer over a low heat, and a heat diffuser will help to prevent burning on the base of the karahi or wok.

Table Sizzler

This heated appliance allows food that is still cooking to be brought to the dinner table ready for serving. It is very useful when you are entertaining.

Knives

Good kitchen knives in a range of sizes are essential. Always keep knives sharp to make chopping easier and to ensure neat edges.

Colander and Sieve

Use for draining boiled rice and vegetables, and for straining ingredients. Choose a long-handled, sturdy colander and sieve made from stainless steel, as these allow you to stand back to pour steaming rice out of a pan, and will not discolour like plastic ones.

Tongs

These are very useful for turning chicken portions and for picking up meat pieces when they are browning.

Slotted Spoon

Stirring cooked, drained rice with a slotted spoon will produce soft, fluffy rice by allowing air in between the grains; the slots in the spoon prevent the grains from breaking as the rice is moved around the pan. The spoon also enables foods to be removed from hot oil or other liquids.

Chapati Spoon

The square, flat-headed chapati spoon is used for turning roasting breads on the hot chapati griddle. A fish slice (spatula) could also be used.

Chapati Rolling Board

This round wooden board on short stubby legs is used to mould breads into shape; the extra height provided by the legs helps to disperse excess dry flour. A wooden pastry board makes an appropriate substitute.

Chapati Rolling Pin

The traditional chapati rolling pin is thinner in shape than Western rolling pins and comes in several different sizes. Use the size that feels most comfortable in your hands.

Balloon Whisk

A metal whisk is useful for beating yogurt and dairy or coconut cream.

Pastry Brush

Use for brushing and basting meats and vegetables lightly with oil before and during grilling (broiling).

Stainless Steel Grater

Use to grate fresh root spices such as ginger and horseradish. Nutmegs can be grated on a special nutmeg grater.

HERBS, SPICES & AROMATICS

Spices are integral to both the flavour and aroma of a dish. Some spices are used for the taste they impart, while others, known as aromatics, are used for their aroma. One individual spice can completely alter the taste of a dish, and a combination of several spices will also affect its colour and texture. In some Indian dishes, as many as 15 spices may be blended to flavour a single dish.

The quantities of spices and salt specified in recipes are measured to achieve a balance of flavours, although you can increase or decrease the quantities according to taste. This is particularly true of fresh chillies and chilli powder: experiment with quantities, adding less or more than specified.

Fresh and dried herbs play an important part in the combinations of colour, flavour, aroma and texture that make up a curry. Fresh herbs require only a minimal amount of cooking, and they retain a marvellous intensity of flavour and fragrance.

ANISEED

These liquorice-flavoured seeds are used in many fried and deep-fried Indian dishes as an aid to digestion. Dry-frying heightens the smell and changes the taste to bitter sweet. It also makes the seeds brittle and much easier to crush. Store the seeds in an airtight jar and use within 6 months.

AJOWAN

The tiny, oval, grey-green seeds of Ajowan look like miniature cumin seeds and their fragrance is similar. When crushed, they have a strong and distinctive thyme-like bouquet. They can be used as a substitute for thyme, but use them sparingly as they are stronger in flavour. This spice is popular in the delicate vegetarian dishes from the state of Gujarat. The seeds will keep for up to a year if stored in an airtight jar.

ASAFOETIDA

This seasoning is a resin with an acrid and very bitter taste and a strong odour. It is used primarily as a digestive and anti-flatulent, and only minute quantities are used in recipes. A pinch of it is thrown into very hot oil and allowed to fry for a second or two before other foods are added. Store in a glass jar with a strong airtight seal to prevent the smell dispersing into other ingredients in the pantry.

BAY LEAVES

Indian bay leaves come from the cassia tree, which is similar to the tree from which cinnamon is taken. Bay leaves sold in the West are taken from the laurel tree. When used fresh, bay leaves have a deliciously sweet flavour. The dried leaves are a dull sage green in colour and are quite brittle. They keep for up to 6 months if stored in a cool, dark place in an airtight jar. Bay leaves are used in meat and rice dishes and are removed from the dish before serving.

CARDAMOM PODS

This spice is native to India, where it is considered the most prized spice after saffron. The pods can be used whole or the husks can be removed to release the seeds; whole pods should be always removed from the dish before serving. They have a slightly pungent but very aromatic taste. They come in three varieties: green, white and black. The green and white pods can be used for both sweet and savoury dishes or to flavour rice. The black pods are used only for savoury dishes.

CHILLIES

These hot peppers belong to the genus capsicum, along with sweet (bell) peppers. Some varieties are extremely fiery and all chillies should be used with caution. Much of the heat of fresh chillies is contained in the seeds, and the heat can be toned down by removing these before use. Chillies are perfect for hot climates because they cause blood to rush to the surface of the skin, promoting instant cooling.

Chillies vary in size and colour, but, as a rule, dark green chillies are hotter than light green ones. Red chillies are usually hotter still, and some will darken to brown or black when fully ripe. Shape and colour give no sure indication of the hotness, and it is wise to be wary of any unfamiliar variety. Dried chillies can be used whole or crushed.

Chilli powder is a fiery ground spice that should be used with great caution. The heat varies from brand to brand, so adjust quantities to suit your taste buds. Some brands include other spices and herbs, as well as ground chillies, and these may not be appropriate to the dish you are cooking. Always check the label carefully.

PREPARING CHILLIES

For a fairly hot dish, use 2 or more chillies. Use less if you prefer a milder curry. All chillies contain capsaicin, an oily substance that can cause intense irritation to sensitive skin. If you get capsaicin on your hands and transfer it to your eyes by rubbing, you will experience considerable pain. Wash your hands with warm soapy water after handling. Dry your hands and rub a little oil into the skin to remove any stinging juices. If you have sensitive skin, you may prefer to wear rubber (latex) gloves to help protect your hands when preparing chillies.

To prepare fresh chillies, cut the chillies in half lengthways. Remove the membranes and seeds (where much of the heat resides). Cut the chilli flesh lengthways into long, thin strips. If required, cut the strips crossways into small dice.

To prepare dried chillies, remove the stems and seeds, then break each chilli into two or three pieces. Put the pieces in a small bowl and cover with hot water. Leave to stand for 30 minutes, then drain (use the soaking water in the recipe, if appropriate). Use the chilli pieces as they are, or chop them finely.

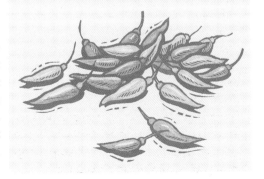

CINNAMON

One of the earliest known spices, cinnamon has a highly aromatic, sweet, warm flavour. It is sold ready-ground and as sticks, which are quill-like shapes rolled from the bark of the cinnamon tree. Use cinnamon sticks whole or broken, as directed in individual recipes, and remove them from the food before serving. Ground cinnamon is a useful pantry staple.

CLOVES

Originally found in the Spice Islands of Indonesia, cloves were taken to the Seychelles and Mauritius early in the 18th century. Cloves are the unopened flower buds of a tree that belongs to the myrtle family. They have an aromatic and even fiery flavour and an intense fragrance. They are used to flavour both sweet and savoury dishes. Cloves are usually added whole and should be removed before serving. Their warm flavour complements all rich meats, and they need no preparation. Ground cloves are often one of the ingredients that are included in spice mixtures.

CORIANDER

There is no substitute for fresh coriander (cilantro), and the more that is used in Indian cooking the better. Coriander imparts a wonderful aroma and flavour, and is used both as an ingredient in cooking, and sprinkled over dishes as a garnish. Chopped coriander can be frozen successfully; the frozen coriander does not need to be defrosted before use. Coriander

seeds and ground coriander powder are used for flavouring. The seeds have a pungent, slightly lemony flavour and are used coarsely ground in meat, fish and poultry dishes. Ground coriander, which is a brownish powder, is an important constituent of any curry spice mixture.

FREEZING FRESH CORIANDER

Fresh coriander (cilantro) is widely used in Indian cooking. Its flavour and aroma make it an important ingredient, and the leaves make an attractive garnish. Fresh coriander tends to deteriorate quickly, but it is very simple to freeze any that is not required immediately.

1 Cut off the roots and any thick stalks, retaining the fine stalks.

2 Wash the leaves in cold water and leave in a strainer to drain.

3 When the leaves are dry, chop them finely using a sharp knife and store them in small quantities in plastic bags or airtight containers in the freezer.

CUMIN

White cumin seeds are oval, ridged and greenish-brown in colour. They have a strong aroma and flavour with a slightly bitter and pungent taste. The bitterness is particularly noticeable in the ground spice, and it is frequently used with coriander, which counteracts the bitterness. Ready-ground cumin powder is widely available, but it should be bought in small quantities as it loses its flavour rapidly.

Black cumin seeds are smaller than the white ones, and they have a sweeter aroma. They are sometimes confused with nigella seeds. Black cumin is one of the ingredients used to make garam masala, and they can be used to flavour curries and rice.

CURRY LEAVES

Bright green and shiny, curry leaves are similar in appearance to bay leaves but they have a different flavour. The leaves of a hardwood tree that is indigenous to India, they are widely used in Indian cooking, particularly in southern and western India (although not in Goa) and in Sri Lanka. Curry leaves have a warm fragrance with a subtle hint of sweet, green pepper or tangerine. The leaves release their full flavour when bruised and impart a highly distinctive flavour to curries.

Curry leaves are usually sold dried, but occasionally fresh ones can be found in Indian food stores. Fresh leaves freeze well, and the dried leaves make a poor substitute because they rapidly lose their fragrance.

FENNEL SEEDS

Similar in appearance to cumin, fennel seeds have a sweet taste and are used to flavour curries. They can be chewed as a mouth-freshener after a spicy meal.

FENUGREEK

Fresh fenugreek is usually sold in bunches. It has very small leaves and is used to flavour meat and vegetarian dishes. Always discard the stalks, which will impart an unpleasant bitterness to a dish if used. Fenugreek seeds are flat, extremely pungent and slightly bitter. They only appear in a few recipes, where they are added whole, mainly for taste; these should be used cautiously. Dried fenugreek leaves are sold in Indian food stores. Store them in an airtight jar, in a cool, dark place; they will keep for about 12 months. Fenugreek seeds are small and pungent and are widely used in spice mixtures.

GARLIC

Widely available fresh and dried, garlic is used for its strong, aromatic flavour, and is a standard ingredient, along with ginger, in most curries. Fresh garlic can be pulped, crushed or chopped, or the cloves can be used whole. Garlic powder is mainly used in spice mixtures.

PULPING GARLIC

Fresh garlic is used so often in Indian cooking that you may find it more practical to prepare garlic in bulk and store it in the refrigerator or freezer until it is needed.

Separate the garlic bulb into cloves and peel off the papery skin. Process the whole cloves in a food processor until smooth. Freeze the garlic pulp in ice cube trays kept specially for this purpose. Put 5ml/1 tsp in each compartment, freeze, remove from the tray and store in the freezer in a sealed plastic bag. Or store the pulp in an airtight container in the refrigerator for 3–4 weeks.

GINGER

One of the most popular spices in India and also one of the oldest, fresh root ginger is an important ingredient in many Indian curries. Its refreshing scent is reminiscent of citrus, and it has a pleasant, sharp flavour. The root should be plump with a fairly smooth skin, which is peeled off before use. Young root ginger is tender and mild, whereas older roots are quite fibrous, with a more pungent flavour. Dried powdered ginger is a useful standby, but the flavour is not quite the same. It is often blended with other spices to make curry powder.

PREPARING FRESH ROOT GINGER

Fresh root ginger has a delightfully clean and pungent taste, and it is very easy to prepare. Pulping fresh root ginger can be a little time-consuming, so prepare a large quantity and store it in the freezer until needed. Fresh ginger is widely available from supermarkets and Indian markets.

To grate ginger, *carefully remove the papery skin using a sharp knife or vegetable peeler. Grate the peeled ginger using the fine side of a stainless steel cheese grater.*

To chop ginger, *remove the skin with a sharp knife or vegetable peeler. Slice the ginger into matchstick strips, or chop into small pieces, as required.*

To pulp fresh root ginger, *peel off the tough outer skin using a sharp knife or a vegetable peeler. Roughly chop the flesh, then process in a food processor, adding a little water to get a smooth consistency. Store in the refrigerator for 3–4 weeks.*

To freeze ginger, *pulp the fresh root ginger and freeze in ice cube trays kept specially for this purpose.*

MINT

There are many varieties of mint available, and the stronger-flavoured types tend to be used in Indian cooking. These taste slightly sweet and have a cool aftertaste. Mint has a fresh, stimulating aroma and is traditionally used with lamb, as well as for flavouring vegetables. It is used for making chutneys and refreshing raitas, and as a garnish. Mint is added at the end of cooking time in order to retain its flavour.

MUSTARD SEEDS

Whole black and brown mustard seeds are indigenous to India and appear often in Indian cooking. In their raw state, the seeds have no aroma, but when roasted or fried in ghee or hot oil until they pop and crackle, they release a rich, nutty flavour and aroma. Mustard seeds are commonly used with vegetables and dhal dishes.

NIGELLA SEEDS

This aromatic spice has a sharp and tingling taste. It is frequently used in vegetarian dishes and also goes well with fish.

NUTMEG

Whole nutmeg should be grated on a special nutmeg grater to release its sweet, nutty flavour. Ground nutmeg imparts a similar, though less intense, flavour and makes a very useful pantry standby.

FRYING MUSTARD SEEDS

Mustard seeds release their aroma when heated, so they should be fried before they are added to a dish.

Heat a little ghee or vegetable oil in a wok, karahi or large pan, and add the mustard seeds. Shake the pan over the heat until the seeds start to change colour. Stir the seeds from time to time so that they heat right through. Use the pan lid to stop the seeds jumping out of the pan when they start to splutter and pop.

ONION SEEDS

These black, triangular-shaped, aromatic seeds are used in pickles and to flavour vegetable curries and lentil dishes.

PAPRIKA

A rich red powder with a mild, rather sweet taste, paprika is often used in place of, or alongside, chillies in westernized Indian cooking to add colour to a dish.

PEPPERCORNS

Black peppercorns are native to India. They are used both whole and ground in Indian cooking, although whole peppercorns are always removed before serving. They are an essential ingredient in garam masala.

SAFFRON

Saffron is the dried stigmas of the saffron crocus, which is native to Asia Minor. It is the world's most expensive spice: to produce 450g/1lb of saffron, 60,000 stigmas are required. Fortunately, only a small quantity of saffron is needed to flavour and colour a dish, whether sweet or savoury. Saffron is sold as threads and as a powder. It has a beautiful flavour and aroma. Store saffron in a airtight jar away from light, which can bleach it.

TURMERIC

A member of the ginger family but without ginger's characteristic heat, turmeric is a rhizome that is indigenous to Asia. It is sometimes referred to as Indian saffron, as it shares saffron's ability to colour food yellow, although it lacks the subtlety of saffron. Fresh turmeric adds a warm and slightly musky flavour to food, but it has a strong, bitter flavour and should be used sparingly. Turmeric has a natural affinity with fish and is also used in rice, dhal and vegetable dishes. The yellow colour of some pickles and chutneys, such as piccalilli, comes from turmeric.

INFUSING SAFFRON

Some spices such as saffron are always infused in a warm liquid before use. When saffron is infused, it not only imparts a wonderful aroma but also a vibrant yellow colour.

1 Warm a small quantity of milk, water or liquid from the recipe in a small pan. Add the saffron in the warm liquid and leave to infuse for about 5 minutes.

2 Add the saffron and soaking liquid to the other ingredients. (Don't strain the liquid – both strands and liquid are used in the recipe.)

CURRY POWDERS & PASTES

Freshly made blends of herbs, spices and aromatics are used as the basis of any curry. Traditional Indian households would blend individual spices as needed, but for convenience you may prefer to prepare a quantity in advance. Many of the most commonly used spice powders and pastes are now available ready-made in supermarkets and make a good standby.

Traditionally, spice mixtures would usually be prepared and mixed as required on a daily basis. However, this can prove time-consuming, and many powders and pastes can be made in advance and stored in an airtight jar in a cool place, away from direct sunlight, for several days or weeks.

CURRY POWDER

This is a basic recipe for a dry spice blend for use in any curry dish. It is a mild recipe, but you could increase the quantity of dried chilli for a hotter taste, if liked.

Makes about 115g/4oz/½ cup
50g/2oz/½ cup coriander seeds
60ml/4 tbsp cumin seeds
30ml/2 tbsp fennel seeds
30ml/2 tbsp fenugreek seeds
4 dried red chillies, or more to taste
5 curry leaves
15ml/1 tbsp chilli powder
15ml/1 tbsp ground turmeric
2.5ml/½ tsp salt

1 Dry-fry the whole spices in a large heavy pan for 8–10 minutes, shaking the pan until the spices darken and release a rich aroma. Allow to cool.

2 Put the dry-fried whole spices in a spice mill and grind to a fine powder.

3 In a large mixing bowl, combine the ground roasted whole spices with the chilli powder, ground turmeric and salt. Store the curry powder in an airtight container.

CURRY PASTE

This is a wet blend of spices cooked with oil and vinegar. It is a quick and convenient way of adding spices to a curry. As only a small amount of paste is added at a time, a little curry paste will last a long time. Store in the refrigerator and use as required.

Makes about 600ml/1 pint/2½ cups
50g/2oz/½ cup coriander seeds
60ml/4 tbsp cumin seeds
30ml/2 tbsp fennel seeds
30ml/2 tbsp fenugreek seeds
4 dried red chillies
5 curry leaves
15ml/1 tbsp chilli powder
15ml/1 tbsp ground turmeric
150ml/¼ pint/⅔ cup wine vinegar
250ml/8fl oz/1 cup vegetable oil, plus extra

1 Grind the whole spices to a powder in a spice mill. Transfer to a bowl and add the remaining ground spices.

2 Mix the spices until well blended, then add the wine vinegar and stir. Add about 75ml/5 tbsp water and stir well to form a smooth paste.

3 Heat the oil in a wok, karahi or large pan and stir-fry the spice paste for about 10 minutes, or until all the water has been absorbed. When the oil rises to the surface, the paste is cooked. Allow to cool slightly before spooning the paste into airtight jars.

4 Heat a little more oil and pour on top of the paste, then seal the jar. This will help to preserve the mixture and, as the oil stays on top as the paste is used, it will stop any mould from forming during storage. Store in the refrigerator.

DHANA JEERA POWDER

This classic spice mixture is made from ground roasted coriander and cumin seeds. The proportions are generally two parts coriander to one part cumin.

MASALAS

These are blends of spices that can be a dry mixture or a paste. The flavours can be mild and fragrant or more highly spiced. This depends largely on the cook and the dish in which the masala is to be used. The spices are usually dry-fried before grinding, which greatly enhances the flavour.

There are many different masala spice blends, the best known of which is probably garam masala. Other variations, which all have their own unique flavour and aroma, include tandoori masala, Kashmiri masala, Madras masala, sambar masala, dhansak masala and green masala. These mixtures are sold commercially, as pastes ready-made in jars. They can be substituted for garam masala and make useful pantry standbys.

Garam Masala

This spice mix is used mainly for meat, although it can be used in poultry and rice dishes. The aroma is generally considered too strong for fish or vegetable dishes. Garam means hot and masala means spices, and this mixture uses spices that are known to heat the body. There is no set recipe, but a typical mixture might include black cumin seeds, peppercorns, cinnamon, cloves and black cardamom pods.

Makes about 50g/2oz/¼ cup
10 dried red chillies
3 × 2.5cm/1in pieces cinnamon stick
2 curry leaves
30ml/2 tbsp coriander seeds
30ml/2 tbsp cumin seeds
5ml/1 tsp black peppercorns
5ml/1 tsp cloves
5ml/1 tsp fenugreek seeds
5ml/1 tsp black mustard seeds
1.5ml/¼ tsp chilli powder

1 Dry-fry the dried red chillies, cinnamon and curry leaves in a wok, karahi or large pan over a low heat for about 2 minutes.

2 Add the coriander and cumin seeds, black peppercorns, cloves, fenugreek and mustard seeds, and dry-fry for 8–10 minutes, shaking the pan from side to side until the spices begin to darken in colour and release a rich aroma. Allow the mixture to cool.

3 Using either a spice mill or a stainless steel mortar and pestle, grind the roasted spices to a fine powder.

4 Transfer the powder to a glass bowl and mix in the chilli powder. Store in an airtight container in a cool place away from direct light. It will keep for 2–4 months. Once opened, store in the refrigerator.

Tandoori Masala

This versatile spice blend can be used in marinades for meat dishes or added to hot oil to flavour curries. It has a distinctive aroma with a definite taste of cumin and coriander. Ready-made varieties are often bright red and give food a strong reddish-orange colour.

Makes about 50g/2oz/¼ cup
4cm/1½in piece cinnamon stick
20ml/4 tsp cumin seeds
20ml/4 tsp coriander seeds
10ml/2 tsp cloves
10ml/2 tsp chilli powder
10ml/2 tsp ground ginger
10ml/2 tsp ground turmeric
10ml/2 tsp garlic powder
10ml/2 tsp ground mace
10ml/2 tsp salt
1.5ml/¼ tsp red food colouring powder

1 Break up the cinnamon stick and dry-fry the whole spices in a heavy frying pan. Leave the spices to cool slightly.

2 Using a spice mill, grind the cooled spices with the remaining ingredients. Store in an airtight jar in a cool, dark place.

Kashmiri Masala

This aromatic masala is particularly good with prawn (shrimp) and lamb dishes.

Makes about 60ml/4 tbsp
12 green cardamom pods
5cm/1in piece cinnamon stick
30ml/1 tbsp black peppercorns
15ml/1 tbsp black cumin seeds
10ml/2 tsp caraway seeds
5ml/1 tsp ground nutmeg

1 Using a knife, split the cardamom pods and break the cinnamon stick into pieces.

2 Dry-fry the spices, except the nutmeg, tossing them continuously until they give off a rich aroma.

3 Remove the cardamom seeds from their pods and grind all the spices to a very fine powder. Mix in the nutmeg and store in an airtight jar.

Madras Masala

This blend of dry and wet spices is typical of seasoning mixes from south India. The dry spices are roasted and ground before adding garlic, finely grated ginger and vinegar to make a paste, which is then cooked in oil to develop the flavours before being stored in an airtight jar.

Makes about 450g/1lb
120ml/8 tbsp coriander seeds
60ml/4 tbsp cumin seeds
15ml/1 tbsp black peppercorns
15ml/1 tbsp black mustard seeds
165ml/11 tbsp ground turmeric
15–20ml/3–4 tsp chilli powder
15ml/1 tbsp salt
8 garlic cloves, crushed
7.5cm/3in piece fresh root ginger,
    peeled and finely grated
50ml/2fl oz/¼ cup cider vinegar
175ml/6fl oz/¾ cup sunflower oil

1 Briefly dry-fry the coriander, cumin and peppercorns in a large, heavy pan. Add the mustard seeds and toss the mixture until the spices give off an aroma.

2 Using a spice mill, grind the mixture to a fine powder, then add the turmeric, chilli powder and salt. Add the garlic, ginger and sufficient vinegar to make a paste.

3 Heat the oil and fry the paste, stirring and turning continuously, until the oil begins to separate from the spice mixture.

4 Leave the paste to cool and store in an airtight jar away from direct light in a cool place. It will keep for 2–3 weeks.

Sambhar Masala

This classic blend of spices is used widely in south Indian dishes to flavour lentil and vegetable combinations and spicy broths. The powder has a nutty flavour. It also gives a smooth, velvety thickening to the finished sauce. The dhal are readily available in Indian stores and most larger supermarkets.

Makes about 250ml/8fl oz/1 cup
8–10 dried red chillies
90ml/6 tbsp coriander seeds
30ml/2 tbsp cumin seeds
10ml/2 tsp fenugreek seeds
10ml/2 tsp urad dhal (white split
   gram beans)
10ml/2 tsp channa dhal (yellow split peas)
10ml/2 tsp mung dhal (yellow
   mung beans)
25ml/1½ tbsp ground turmeric

1 Discard the stalks and the seeds from the dried chillies, then dry-fry the chillies, coriander, cumin and fenugreek over a medium heat. Toss continuously until the spices give off a rich aroma, then tip into a mixing bowl and set aside.

2 Dry-fry the pulses in the same way until they are toasted. Stir frequently so that they do not burn or stick to the pan.

3 Using a spice mill, grind the toasted spices and pulses to a fine powder, then stir in the turmeric. Store in an airtight jar.

Green Masala

This mild spice paste has a rich jewel-green colour and is tangy with fresh coriander and mint leaves. It makes a wonderful addition to prawn (shrimp), poultry and vegetable dishes, especially those enriched with coconut milk, or as an addition to a simple dhal dish.

Makes about 250ml/8fl oz/1 cup
5ml/1 tsp fenugreek seeds
10 green cardamom pods
6 cloves
10ml/2 tsp ground turmeric
10ml/2 tsp salt
4 cloves garlic, crushed
5cm/2in piece fresh root ginger, peeled
   and finely grated
50g/2oz fresh mint leaves
50g/2oz fresh coriander (cilantro)
1 small green (bell) pepper, seeded
   and chopped (optional)
50ml/2fl oz/¼ cup cider vinegar
120ml/4fl oz/½ cup mixed sunflower
   and sesame oil

1 Soak the feungreek seeds in water for about 8 hours, or overnight.

2 Next day, bruise the cardamom pods and dry-fry them in a heavy pan with the cloves until they give off a rich aroma.

3 Grind the roasted spices to a powder and add the turmeric and salt.

4 Drain the fenugreek seeds and put them in a food processor or blender with the garlic, ginger, mint, coriander, green pepper, if using, and the vinegar. Blend the mixture to a smooth paste, then add the salt and ground spices. Store in an airtight jar.

Chat Masala

Chat is an Indian salad snack sold on street stalls. It might consist of banana, papaya, guavas and chikoo or apples. This recipe is for the spicy and rather tart mixture used to flavour the salad, which can also be served as a first course before a main meal. The whole spices are ground without dry-frying.

Makes 2¹/₂ tbsp
5ml/1 tsp black peppercorns
5ml/1 tsp cumin seeds
5ml/1 tsp ajowan seeds
5ml/1 tsp pomegranate seeds
5ml/1 tsp mixed black salt and sea salt
1.5ml/¼ tsp asafoetida
5ml/1 tsp mango powder
2.5ml/½ tsp cayenne pepper, or to taste
2.5ml/½ tsp garam masala (optional)

1 Grind the peppercorns with the cumin, ajowan, pomegranate seeds and salt.

2 Add the remaining ingredients, adjusting the quantity of cayenne pepper to taste and omitting the garam masala, if preferred.

TARKA
Also known as a baghar, this is a mixture of spices and flavourings fried in hot ghee or mustard oil to release their flavours. The spices and oil are then quickly poured over or stirred into dhals, vegetable curries and yogurt salads. There are many different variations on this spice mix.

Makes enough for 1 dish
30ml/2 tbsp ghee
10ml/2 tsp black mustard seeds
1.5ml/½ tsp ground asafoetida
about 8 fresh or dried curry leaves

1 Melt the ghee in a heavy pan and have a lid ready. When the ghee is hot, add the mustard seeds and cover the pan at once. (This is important because the seeds will jump when they pop.)

2 Draw the pan off the heat and add the asafoetida and curry leaves. Stir, then pour over the dhal, soup or stew.

Coriander Baghar

This combination of spices, fried in mustard oil, is used in north India cooking as a topping for dahl. In south Indian cooking, black mustard seeds, asafoetida and fresh or dried curry leaves are used.

Makes enough for 1 dish
60ml/4 tbsp mustard oil
15–20ml/3–4 tsp cumin seeds
1 small onion, finely chopped
60ml/4 tbsp finely chopped fresh
    coriander (cilantro)

1 Heat the mustard oil in a heavy pan until just smoking. Remove from the heat and allow the oil to cool briefly.

2 Reheat the oil and fry the cumin seeds until they start to change colour.

3 Add the onion and cook until it turns a light golden brown.

4 Add the chopped coriander leaves and stir for only a few seconds.

5 Pour the spice mixture over the dhal or soup and serve immediately.

BENGALI FIVE SPICES

In this spice mix of Bengali origin, which is sometimes known as *panch phoron*, equal quantities of the whole spices are simply mixed together, without dry-frying or grinding them The spice mixture can be used in either of two ways: it may be fried in oil to impart flavour to the oil before adding the main ingredients, or fried in ghee and stirred into cooked dhal or vegetables just before they are served.

Makes 10 tbsp
30ml/2 tbsp cumin seeds
30ml/2 tbsp fennel seeds
30ml/2 tbsp mustard seeds
30ml/2 tbsp fenugreek seeds
30ml/ 2 tbsp nigella seeds

1 Mix the spices together.

2 Put the mixture into an airtight jar and store away from strong light.

TIKKA PASTE

This is a delicious, versatile paste. It has a slightly sour flavour, and can be used in a variety of Indian dishes, including chicken tikka, tandoori chicken and tikka masala. The paste should be used sparingly as it is quite strong and a little bit goes a long way. Store the paste in airtight glass jars in the refrigerator until it is required.

Makes about 475ml/16fl oz/2 cups
30ml/2 tbsp coriander seeds
30ml/2 tbsp cumin seeds
25ml/1½ tbsp garlic powder
30ml/2 tbsp paprika
15ml/1 tbsp garam masala
15ml/1 tbsp ground ginger
10ml/2 tsp chilli powder
2.5ml/½ tsp ground turmeric
15ml/1 tbsp dried mint
1.5ml/¼ tsp salt
5ml/1 tsp lemon juice
a few drops of red food colouring
a few drops of yellow food colouring
150ml/¼ pint/⅔ cup wine vinegar
150ml/¼ pint/⅔ cup vegetable oil

1 Grind the coriander and cumin seeds to a fine powder using a spice mill or mortar and pestle. Spoon the mixture into a bowl and add the remaining spices, the mint and salt, stirring well.

2 Mix the spice powder with the lemon juice, food colourings and wine vinegar and add 30ml/2 tbsp water to form a thin paste.

3 Heat the oil in a large pan, wok or karahi, and stir-fry the paste for 10 minutes until all the water has been absorbed. When the oil rises to the surface, the paste is cooked. Allow to cool before spooning into airtight jars. The paste will keep in the refrigerator for 3–4 weeks after opening.

ADDITIONAL INGREDIENTS

Besides the essential spices, herbs and aromatics that give Indian dishes their unique flavour and aroma, there are several other ingredients that are central to Indian cooking. Among the additional ingredients listed here are the different types of cooking oils, and thickening and souring agents, such as yogurt. Nuts and seeds are popular in Indian cuisine and are often used as a garnish.

ALMONDS

In the West, almonds are readily available whole, sliced, ground and as thin slivers. The whole kernels should be soaked in boiling water before use to remove the thin red skin; once blanched, they can be eaten raw. Almonds have a unique aroma, and they impart a sumptuous richness to curries. They make an effective thickener for sauces and are also used for garnishing. Almonds are considered a delicacy in India and, because they are not indigenous, they are very expensive to buy. They are often added to creamy, mild curries.

CASHEW NUTS

These pale, full-flavoured nuts can be used raw or dry-fried in Indian cooking. Cashew nuts are ground and used in mild korma dishes to enrich and thicken the sauce. They can also be toasted and sprinkled over pulaos and biryanis, as a garnish. In India, cashew nuts are often used in vegetable and rice dishes as a substitute for the more expensive almonds.

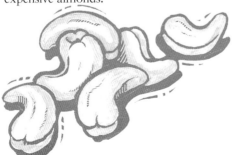

PISTACHIO NUTS

These small, greenish-purple nuts are not indigenous to India, but they are frequently used as a thickening agent. They have a characteristic rich and creamy flavour. Pistachio nuts are also popularly used in sweets (candies), such as burfi, and desserts, such as the classic Indian ice cream, kulfi. Raw or toasted pistachio nuts make an attractive garnish to many dishes.

POPPY SEEDS

These seeds are usually dry-fried to bring out their full, nutty flavour. They can be sprinkled over dry meat and vegetable dishes, or ground and added to curries to thicken sauces.

SESAME SEEDS

These small, pear-shaped seeds probably originated in Africa, but they have been cultivated in India since ancient times. The seeds are usually white, but they can be cream, brown, red or black. Raw sesame seeds have very little aroma and taste until they have been dry-fried, when they take on a slightly nutty taste. The toasted seeds can be ground with a mortar and pestle, or in a spice mill, and used to enrich curries. They are also added to chutneys.

The high fat content of sesame seeds means that they do not keep well. Buy the seeds in small quantities and store them in an airtight jar in a cool, dark place.

TAMARIND

The brown, crescent-shaped fruit pods of the tamarind tree are 15–20cm/6–8in long. Inside the thin brittle pod, the squarish, dark brown, shiny seeds are surrounded by a sticky pulp. Tamarind is cultivated in India, as well as in other parts of South-east Asia, East Africa and the West Indies, and it is undoubtably one of the natural treasures of the East. The high tartaric acid content makes tamarind an excellent souring agent, and for this purpose it has no substitute. It does not have a strong aroma, but the flavour is quite wonderful – tart without being bitter, fruity and refreshing.

Tamarind is usually sold compressed in blocks or dried in slices. Fresh tamarind and concentrated paste are also available. Both the blocks and the paste store well and will last for up to a year.

PREPARING COMPRESSED TAMARIND

Asian food stores and supermarkets sell compressed tamarind in a solid block and in this form it looks rather like a packet of dried dates – in fact it is sometimes known as the Indian date.

To prepare compressed tamarind, tear off a piece that is roughly equivalent to 15ml/1 tbsp. Put the tamarind in a jug (pitcher) and add 150ml/¼ pint/⅔ cup warm water. Leave to soak for about 10 minutes. Swirl the tamarind around with your fingers so that the pulp is released from the seeds. Using a nylon sieve (a metal one will react with the acid), strain the juice into a bowl. Discard the contents of the sieve and use the liquid as required. Store any leftover liquid in the refrigerator for use in another recipe.

PREPARING POMEGRANATE SEEDS

Fresh pomegranate seeds can be dried at home. Cut off and discard a slice from the stem end of the fruit. Stand the fruit on a board and make five incisions from top to bottom. Use your fingers to prise open the fruit in wedge-shaped sections and scoop out the seeds, avoiding the bitter membrane. Spread out the seeds on a baking sheet or ovenproof dish and dry them in the sun or in a cool oven, until they harden. Use a pestle and mortar to crush the seeds, if necessary.

POMEGRANATE SEEDS

These dried seeds, known as *anardana* in India, impart a delicious tangy flavour to chutneys, dhals and curries. They can be extracted from fresh pomegranates or, for convenience, they can be bought in jars from Asian food stores, either whole or in powdered form. The seeds are reddish-brown in colour and tend to form clumps when whole, rather like reddish-black raisins. When buying, choose seeds that are dark in colour and only buy in small quantities as they should be used sparingly.

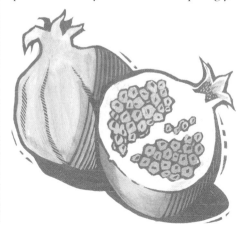

DRY MANGO POWDER

Mangoes are indigenous to India, and they have many uses in Indian cooking. The fruit is used in curries at different stages of ripeness, but the unripe fruit is also sun-dried and ground into a dry powder called *amchur*. The powder has a sour taste and is sprinkled over dishes as a garnish; it is not used in cooking.

GHEE AND COOKING OILS

Clarified butter, known as ghee, is used in many Indian dishes and is particularly used for frying meat. It can be bought in jars or cans in some supermarkets, or in Indian food stores. To prepare ghee, butter made from cow or water buffalo milk is melted and simmered to boil off all the water. The ghee solidifies as it cools, but remains creamy like soft margarine. It has a unique nutty flavour for which there is no real substitute. In the days before refrigeration, making ghee was a way of keeping butter fresh in a hot climate. It will keep for several weeks at room temperature, and for many months if kept in the refrigerator.

Indian cooks, like cooks all over the world, have become conscious of the need to reduce the amount of saturated fat in our diet. Ghee is often now kept for special occasions, and oil is used for frying instead. Sunflower oil is a popular choice because it is low in cholesterol and can be reheated without ill effects. Corn oil is also suitable.

In India, the type of oil that is used in the local cuisine reflects what grows in the region. Coconut palms grow on the south and west coasts, and coconut oil is the standard oil used in coastal cusine. Mustard grows widely in eastern India, in the Punjab and Bengal. Dishes from those areas have the distinct pungent taste and aroma of mustard oil. Groundnut (peanut) oil is used in Gujarat and Maharashtra.

YOGURT

In India, yogurt is known as curd. It is eaten in one form or another at almost every meal. It can be used as a marinade for tenderizing meat or added to sauces to give them a thick and creamy texture, but it is most often used as a souring agent, particularly in the dairy-dominated north of India. Yogurt is the key ingredient in raitas, and also in the popular Indian drink, *lassi*.

Yogurt will curdle quickly when heated, and it should be used with care in recipes: add only a spoonful at a time, stir well and allow the sauce to simmer for 5 minutes before adding the next spoonful. In India, yogurt would be made at home on a daily basis, although ready-made natural (plain) yogurt is an acceptable substitute. Always choose live yogurt because of its beneficial effect on the digestive system.

PANEER

This traditional North Indian cheese is made from rich dairy milk. Paneer is white in colour and smooth-textured. It is usually available from Indian food stores and large supermarkets, but tofu and beancurd are adequate substitutes.

MAKING PANEER
Paneer is easy to make and adventurous cooks may prefer to make their own.
Bring 1 litre/1¾ pints/4 cups milk to the boil over a low heat. Add 30ml/2 tbsp lemon juice and stir gently until the milk thickens and begins to curdle. Strain the curdled milk through a sieve lined with muslin (cheesecloth). Set the curd aside for 1½–2 hours under a heavy weight to press it into a flat shape, about 1cm/½in thick. Cut into wedges and use as required. Paneer will keep for up to a week in the refrigerator.

JAGGERY

Also known as palm sugar, jaggery is dehydrated sugar cane juice. It is one of the by-products that are formed during the manufacture of sugar from sugar cane. Jaggery is sometimes used in Indian cookery in place of sugar. It has a distinct musky flavour of its own that is different from sugar. It goes well with lentils and tamarind. In Indian food stores, jaggery is sold in pieces that are cut off from larger blocks. It is mustard yellow or amber in colour, and sticky. You should look for the kind that crumbles easily and is not rock hard. Store the jaggery in an airtight container and use it within 6 months.

EDIBLE SILVER FOIL

Used as a garnish for sweets (candies), cakes, and savoury dishes such as biryanis and pulaos, edible silver foil is very popular in India. It is made by beating small balls of silver placed between sheets of tissue paper until they are wafer-thin.

COCONUT

Used in both sweet and savoury Indian dishes, fresh coconut is available from Indian food stores and supermarkets. If buying a whole coconut, make sure that it has no cracks and there is no mould on it, and shake it to make sure it is heavy with liquid. To break a coconut, hold it over the sink and hit it around the centre with the blunt side of a heavy cleaver or the claw end of a hammer. The coconut should crack and break into two halves. Prise off the flesh from the hard shell with a knife.

Desiccated (dry, unsweetened, shredded) coconut, and creamed coconut and coconut cream, which are all made from grated coconut, make acceptable substitutes in most recipes if fresh coconut is unavailable. Coconut milk is used in Indian curries to thicken and enrich sauces. In Western supermarkets, it is often sold in cans and powdered form, as a convenient alternative to the fresh fruit; the powdered milk has to be blended with hot water before use. Coconut milk can be made at home from desiccated coconut. Coconut cream is used to add fragrance and aroma to dishes, while creamed coconut adds richness.

MAKING COCONUT MILK

You can make as much milk as you like from this recipe by adapting the quantities accordingly. However, this method is much better suited to making large quantities.

1 Tip 225g/8oz/2⅔ cups desiccated (dry, unsweetened, shredded) coconut into a food processor and pour over 450ml/ ¾ pint/scant 2 cups boiling water. Process for 20–30 seconds, then cool.

2 Place a strainer lined with muslin (cheesecloth) over a bowl in the kitchen sink. Ladle some of the softened coconut into the muslin. Bring up the ends of the cloth and twist it over the sieve to extract the liquid.

3 Use the milk as directed in recipes. Coconut milk will keep for 1–2 days in the refrigerator, or it can be frozen for use on a later occasion.

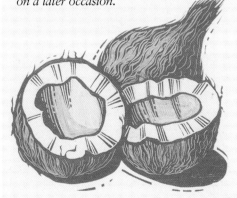

FRUITS

Indians love fruit, and nothing can beat a simple dessert of perfectly ripe, juicy fruit at the end of a meal. As well as eating the fruit raw, Indian cooks use them together with spices, chilli and coconut milk in all kinds of savoury dishes. The exotic fruits listed here are all native to India, and they are as diverse in their colour and shape as they are in their flavour.

BANANAS
The soft and creamy flesh of bananas is high in starch and is an excellent source of energy, as well as potassium and vitamins A and C. Indian cuisine uses several varieties of banana in vegetarian curries, including plantains, green bananas and sweet red-skinned bananas.

LEMONS AND LIMES
These citrus fruits are indigenous to India, although limes, which in India are confusingly called lemons, are the most commonly available of the two. Both fruits are frequently used as souring agents and are added to curries at the end of the cooking process; adding them any sooner would prevent any meat in the dish from becoming tender while it cooks.

MANGOES
Ripe, fresh mangoes grow in India throughout the summer months, and they come in many different shapes, sizes and colours. They are rich in vitamins, especially A and C, and are a good source of beta-carotene. They can be eaten raw, or used in sweet dishes. Unripe green mangoes, sold in the springtime, are used to make tangy pickles and chutneys, and they are added to curries as a souring agent for seasoning. Some Indian dishes require mango pulp. This is available ready-made in cans, but you can also make fresh pulp at home.

PAPAYAS
Also known as pawpaw, these pear-shaped fruits are native to tropical America and were not introduced to Asia until the 17th century. When ripe, the green skin turns a speckled yellow and the pulp is a vibrant orange-pink. The edible small black seeds taste peppery when dried. Peel off the skin using a sharp knife and eat the creamy flesh of the ripe fruit raw. The unripe green fruit is used in cooking: one of the unique properties of papaya is that it will help to tenderize meat.

PINEAPPLES
These distinctive-looking fruits have a sweet, golden and exceedingly juicy flesh. Unlike most other fruits, pineapples do not ripen after picking, although leaving a slightly unripe fruit at room temperature will help to reduce its acidity. Pineapples are cultivated in India, mainly in the south, and are gently cooked with spices to make palate-cleansing side dishes.

VEGETABLES

M any Indians are vegetarian, particularly those living in the state of Gujarat. Their cuisine specializes in a huge range of excellent vegetable dishes, using everything from cauliflower, potatoes and peas to the more exotic and unusual varieties, such as okra, bottle gourds and aubergines. In the meat-eating areas, too, vegetables are extensively and creatively used.

AUBERGINES/EGGPLANT
Available in many different varieties, the shiny deep purple aubergine is the most common and widely used type in Indian cooking. Aubergines have a strong flavour, and some have a slightly bitter taste. The cut flesh may be sprinkled with salt to extract these bitter juices.

BOTTLE GOURDS
One of the many bitter vegetables used in Indian cooking, this long, knobbly green vegetable comes from Kenya and has a strong, bitter taste. It is known to have properties that purify the blood. To prepare a gourd, peel the ridged skin with a sharp knife, scrape away and discard the seeds and chop the flesh.

CORN
Although it originated in South America, corn is now produced worldwide, and it is grown extensively in North India. It has a delicious sweet, juicy flavour, which is at its best just after picking.

OKRA
Also known as ladies' fingers, okra is a popular ingredient in Indian vegetable curries. They are also delicious fried and seasoned with spices. These small, green, five-sided pods are indigenous to India. They have a very distinctive flavour and a sticky, pulpy texture when they are cooked.

ONIONS
A versatile vegetable belonging to the allium family, onions have a strong pungent flavour and aroma. Globe onions are the most commonly used variety for Indian cooking. Spring onions (scallions), which have a milder taste, are also used in some dishes to add colour.

PEPPERS/BELL PEPPERS
Large, hollow pods belonging to the capsicum family, peppers are available in a variety of colours – red, green, yellow or orange. The red ones are the sweetest. Peppers are used in a wide variety of dishes, adding both colour and flavour.

SPINACH
Available all year round, this leafy green vegetable has a mild, delicate flavour. The leaves vary in size, and only the very large thick leaves need to be trimmed of their stalks. Spinach is a favourite vegetable in Indian cooking, and it is cooked in many different ways – with other vegetables, meat and with beans, peas and lentils.

TOMATOES
These are an essential ingredient in Indian cooking, and they are added to curries, chutneys and relishes. Salad tomatoes are quite adequate, but they are usually peeled before use. Use canned tomatoes in sauces and curries for their rich colour.

BEANS & LENTILS

These important ingredients play a key role in Indian cooking. Some are eaten whole, while others are cooked to a purée and enjoyed in soups or dhals. Beans and lentils are an excellent source of protein and fibre, and they are delicious combined with vegetables or meat. Beans and chickpeas should be soaked before cooking, while lentils can be cooked straight from their dried form.

BLACK-EYED BEANS

These beans are small and cream-coloured, with a black spot or "eye". When cooked, black-eyed beans (peas) have a tender, creamy texture and a mild, smoky flavour. They are used widely in Indian cooking, often being added to green vegetables, such as spinach, turnip or fenugreek greens, to make a nutritious vegetarian dish.

CHICKPEAS

These round, beige-coloured pulses have a strong, nutty flavour when cooked. As well as being used for curries, they are ground into a flour, called besan or gram flour, that is widely used in many Indian dishes, such as pakoras and bhajias. They are also added to Indian snacks. You can remove the skins from cooked chickpeas by rubbing the peas gently between your palms.

CHANA DHAL

This round, yellow split lentil is similar in appearance to the yellow split pea, which will make a good substitute. It is cooked in a variety of vegetable dishes and is also deep-fried and mixed with spices to make the Indian snack Bombay mix. Chana dhal can be used as a binding agent.

FLAGEOLET BEANS

These small oval beans can be either white or pale green in colour. They have a very mild, refreshing flavour.

GREEN LENTILS

Also known as continental lentils, green lentils are whole and still have their skins on. They have quite a strong flavour and retain their shape during cooking. These lentils are good for sprouting.

PREPARING AND COOKING BEANS AND PEAS

Beans and chickpeas should be boiled for at least 10 minutes before cooking to destroy the potentially harmful toxins that they contain.

Wash the beans or chickpeas under cold running water, then place in a large bowl of fresh cold water and leave to soak overnight. Next day, discard any pulses that float to the surface.

Drain the beans or chickpeas and rinse them again. Put in a large pan and cover with plenty of fresh cold water. Bring to the boil and boil rapidly for 10–15 minutes. Reduce the heat and simmer until tender. Drain and use as required.

HARICOT BEANS

These small, white oval beans come in several varieties. Known as navy beans in the United States, they are ideal for Indian cooking because they retain their shape and absorb the flavours of other ingredients.

KIDNEY BEANS

These dark red-brown kidney-shaped beans originated in Central and South America, but today they are grown all round the world. They have a strong nutty aroma, a slightly sweet flavour and a firm texture. Their nice, rich glossy colour lends itself to the dish in which they are cooked.

In India, these beans are particularly popular in the north-west region of the Punjab, where red kidney bean stew is a staple food. Dried kidney beans should always be soaked in water overnight and then thoroughly cooked to destroy any harmful toxins.

MUNG BEANS

These small, round green beans have a sweet nutty flavour and a creamy texture. They are indigenous to India, and are particularly popular in the north of the country, where they are served several times a week and in many different ways. Mung beans are particularly good for sprouting to produce beansprouts. Split mung beans are available as well as whole ones, and these are often cooked with rice.

RED SPLIT LENTILS

Red lentils grow in the colder climate of northern India. The whole lentils have a dark brown or greenish-black skin, and inside this is the reddish-orange- pulse with which we are more familiar. In India you can buy the lentils unhulled or with their hulls on. Hulled, split lentils are the most commonly used. They cook quickly and are excellent for vegetarian stews and soups.

TUVAR DHAL

A dull, orange-coloured split pea with a distinctive earthy flavour. Tuvar dhal is available plain and in an oily variety.

URID DHAL

This lentil is available split, either with the blackish hull retained or removed. It has quite a dry texture when cooked. In south India, it is also used as a seasoning. When the lentils are tossed into hot oil, they turn red and nutty. Anything stir-fried in the oil will pick up the nutty flavour and aroma.

SPROUTING BEANS AND PEAS

Most varieties of beans and peas are suitable for sprouting, and mung beans are particularly ideal.

Place 2 or 3 tablespoons of beans in a jar and cover with 4 times their volume of lukewarm water. Cover the jar with muslin (cheesecloth) and secure with an elastic band. Leave to soak overnight. Next day, drain off any excess water through the cloth top and rinse the beans well. Leave the jar in a warm place away from direct sunlight. Rinse the beans 2 or 3 times during the day. The sprouts will soon be ready to eat.

RICE & RICE PRODUCTS

This staple grain is served with almost every meal in some parts of India, so it is no surprise that the Indians have created a variety of ways of cooking it, each quite distinctive. Plain boiled rice is an everyday accompaniment; for special occasions and entertaining, it is often combined with other ingredients and served as a pulao or as fried rice.

There is no definitive way to cook plain rice, but whatever the recipe, the aim is to produce dry, separate-grained rice that is cooked through yet still retains some bite. The secret is the amount of water added: the rice must be able to absorb it all.

BASMATI RICE
Known as the prince of rices, basmati is the recommended rice for Indian curries – not only because it is easy to cook and produces an excellent finished result, but also because it has a cooling effect on hot and spicy curries. Basmati is a slender, long grain, milled rice grown in northern India, the Punjab, parts of Pakistan and in the foothills of the Himalayas. Its name means fragrant, and it has a distinctive and appealing aroma. After harvesting it is aged for a year, which gives it its characteristic flavour and light, fluffy texture. Basmati rice can be used in almost any savoury dish, particularly curries or pulaos, and it is the essential ingredient in biryanis.

BROWN BASMATI RICE
Like all types of brown rice, brown basmati is unrefined and has not had the bran removed. It has the same flavour as white basmati, with the texture typical of brown rice. In India, brown rice is often disliked and white rice is invariably used.

PATNA RICE
This rice takes its name from Patna in eastern India. At one time, most of the long grain rice sold in Europe came from Patna, and the term was used loosely to mean any long grain rice, whatever its origin. The custom still persists in parts of the United States, but elsewhere Patna is used to describe the specific variety of rice grown in the eastern state of Bihar. Patna rice is used in the same way as other long grain rices, and is suitable for use wherever plain boiled rice is called for.

TO FLAVOUR RICE
If you want to flavour the rice, the absorption method of cooking provides the perfect opportunity to do so. Lemon grass, curry leaves and whole spices can be added with the liquid, which can be water, stock, coconut milk or a mixture of these. This method of cooking rice is the basis of several pulao-style dishes, where onions, garlic and spices are fried before the rice and liquid are added.

Dehra Dun

This long grain, non-sticky Indian rice is not generally available outside India, except from specialist stores.

Puffed Rice

This popular snack, which looks something like popcorn, is sold at roadside stalls all over India. It is made by drying freshly harvested rice in its husk, then tossing the husks into a really hot karahi so that the grains pop out and puff up. A bag of puffed rice needs to be used up quickly once it has been opened because it loses its crispness when exposed to the air. Puffed rice is sometimes mixed with nuts or chutney for a savoury snack, or rolled in melted jaggery to make sweet balls.

Rice Noodles

These look rather like thick vermicelli, and they are made into dishes in much the same way. They are made by cooking rice flour in water to make a soft spongy dough. This dough is then pushed through a perforated press, which shapes the noodles. In India cooks make their own fresh noodles, but in the West dried ones are more readily available. Rice noodles are first stir-fried in ghee or oil, and then flavoured with sweetened coconut milk and cardamom, or with a mixture of spices.

Flaked Rice

Rice flakes are made by flattening cooked rice with rollers until the grains are wafer-thin. Depending on the weight of the rollers, medium or fine flakes are produced. Flakes are ideal for making a quick meal. They have a bland taste, but can be quickly fried and seasoned with chillies and other spices.

Cooking Basmati Rice

Always make sure you use a lid that fits tightly on your rice pan. If you do not have a tight-fitting lid, you can either wrap a dishtowel around the lid or put some foil between the lid and the pan to make a snug fit. Try not to remove the lid until the rice is cooked. (The advantage of using just a lid is that you can tell when the rice is ready because steam begins to escape, visibly and rapidly.)

As a rough guide, allow 75g/3oz/ scant ½ cup rice per person, and 1½-2 times its volume of water. Rinsing the rice before it is cooked is not essential, but it does help to remove excess starch.

If there is time, leave the rice to soak for 30 minutes in cold water before cooking. After soaking, drain the rice thoroughly.

1 *Put the rice into a bowl and cover with cold water. Swirl the grains between your fingers until the water becomes cloudy.*

2 *Allow the rice to settle, then tip the bowl and drain the water away. Repeat several times until the water runs clear.*

3 *Put the rinsed rice into a pan and pour in the measured water. Bring to the boil, then reduce the heat to the lowest setting.*

4 *Cover and cook until all the liquid has been absorbed. This can take up to 25 minutes, depending on the type of rice.*

5 *Remove the pan from the heat and leave to stand, covered with the lid or with a dishtowel, for 5 minutes. Steam holes will have appeared on the surface of the rice. If the grains are not completely tender, replace the cover tightly and leave the rice to stand for 5 minutes more.*

Breads

There are all kinds of breads in India, and they are an integral part of any meal. Chapatis and pooris go very well with most meat dishes, vegetables and pulses. Most traditional Indian breads are unleavened, that is, made without any raising agent, and are made with a finely ground wholemeal (whole-wheat) flour, known as chapati flour or atta.

Throughout India, breads vary from region to region, depending on whatever local ingredients are available. Some breads are cooked dry on a hot griddle, some are fried with a little oil, and others are deep-fried to make small savoury puffs. To enjoy Indian breads at their best, they should be made just before you are ready to serve the meal, so that they can be eaten hot.

Chapatis

The favourite bread of central and southern India is the chapati, a thin, flat, unleavened bread made from ground wholemeal flour. Chapatis are cooked on a hot *tava*, a concave-shaped Indian griddle. Chapatis have a light texture and fairly bland flavour, which makes them an ideal accompaniment for highly spiced curry dishes. Spices can be added to the flour to give more flavour.

Naan

Probably the best-known Indian bread outside India is naan, from the north of the country. Naan is made with plain (all-purpose) flour, yogurt and yeast; some contemporary recipes favour the use of a chemical raising agent such as bicarbonate of soda (baking soda) or self-raising (self-rising) flour as a leaven in place of yeast. Yogurt is important for the fermentation of the dough, and some naan are made entirely using a yogurt fermentation, which gives the bread its characteristic light, puffy texture and soft crust. The flavour comes partly from the soured yogurt and partly from the *tandoor*, which is the clay oven, sunk into the ground, in which the bread is traditionally cooked. The bread is flattened against the blisteringly hot walls of the oven and the pull of gravity produces the characteristic teardrop shape. As the dough scorches and puffs up, it produces a bread that is soft and crisp. Naan can be eaten with almost any meat or vegetable dish and is particularly nice with kababs. There are many types of flavoured naan sold commercially, including plain, coriander (cilantro) and garlic, and masala naan.

Rotis

There are many variations of chapatis, including rotis and dana rotis. Rotis are the everyday bread in most Punjabi villages. They are unleavened breads, made using chapati flour to which ghee, oil, celery seeds and/or fresh coriander are added. Rotis are rolled out thinly and cooked like chapatis.

PARATHAS

A paratha is similar to a chapati except that it contains ghee (clarified butter), which gives the bread a richer flavour and flakier texture, and a golden appearance. Parathas are much thicker than chapatis and they are shallow-fried. Plain parathas are often eaten for lunch, and they go well with most vegetable dishes and with kababs. They can be stuffed with various fillings, the most popular being spiced potato. Stuffed parathas are often served as a snack.

POORIS

Another popular variation on the chapati is the poori, which is a small, puffy bread. Balls of dough made from chapati flour are rolled out and deep-fried. Pooris are best eaten sizzling hot and are traditionally served for breakfast in India. They can be plain or flavoured with spices, such as cumin, turmeric and chilli powder, which are mixed into the dough. Pooris are often served with fish or vegetable curries.

POPPADUMS

These large, thin, crisp disks are now widely available outside India. They can be bought ready-cooked or ready-to-cook. In India, they are often served with vegetarian meals, and they are also good as a snack served with drinks. They are sold in markets and by street vendors, and they are available plain or flavoured with spices or seasoned with ground red or black pepper. The dough is generally made from dried beans, or split peas, but it can also be made from potatoes or sago. It is thinly rolled and left to dry in the sun. Poppadums are cooked either by deep-frying or by placing them under a hot grill (broiler).

FLOURS

Wholemeal (whole-wheat) flour is the most widely used in India, but flours are also made from rice, corn, chickpeas and the native Indian plants jowa and bajra.

Gram flour is made from ground chickpeas. It is also known as besan. Missi rotis, the spicy, unleavened breads from northern India, are made using gram flour or a mixture of wholemeal and gram flours.

Chapati flour is a very fine wholemeal flour that is normally found only in Indian food stores. It is also known as atta. As well as being used for making chapatis, it is also the type of flour used for making rotis and other flatbreads.

Jowar flour is made from the jowar plant, which grows over most of southern India. The flour, ground from the pretty pale yellow grains, is a creamy white colour. The flatbreads usually made from this flour, called bhakris, are roasted on a griddle and traditionally served with a coconut, garlic and red chilli chutney.

Bajra flour is made from the bajra plant, which grows along the west coast of India. It is a grey colour and has a strong nutty aroma and a distinct flavour. Bajra bread, or rotia, is cooked on a griddle.

Rice flour is white and powdery and is used as a thickening agent, or to make dough or batter.

Cornmeal is made from maize (corn) and is coarse, grainy and pale yellow in colour. It is used to make rotis, and may be added to batters.

SOUPS
& APPETIZERS

It is not traditional for an Indian meal to start with an appetizer, however there are plenty of dishes that lend themselves perfectly to fill this role. Many Indian snacks, such as deep-fried onion bhajias, samosas and koftas, are ideal for serving at the start of a meal. These spicy morsels will whet the appetite without the risk of filling you up before the main meal. Soups do not feature in original Indian cuisine, and the various broths included here have been developed since the time of the British Raj to cater for the tastes of Westerners.

SOUTH INDIAN PEPPER WATER

This is a highly soothing broth for winter evenings is also known as Mulla-ga-tani. It can be served with the whole spices still in the soup or strained first and then reheated if you so wish. The amount of lemon juice may be adjusted to taste, but this dish should be distinctly sour, so don't be too cautious.

SERVES 4–6

INGREDIENTS
30ml/2 tbsp vegetable oil
2.5ml/½ tsp ground black pepper
5ml/1 tsp cumin seeds
2.5ml/½ tsp mustard seeds
1.5ml/¼ tsp asafoetida
2 dried red chillies
4–6 curry leaves
2.5ml/½ tsp ground turmeric
2 garlic cloves, crushed
300ml/½ pint/1¼ cups tomato juice
juice of 2 lemons
120ml/4fl oz/½ cup water
salt
chopped fresh coriander (cilantro), to garnish (optional)

1   In a large pan, heat the vegetable oil, then add the ground black pepper, cumin seeds, mustard seeds, asafoetida, dried red chillies, curry leaves, turmeric and crushed garlic. Fry, stirring continuously, until the chillies are nearly black and the garlic has turned golden brown.

2   Lower the heat and add the tomato juice, most of the lemon juice and the water to the pan. Season with salt to taste. Bring the mixture to the boil, then simmer gently for about 10 minutes. Taste the soup and add more lemon juice if you wish. Ladle the soup into warmed individual soup bowls and serve immediately, sprinkled with chopped fresh coriander, if using.

CHICKEN MULLIGATAWNY

Based on the original Pepper Water, this classic spicy soup was created by non-vegetarian chefs during the British Raj. The recipe was then imported to the West, and today is featured on many restaurant menus where it is often simply called Mulligatawny Soup, though it does not always contain chicken.

SERVES 4–6

INGREDIENTS
900g/2lbs/6½ cups skinned, boned and cubed chicken
600ml/1 pint/2½ cups water
6 cardamom pods
1 cinnamon stick, 5cm/2in long
4–6 curry leaves
15ml/1 tbsp ground coriander
5ml/1 tsp ground cumin
2.5ml/½ tsp ground turmeric
3 garlic cloves, crushed
12 whole black peppercorns
4 cloves
1 onion, finely chopped
115g/4oz/½ cup creamed coconut
salt
juice of 2 lemons
deep-fried onions, to garnish

1 Place the cubed chicken in a large pan with the water and cook until the chicken is tender. Skim the surface, then remove the chicken with a slotted spoon, place in a dish and keep warm in a low oven.

2 Reheat the water in the pan. Add all the remaining ingredients, except the chicken and the deep-fried onions and season. Simmer for 10–15 minutes, then strain and return the chicken to the soup. Reheat the soup, add more salt if necessary and serve in warmed soup bowls, garnished with the deep-fried onions.

CHICKEN & ALMOND SOUP

This unusual soup makes an excellent appetizer and, when served with naan bread, will make a satisfying lunch or supper dish.

SERVES 4

INGREDIENTS
75g/3oz/6 tbsp unsalted (sweet) butter
1 leek, chopped
2.5ml/½ tsp fresh root ginger
75g/3oz/1 cup ground almonds
5ml/1 tsp salt
2.5ml/½ tsp crushed black peppercorns
1 fresh green chilli, chopped
1 carrot, sliced
50g/2oz/½ cup frozen peas
115g/4oz/¾ cup skinned, boned and cubed chicken
15ml/1 tbsp chopped fresh coriander (cilantro)
450ml/¾ pint/scant 2 cups water
250ml/8fl oz/1 cup single (light) cream
4 coriander (cilantro) sprigs, to garnish

1 Melt the butter in a large karahi or deep round-based frying pan, and sauté the leek with the ginger until soft. Lower the heat and add the ground almonds, salt, peppercorns, chilli, carrot, peas and chicken. Fry for about 10 minutes or until the chicken is cooked, stirring constantly. Add the coriander.

2 Remove the pan from the heat and allow the chicken and vegetables to cool slightly. Transfer the mixture to a food processor or blender and process for about 1½ minutes. Pour in the water and blend for a further 30 seconds.

3 Pour the mixture back into the pan and bring to the boil, stirring occasionally. Lower the heat and gradually stir in the cream. Cook gently for a further 2 minutes, stirring, then serve in warmed bowls, garnished with coriander.

YOGURT SOUP

*Some communities in India add sugar to this tasty, hot soup. Onion bhajias can
be added to the soup, transforming it into a delicious main dish.*

SERVES 4–6

INGREDIENTS
450ml/¾ pint/scant 2 cups natural (plain) yogurt, beaten
25g/1oz/¼ cup gram flour (besan)
2.5ml/½ tsp chilli powder
2.5ml/½ tsp ground turmeric
salt
2–3 fresh green chillies, finely chopped
60ml/4 tbsp vegetable oil
4 dried red chillies
5ml/1 tsp cumin seeds
3 garlic cloves, crushed
5cm/2in piece fresh root ginger, crushed
3–4 curry leaves
15ml/1 tbsp chopped fresh coriander (cilantro)

1 In a bowl, mix together the yogurt, gram flour, chilli powder, turmeric and salt to taste, and then pass through a strainer into a heavy pan. Add the fresh green chillies and cook gently over a low heat for about 10 minutes, stirring occasionally. Be careful not to let the soup boil.

2 Heat the oil in a frying pan and fry the dried red chillies and cumin seeds with the garlic and ginger, stirring frequently, until the chillies turn black. Add the curry leaves and fresh coriander to the pan and stir to combine.

3 Pour most of the oil and the spices over the yogurt soup, reserving the remainder, cover the soup and leave to rest for 5 minutes off the heat. Mix well and gently reheat for a further 5 minutes. Serve hot in warmed individual soup bowls, drizzled with the remaining oil and spices.

Fragrant Beetroot Soup with Spiced Lamb Kubbeh

This tangy soup, from Cochin in the state of Kerala in south-west India, is served with spicy, lamb-filled dumplings and a dollop of fragrant green herb paste.

Serves 4–6

Ingredients
15ml/1 tbsp vegetable oil
½ onion, finely chopped
6 garlic cloves
1 carrot, diced
1 courgette (zucchini), diced
½ celery stick, diced (optional)
4–5 cardamom pods
2.5ml/½ tsp curry powder
4 vacuum-packed cooked, not pickled, beetroot (beets), finely diced and juice reserved
1 litre/1¾ pints/4 cups vegetable stock
400g/14oz can tomatoes, chopped
45–60ml/3–4 tbsp chopped fresh coriander (cilantro) leaves
2 bay leaves
15ml/1 tbsp sugar
salt and ground black pepper
15–30ml/1–2 tbsp white wine vinegar, to serve

For the kubbeh
2 large pinches saffron
15ml/1 tbsp hot water
15ml/1 tbsp vegetable oil
1 large onion, chopped
250g/9oz lean minced (ground) lamb
5ml/1 tsp vinegar
½ bunch fresh mint, chopped
115g/4oz/1 cup plain (all-purpose) flour, plus extra for dusting
2–3 pinches salt
2.5–5ml/½–1 tsp ground turmeric
45–60ml/3–4 tbsp cold water

FOR THE GINGER AND CORIANDER PASTE
4 garlic cloves, chopped
15–25ml/1–1½ tbsp chopped fresh root ginger
½–4 fresh mild chillies, depending on type, for mild piquancy
½ large bunch fresh coriander (cilantro)
30ml/2 tbsp white wine vinegar
extra virgin olive oil

1 To make the kubbeh filling, place the saffron and hot water in a small bowl and leave to infuse. Meanwhile, heat the oil in a pan, and fry the onion until softened. Put the onion and saffron water in a food processor and blend. Add the lamb, season and blend again. Add the vinegar and mint, then chill.

2 To make the kubbeh dough, put the flour, salt and ground turmeric in a food processor, then slowly add the cold water, processing, until the mixture forms a sticky dough. Knead the dough on a floured surface for 5 minutes, seal in a plastic bag and leave to stand for about 30 minutes.

3 Divide the dough into 12–15 pieces and then roll each piece into a ball. Using a pasta machine or rolling pin, roll each ball into very thin rounds.

4 Lay the rounds on a well-floured surface, place a spoonful of filling in the middle of each. Dampen the edges of the dough, bring them together and seal. Set aside on a floured surface.

5 To make the ginger and coriander paste, put the garlic, ginger and chillies in a food processor and process briefly. Add the coriander, vinegar, a little oil and salt and process to a purée, adding more oil if needed. Set aside.

6 To make the soup, heat the oil in a large, heavy pan, add the onion and fry for about 10 minutes, or until softened but not browned. Add half the garlic, the carrot, courgette, celery, if using, cardamom pods and curry powder, and cook for 2–3 minutes, stirring occasionally.

7 Add 3 of the diced beetroot, the vegetable stock, chopped tomatoes, coriander, bay leaves and sugar to the pan. Bring the mixture to the boil, then reduce the heat and simmer the soup gently for about 20 minutes.

8 Add the remaining beetroot and the beetroot juice to the soup. Season with salt and ground black pepper to taste and set aside until ready to serve.

9 To serve, reheat the soup and poach the dumplings in a large pan of salted gently boiling water for about 4 minutes. Using a slotted spoon, remove each dumpling from the water and place on a plate.

10 Ladle the soup into individual bowls, adding a dash of vinegar to each bowl. Place 2–3 dumplings in each bowl and top with a small spoonful of the ginger and coriander paste. Serve immediately.

COOK'S TIP
If you do not use all the ginger and coriander paste, serve any leftovers as a relish to accompany other Indian dishes. It can be stored in the refrigerator in an airtight container for up to one week.

CRISP FRIED AUBERGINE

The vegetarian community in Bengal will happily eat begun bhaja, *fried aubergine, and a lentil dish with rice for a main meal, but they also make an ideal appetizer served with chutney. Choose the large variety of aubergine with an unblemished, glossy skin. There is no need to salt the aubergine before cooking it.*

SERVES 4

INGREDIENTS
50g/2oz/½ cup gram flour (besan)
15ml/1tbsp semolina or ground rice
2.5ml/½ tsp onion seeds
5ml/1 tsp cumin seeds
2.5ml/½ tsp fennel seeds or aniseeds
2.5–5ml/½–1 tsp hot chilli powder
2.5ml/½ tsp salt, or to taste
1 large aubergine (eggplant)
vegetable oil, for deep-frying

1 Sift the gram flour into a large mixing bowl and mix in the semolina or ground rice, onion seeds, cumin seeds, fennel seeds or aniseeds, chilli powder and salt.

2 Halve the aubergine lengthways and cut each half into 5mm/¼in thick slices. Rinse the slices and shake off the excess water, but do not pat dry. With some of the water still clinging to the slices, add them to the spiced gram flour mixture. Toss until they are evenly coated with the mixture. Use a spoon if necessary to ensure that all the flour is used up.

3 Heat the oil in a deep-fat fryer or other suitable pan over a medium-high heat. If you have a cook's thermometer, check that the oil has reached 190°C/375°F. Alternatively, drop a small piece of day-old bread into the oil. If it floats immediately, then the oil has reached the right temperature.

4 Fry the spice-coated aubergine slices in a single layer. Avoid overcrowding the pan as this will lower the oil temperature, resulting in a soggy texture. Fry until the aubergines are crisp and well browned on both sides. Remove with a slotted spoon, drain on kitchen paper and serve.

ONION BHAJIAS

Bhajias are a classic snack of India and are often served as appetizers in the West. The same batter may be used with a variety of other vegetables, such as cauliflower and broccoli florets, sliced (bell) peppers or fennel bulbs.

MAKES 20–25

INGREDIENTS
225g/8oz/2 cups gram flour (besan)
2.5ml/½ tsp chilli powder
5ml/1 tsp ground turmeric
5ml/1 tsp baking powder
1.5ml/¼ tsp asafoetida
salt
2.5ml/½ tsp each, nigella, fennel, cumin and onion seeds,
   coarsely crushed
2 large onions, finely sliced
2 green chillies, finely chopped
50g/2oz/2 cups fresh coriander (cilantro), chopped
cold water, to mix
vegetable oil, for deep-frying

1 In a bowl, mix together the gram flour, chilli powder, turmeric, baking powder, asafoetida and salt to taste. Sift into a large mixing bowl.

2 Add the coarsely crushed seeds, onion, green chillies and fresh coriander to the bowl and toss together until well combined. Very gradually mix in enough cold water to make a thick batter.

3 Heat enough oil in a karahi or wok for deep-frying. Drop spoonfuls of the bhajias mixture into the hot oil and fry until golden brown. Leave enough space to turn the bhajias. As they are cooked, remove the bhajias with a slotted spoon. Drain well on kitchen paper and serve hot.

SAMOSAS

The origin of samosas can be attributed to the western states of Maharashtra and Gujarat, which are famous for these fabulous crispy pastries with spiced vegetable fillings. The original samosa is vegetarian, but meat fillings are also used.

MAKES 30

INGREDIENTS
1 packet spring roll pastry, thawed and wrapped in a damp dishtowel
vegetable oil, for deep-frying
coriander (cilantro) chutney, to serve

FOR THE FILLING
3 large potatoes, boiled and mashed
75g/3oz/¾ cup frozen peas, thawed and cooked
50g/2oz/⅓ cup canned corn, drained
5ml/1 tsp ground coriander
5ml/1 tsp ground cumin
5ml/1 tsp amchur (dried mango powder)
1 small red onion, finely chopped
2 fresh green chillies, finely chopped
30ml/2 tbsp each fresh coriander (cilantro) and mint leaves, chopped
juice of 1 lemon, to taste
salt

1 Put the filling ingredients in a large mixing bowl and toss together until combined. Adjust the seasoning with salt and lemon juice, if necessary. Working with one strip of pastry at a time, place 15ml/1 tbsp of the filling mixture at one end of the strip and fold the pastry diagonally to form a triangular-shaped parcel. Repeat with the other strips.

2 Heat enough oil in a wok or karahi for deep-frying and fry the samosas in small batches until they are golden. Serve hot with coriander chutney for dipping.

Indian Potato Pancakes

Although called a pancake, these crispy spiced cakes are more like a bhajia, although they are shallow-fried instead of being deep-fried. They make an ideal appetizer.

MAKES 10

INGREDIENTS
300g/11oz potatoes, peeled and grated
25ml/1½ tsp garam masala or curry powder
4 spring onions (scallions), finely chopped
1 large egg white, lightly beaten
30ml/2 tbsp vegetable oil
salt and ground black pepper
chutney and relishes, to serve

1 Using your hands, squeeze the excess liquid from the grated potatoes and pat dry with kitchen paper. Place the dry, grated potatoes in a bowl and add the garam masala or curry powder, spring onions and egg white and season with salt and pepper. Stir well to combine.

2 Heat a non-stick frying pan over a medium heat and add the vegetable oil. Drop tablespoonfuls of the potato mixture on to the pan and flatten out with the back of a spoon (you will need to cook the pancakes in two batches).

3 Cook the pancakes for a few minutes, then flip them over with a wooden spatula. Cook the second side for a further 3 minutes. Carefully lift the pancakes from the pan and drain on kitchen paper. Serve with chutney and relishes.

COOK'S TIPS
• *Many food processors have a grating blade that will make quick work of grating the potatoes. Make sure you use a grater with coarse blade.*
• *Don't grate the potatoes too soon before use as the flesh will quickly turn brown.*

POTATO CAKES WITH STUFFING

Only a few communities in India make these unusual potato cakes known as petis.
They can also be served as a main meal with a tomato salad.

MAKES 8–10

INGREDIENTS
15ml/1 tbsp vegetable oil
1 large onion, finely chopped
2 cloves garlic, finely crushed
5cm/2in piece fresh root ginger, finely crushed
5ml/1 tsp ground coriander
5ml/1 tsp ground cumin
2 fresh green chillies, finely chopped
30ml/2 tbsp each, chopped fresh coriander (cilantro) and mint
225g/8oz/2 cups lean minced (ground) beef or lamb
50g/2oz/½ cup frozen peas, thawed
juice of 1 lemon
900g/2lb potatoes, boiled and mashed
2 eggs, beaten
breadcrumbs, for coating
vegetable oil, for shallow-frying
salt
salad leaves and lemon wedges, to serve

1 Heat the oil and add the onion, garlic, ginger, coriander, cumin, chillies and herbs. Fry until the onion is translucent. Add the meat and peas and fry until the meat is cooked, then add lemon juice and salt to taste.

2 Divide the mashed potato into 8–10 portions, then press each one flat. Place a spoonful of the meat in the centre of each and gather the sides together to enclose the filling. Flatten, then dip in beaten egg and coat in breadcrumbs. Chill for 1 hour.

3 Heat the oil in a frying pan and shallow-fry the cakes until golden brown all over. Serve on a bed of salad leaves with lemon wedges for squeezing over.

SPLIT PEA FRITTERS

These delicious spicy fritters are called piaju. *Serve them with a wedge of lemon for squeezing over and a spoonful of hot, fragrant chutney.*

SERVES 6

INGREDIENTS
250g/9oz/generous1 cup yellow split peas or red lentils, soaked overnight
3–5 garlic cloves, chopped
30ml/2 tbsp roughly chopped fresh root ginger
120ml/8 tbsp chopped fresh coriander (cilantro) leaves
2.5–5ml/½–1 tsp ground cumin
1.5–2.5ml/¼–½ tsp ground turmeric
large pinch of cayenne pepper or ½–1 fresh green chilli, chopped
120ml/8 tbsp gram (besan) flour, plus extra
5ml/1 tsp baking powder
30ml/2 tbsp couscous, plus extra
2 large or 3 small onions, chopped
vegetable oil, for frying
salt and ground black pepper
lemon wedges, to serve

> ### VARIATION
> *Use red lentils in place of the split peas, if you like.*
> *Soak them overnight, then continue as above.*

1 Drain the split peas in a colander, reserving a little of the soaking water. Put the garlic and ginger in a food processor or blender and process until finely minced. Add the drained split peas, 15–30ml/1–2 tbsp of the reserved soaking water and the chopped coriander, and process to form a purée.

2 Add the cumin, turmeric, cayenne pepper or green chilli, 2.5ml/½ tsp salt, 2.5ml/½ tsp pepper, the gram flour, baking powder and couscous to the mixture and stir together. The mixture should form a thick paste. If it seems too thick, add a spoonful of soaking water and if it is too watery, add a little more flour or couscous. Add the chopped onions and stir to combine.

3 Heat the vegetable oil in a wide, deep frying pan, to a depth of about 5cm/ 2in, until it is hot enough to brown a cube of bread in 30 seconds. Using 2 tablespoons, form the mixture into two-bitesize balls and slip each one gently into the hot oil. Cook until golden brown on the underside then turn and cook the second side until golden brown.

4 Remove the fritters from the pan with a slotted spoon and drain well on kitchen paper. Transfer to a baking sheet and keep warm in the oven while you cook the remaining mixture in the same way. Serve the fritters hot or at room temperature with the lemon wedges for squeezing over.

SPICY CHICKEN KOFTAS WITH PANEER

This rather unusual appetizer, combining chicken with fresh paneer cheese, looks most elegant when served in small individual karahis.

SERVES 6

INGREDIENTS

450g/1lb/3¼ cups cubed chicken
5ml/1 tsp crushed garlic
5ml/1 tsp grated fresh root ginger
7.5ml/1½ tsp ground coriander
7.5ml/1½ tsp chilli powder
2.5ml/½ tsp ground fenugreek
1.5ml/¼ tsp ground turmeric
5ml/1 tsp salt
30ml/2 tbsp chopped fresh coriander (cilantro)
2 fresh green chillies, chopped
600ml/1 pint/2½ cups water
corn oil, for frying
mint sprigs, to garnish
1 dried red chilli, crushed, to garnish (optional)

FOR THE PANEER MIXTURE

1 onion, sliced
1 red (bell) pepper, seeded and cut into strips
1 green (bell) pepper, seeded and cut into strips
175g/6oz paneer, cubed
175g/6oz/1 cup cooked corn, or canned corn, drained

1 To make the kofta, put the chicken, garlic, ginger, coriander, chilli powder, fenugreek, turmeric, salt, coriander, chillies and water into a pan. Bring to the boil slowly, over a medium heat, and cook until the liquid has evaporated.

2 Remove the mixture from the heat and allow to cool slightly. Put the cooled mixture into a food processor or blender and process for about 2 minutes, stopping once or twice to loosen the mixture with a spoon.

3 Scrape the kofta mixture into a large mixing bowl. Taking a little of the mixture at a time, carefully shape it into small balls using your hands. You should be able to make about 12 koftas.

4 Heat the corn oil in a karahi or deep round-based frying pan over a high heat. Reduce the heat slightly and gently add the koftas to the oil. Using a slotted spoon, move the koftas around to ensure that they cook evenly. When the koftas are lightly browned, remove from the pan with a slotted spoon and drain well on kitchen paper. Set to one side.

5 Make the paneer mixture. Heat the oil still remaining in the karahi, and flash fry the onion, peppers, paneer and corn for 3 minutes over a high heat.

6 Divide the paneer mixture among six individual karahis. Add two koftas to each dish, and garnish with mint sprigs and crushed red chilli, if using.

KOFTAS

Serve these tasty meatballs piping hot with naan bread, raita and a tomato salad for a substantial appetizer, or simply provide some fresh coriander relish as an accompaniment for a lighter start to a meal.

MAKES 20–25

INGREDIENTS
450g/1lb lean minced (ground) beef or lamb
30ml/2 tbsp grated fresh root ginger
30ml/2 tbsp crushed garlic
4 fresh green chillies, finely chopped
1 small onion, finely chopped
1 egg
2.5ml/½ tsp ground turmeric
5ml/1 tsp garam masala
50g/2oz/2 cups fresh coriander (cilantro), chopped
4–6 fresh mint leaves, chopped, or 2.5ml/½ tsp mint sauce
175g/6oz potato, peeled
salt
vegetable oil, for deep-frying

1 Place the beef or lamb in a large bowl and add the ginger, garlic, chillies, onion, egg, turmeric, garam masala, coriander and mint or mint sauce. Grate the potato into the bowl, and season with salt. Knead together to form a soft dough. Shape the mixture into portions the size of golf balls. Set aside on a plate and leave to rest for about 25 minutes.

2 In a karahi or wok, heat the oil to medium-hot and fry the koftas in small batches until they are golden brown, turning so they cook evenly. Remove the koftas from the pan with a slotted spoon, drain well on kitchen paper and serve hot.

SPICY OMELETTE

This irresistible omelette, which is Parsee in origin, is now popular in western India. The flavours of Parsee food appeal to both Eastern and Western palates. Serve this omelette with crisp green salad leaves.

SERVES 4–6

INGREDIENTS
30ml/2 tbsp vegetable oil
1 onion, finely chopped
2.5ml/½ tsp ground cumin
1 garlic clove, crushed
1–2 fresh green chillies, finely chopped
a few coriander (cilantro) sprigs, chopped, plus extra,
* to garnish*
1 firm tomato, chopped
1 small potato, cubed and boiled
25g/1oz/¼ cup cooked peas
25g/1oz/¼ cup cooked corn, or canned corn, drained
2 eggs, beaten
25g/1oz/¼ cup grated Cheddar cheese
salt and ground black pepper

1 Heat the vegetable oil in a wok, karahi or large pan, then add the onion, cumin, garlic, chillies, coriander, tomato, potato, peas and corn and fry until they are well blended but the potato and tomato are still firm. Season to taste.

2 Increase the heat and pour the beaten eggs into the pan. Reduce the heat, cover and cook until the underside is brown. Turn the omelette over and sprinkle with the grated cheese. Place under a hot grill (broiler) and cook until the egg sets and the cheese has melted. Garnish with sprigs of coriander.

EGGS BAKED ON CHIPSTICKS

This is an unusual and delicious way of combining eggs with potato sticks. The potato sticks are cooked with spices to form a pancake. Eggs are then placed on top of the potato pancake and gently cooked. Serve with chapatis and salad.

SERVES 4–6

INGREDIENTS
225g/8oz salted chipsticks
2 fresh green chillies, finely chopped
a few coriander (cilantro) sprigs, chopped
1.5ml/¼ tsp ground turmeric
60ml/4 tbsp vegetable oil
75ml/5 tbsp water
6 eggs
3 spring onions (scallions), finely chopped
salt and ground black pepper

1 In a bowl, combine the chipsticks, chopped chillies, coriander and turmeric. Heat 30ml/2 tbsp of the vegetable oil in a heavy frying pan. Add the chipstick mixture and water. Cook until the chipsticks turn soft, and then crisp.

2 Place a dinner plate over the frying pan and hold in place as you turn the pan over and carefully transfer the chipstick pancake on to the plate. Heat the remaining vegetable oil in the pan and carefully slide the pancake back into the frying pan to brown the other side.

3 Gently break the eggs over the pancake, cover the frying pan and allow the eggs to set over a low heat. Season well and sprinkle with spring onions. Cook until the base is crisp. Serve hot.

COOK'S TIP
Make sure you use plain salted chipsticks for this dish. Flavoured varieties will give a peculiar result.

CHICKEN TIKKA

This chicken dish is an extremely popular Indian appetizer and is quick and easy to prepare and cook. This dish can also be served as a main course for four with extra salad as part of the garnish.

SERVES 6

INGREDIENTS
450g/1lb/3¼ cups cubed chicken
5ml/1 tsp grated fresh root ginger
5ml/1 tsp crushed garlic
5ml/1 tsp chilli powder
1.5ml/¼ tsp ground turmeric
5ml/1 tsp salt
150ml/¼ pint/⅔ cup natural (plain) low-fat yogurt
60ml/4 tbsp lemon juice
15ml/1 tbsp chopped fresh coriander (cilantro)
15ml/1 tbsp vegetable oil

FOR THE GARNISH
mixed salad
1 small onion, cut into rings
fresh coriander (cilantro) leaves
lime wedges

1 In a large bowl, mix together the cubed chicken, fresh root ginger, garlic, chilli powder, turmeric, salt, yogurt, lemon juice and fresh coriander and leave to marinate for at least 2 hours.

2 Place the marinated chicken mixture in a grill (broiling) pan or in a flameproof dish lined with foil and baste with the vegetable oil.

3 Preheat the grill (broiler) to medium. Grill (broil) the chicken for 15 minutes, or until it is cooked through, turning and basting 2–3 times. Serve immediately with mixed salad and onion rings with coriander scattered over and lime wedges.

Tandoori Masala Spring Lamb Chops

These spicy lean and trimmed lamb chops are marinated for three hours and then cooked in the oven using very little cooking oil. They make an excellent appetizer, served with a salad, and would also serve three as a main course with a rice cooked with spices as an accompaniment.

SERVES 6

INGREDIENTS
6 spring lamb chops
30ml/2 tbsp natural (plain) low-fat yogurt
15ml/1 tbsp tomato purée (paste)
10ml/2 tsp ground coriander
5ml/1 tsp grated fresh root ginger
5ml/1 tsp crushed garlic
5ml/1 tsp chilli powder
a few drops of red food colouring (optional)
5ml/1 tsp salt
15ml/1 tbsp corn oil
45ml/3 tbsp lemon juice
oil, for basting

TO GARNISH
lettuce leaves (optional)
1 small onion, sliced
fresh coriander (cilantro) sprigs
lime wedges

> VARIATION
> *If spring lamb chops are not available, choose lamb cutlets instead and trim and cook in the same way.*

1 Rinse the chops and pat dry with kitchen paper. Trim off any fat. In a bowl, mix together the yogurt, tomato purée, ground coriander, ginger, garlic, chilli powder, food colouring, if using, salt, oil and lemon juice.

2 Rub the yogurt mixture over the chops, using your hands, and leave to marinate for at least 3 hours. Preheat the oven to 240°C/475°F/Gas 9.

3 Place the marinated chops in an ovenproof dish. Using a brush, baste the chops with about 5ml/1 tsp oil and cook in the preheated oven for 15 minutes. Lower the heat to 150°C/350°F/Gas 4 and cook for a further 10–15 minutes.

4 Check to see that the chops are cooked and serve immediately on a bed of lettuce leaves, if using, and garnish with sliced onion and fresh coriander sprigs with lime wedges for squeezing over.

VEGETABLE & FRUIT CURRIES

Spiced vegetable dishes feature prominently in Indian cuisine. Some communities, such as the Gujarati, are strict vegetarians, but all Indians enjoy a wide variety of non-meat dishes using either vegetables or fruit combined with various spice mixtures – some subtle and some quite fiery. Humble vegetables, such as potatoes, are transformed into deeply flavoured delicacies, and other more unusual produce, including bitter melons and okra, provide added interest to any meal. Some of the dishes featured here may be served simply with different breads and perhaps a freshly made relish and yogurt dip. Others may be included in a more elaborate meal and served with meat, poultry or fish curries along with rice and other accompaniments.

Courgettes in Spiced Tomato Sauce

The subtle use of spices in a simple tomato sauce, using canned tomatoes, transforms the mild-flavoured courgette into a wonderfully tasty vegetable dish.

SERVES 4

INGREDIENTS
675g/1½lb courgettes (zucchini)
45ml/3 tbsp vegetable oil
2.5ml/½ tsp cumin seeds
2.5ml/½ tsp mustard seeds
1 onion, thinly sliced
2 garlic cloves, crushed
1.5ml/¼ tsp ground turmeric
1.5ml/¼ tsp chilli powder
5ml/1 tsp ground coriander
5ml/1 tsp ground cumin
2.5ml/½ tsp salt
15ml/1 tbsp tomato purée (paste)
400g/14oz can chopped tomatoes
150ml/¼ pint/⅔ cup water
15ml/1 tbsp chopped fresh coriander (cilantro)
5ml/1 tsp garam masala

> COOK'S TIP
> *In India, tender marrow (large zucchini) would be used for this recipe as courgettes are not grown there. Try this recipe with a young marrow in the summer. It will also work well with winter squashes, such as butternut and acorn.*

1 Using a sharp knife, trim the ends from the courgettes then cut them into 1cm/ ½in thick slices. Set aside until required.

2 Heat the vegetable oil in a wok, karahi or large pan. Fry the cumin and mustard seeds for 2 minutes until they begin to splutter, then add the onion and crushed garlic and fry for about 5–6 minutes.

3 Add the ground turmeric, chilli powder, coriander, cumin and salt to the pan and fry for 2–3 minutes, stirring frequently.

4 Add the sliced courgettes to the pan, and cook for about 5 minutes. Add the tomato purée and chopped tomatoes and stir to combine.

5 Add the water to the tomato mixture, then cover the pan and simmer for about 10 minutes until the sauce thickens. Stir in the fresh coriander and garam masala, then cook for about 5 minutes, or until the courgettes are tender. Serve as an accompaniment to any meat, poultry or fish dish.

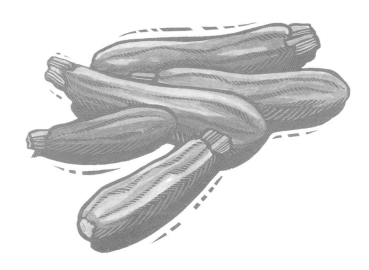

SPICY BITTER MELONS

Bitter melons are widely used in Indian cooking, both on their own and with other vegetables. Their bitter tang adds a wonderful accent to this dish.

SERVES 4

INGREDIENTS
675g/1½lb bitter melons
60ml/4 tbsp oil
2.5ml/½ tsp cumin seeds
6 spring onions (scallions), finely chopped
5 tomatoes, finely chopped
2.5cm/1in piece fresh root ginger, finely chopped
2 garlic cloves, crushed
2 fresh green chillies, finely chopped
2.5ml/½ tsp salt
2.5ml/½ tsp cayenne pepper
5ml/1 tsp ground coriander
5ml/1 tsp ground cumin
25g/1oz/3 tbsp peanuts, crushed
40g/1½oz/3 tbsp brown sugar
15ml/1 tbsp gram flour (besan)
coriander (cilantro) sprigs, to garnish

1 Bring a large pan of lightly salted water to the boil. Peel the bitter melons using a small sharp knife and halve them. Discard the seeds. Cut into 2cm/¾in pieces, then boil for 10–15 minutes, or until tender. Drain well and set aside.

2 Heat the oil in a large pan and fry the cumin seeds for 2 minutes, until they begin to splutter. Add the spring onions and fry for about 3 minutes. Add the tomatoes, ginger, garlic and chillies and cook for 5 minutes. Add the salt, remaining spices, the peanuts and sugar and cook for 2–3 minutes more.

3 Add the bitter melons and mix well. Sprinkle over the gram flour. Cover and simmer over a low heat for 5–8 minutes or until all of the gram flour has been absorbed into the sauce. Serve garnished with coriander sprigs.

CUCUMBER CURRY

This unusual curry makes a pleasant accompaniment to fish dishes when served
hot and may also be served cold for a refreshing alternative.

SERVES 4–6

INGREDIENTS
115g/4oz/½ cup creamed coconut
2.5ml/½ tsp ground turmeric
salt
5ml/1 tsp sugar
1 large cucumber, cut into small pieces
1 large red (bell) pepper, cut into small pieces
50g/2oz/½ cup salted peanuts, coarsely crushed
60ml/4 tbsp vegetable oil
2 dried red chillies
5ml/1 tsp cumin seeds
5ml/1 tsp mustard seeds
4–6 curry leaves
4 garlic cloves, crushed
a few whole salted peanuts, to garnish

1 Bring 120ml/4fl oz/ ½ cup water to the boil in a heavy pan and add the creamed
coconut, turmeric, salt and sugar. Simmer until smooth and thick, then add the
cucumber, red pepper and crushed peanuts to the sauce and simmer for 5 minutes.
Transfer to a heatproof serving dish and keep warm.

2 Heat the oil in a frying pan. Fry the chillies and cumin with the mustard seeds
until they start to pop. Reduce the heat, add the curry leaves and garlic and
cook briefly. Pour over the cucumber and stir. Garnish with peanuts and serve hot.

VARIATION
If you prefer, use 2 courgettes (zucchini) in place of
the cucumber. The delicate flavour of the vegetables,
coconut and spices go together well.

Stuffed Aubergines in Seasoned Tamarind Juice

The traditional way of cooking with tamarind is in a terracotta dish, which brings out the full fruity tartness of the pods. This spicy aubergine dish will add a refreshing tang to any meal. It is good served with chapatis and meat or poultry dishes.

SERVES 4

INGREDIENTS
12 baby aubergines (eggplant)
30ml/2 tbsp vegetable oil
1 small onion, chopped
10ml/2 tsp grated fresh root ginger
10ml/2 tsp crushed garlic
5ml/1 tsp coriander seeds
5ml/1 tsp cumin seeds
10ml/2 tsp white poppy seeds
10ml/2 tsp sesame seeds
10ml/2 tsp desiccated (dry unsweetened shredded) coconut
15ml/1 tbsp dry-roasted skinned peanuts
2.5–5ml/½–1 tsp chilli powder
6–8 curry leaves
1–2 dried red chillies, chopped
2.5ml/½ tsp concentrated tamarind paste
salt

1 Using a sharp knife, make three deep slits lengthways on each aubergine, without cutting through, then soak in salted water for about 20 minutes.

2 Heat half the vegetable oil in a pan and fry the onion for 3–4 minutes. Add the ginger and garlic and cook for about 30 seconds.

3 Add the coriander and cumin seeds to the pan and fry for 30 seconds, then add the poppy seeds, sesame seeds, coconut and peanuts. Fry for 1 minute, stirring. Allow to cool slightly, then grind the spices in a food processor or blender, adding 105ml/7 tbsp warm water. The mixture should form a thick, coarse paste.

4 Mix the chilli powder and 5ml/1 tsp salt into the spice paste. Drain the aubergines and pat dry on kitchen paper. Carefully stuff each of the slits with the spice paste and reserve any paste that has not been used.

5 Heat the remaining oil in a wok, karahi or large pan over a medium heat and add the curry leaves and dried red chillies. Let the chillies blacken, then add the aubergines and the tamarind paste blended with 105ml/7 tbsp hot water. Add any remaining spice paste and stir to mix.

6 Cover the pan and simmer gently for about 15 minutes, or until the stuffed aubergines are cooked through and tender. Serve with chapatis and a meat or poultry dish, if you like.

ROASTED AUBERGINES

This classic dish, made of roasted and mashed aubergines cooked with spring onions, is known as bharta *in the Punjab region of India. The term* bharta *means "to mash". Traditionally, the aubergine is roasted over charcoal, which imparts a smoky flavour.*

SERVES 4

INGREDIENTS
2 large aubergines (eggplant)
45ml/3 tbsp vegetable oil
2.5ml/½ tsp black mustard seeds
1 bunch spring onions (scallions), finely chopped
115g/4oz/1½ cups button (white) mushrooms, halved
2 garlic cloves, crushed
1 fresh red chilli, finely chopped
2.5ml/½ tsp chilli powder
5ml/1 tsp ground cumin
5ml/1 tsp ground coriander
1.5ml/¼ tsp ground turmeric
5ml/1 tsp salt
400g/14oz can chopped tomatoes
15ml/1 tbsp chopped fresh coriander (cilantro), plus a few sprigs to garnish

1 Preheat the oven to 200°C/400°F/Gas 6. Brush the aubergines all over with 15ml/1 tbsp of the oil; prick with a fork. Bake for 30–35 minutes until soft.

2 Meanwhile, heat the remaining oil and fry the black mustard seeds for about 2 minutes until they splutter. Add the onions, mushrooms, garlic and chilli, and fry for 5 minutes more. Stir in the chilli powder, cumin, coriander, turmeric and salt and fry for 3–4 minutes. Add the tomatoes and simmer for 5 minutes.

3 Cut the aubergines in half lengthways and scoop out the soft flesh into a large mixing bowl. Mash the flesh to a course texture, using a fork.

4 Add the aubergines to the pan with the coriander. Bring to the boil and simmer for 5 minutes until the sauce thickens. Serve garnished with coriander.

MUSHROOM CURRY

In India, mushrooms traditionally grow only in the northern state of Kashmir.
However, they are now being cultivated in other northern areas. Serve this curry
with Indian bread such as naan and any dry meat or poultry dish.

SERVES 4

INGREDIENTS
30ml/2 tbsp vegetable oil
2.5ml/½ tsp cumin seeds
1.5ml/¼ tsp black peppercorns
4 cardamom pods
1.5ml/¼ tsp ground turmeric
1 onion, finely chopped
5ml/1 tsp ground cumin
5ml/1 tsp ground coriander
2.5ml/½ tsp garam masala
1 fresh green chilli, finely chopped
2 garlic cloves, crushed
2.5cm/1in piece fresh root ginger, grated
400g/14oz can chopped tomatoes
1.5ml/¼ tsp salt
450g/1lb/6 cups button (white) mushrooms
chopped fresh coriander (cilantro), to garnish

1 Heat the vegetable oil in a wok, karahi or large pan and fry the cumin seeds,
black peppercorns, cardamom pods and turmeric for 2–3 minutes.

2 Add the onion to the pan and fry for 5 minutes or until golden. Stir in the
ground cumin, coriander and garam masala and fry for 2 minutes. Add
the green chilli, garlic and ginger and fry for 2–3 minutes, stirring constantly.
Add the tomatoes and salt. Bring to the boil and simmer for about 5 minutes.

3 Halve the mushrooms, then add them to the pan. Cover and simmer over a low
heat for about 10 minutes. Transfer the curry to a warm serving platter and
garnish with chopped fresh coriander.

STIR-FRIED INDIAN CHEESE WITH MUSHROOMS & PEAS

Indian cheese, known as paneer, *is a very versatile ingredient. It is used in both sweet and savoury dishes. Indian housewives generally make this cheese at home, although in recent years it has become available commercially.*

SERVES 4–6

INGREDIENTS
90ml/6 tbsp ghee or vegetable oil
225g/8oz paneer, cubed
1 onion, finely chopped
a few fresh mint leaves, chopped, plus a few sprigs to garnish
50g/2oz chopped fresh coriander (cilantro)
3 fresh green chillies, chopped
3 garlic cloves
2.5cm/1in piece fresh root ginger, sliced
5ml/1 tsp ground turmeric
5ml/1 tsp chilli powder (optional)
5ml/1 tsp garam masala
225g/8oz/3 cups tiny button (white) mushrooms, washed
225g/8oz/2 cups frozen peas, thawed
175ml/6fl oz/³⁄4 cup natural (plain) yogurt, mixed with
  5ml/1 tsp cornflour (cornstarch)
salt

1 Heat the ghee or oil in a wok, karahi or large pan, and fry the paneer cubes until golden brown on all sides. Remove and drain on kitchen paper.

2 Grind the onion, mint, coriander, chillies, garlic and ginger using a pestle and mortar to a fairly smooth paste. Mix in the turmeric, chilli powder, if using, and garam masala and season with salt.

3 Pour off all but 15ml/1 tbsp of the ghee or oil from the pan. Fry the paste over a medium heat for 8–10 minutes. Add the mushrooms, peas and paneer. Mix well. Cool the mixture slightly and fold in the yogurt. Simmer for about 10 minutes. Garnish with fresh mint and serve immediately.

Karahi Shredded Cabbage with Cumin

Despite the number of dried and fresh chillies included in this cabbage dish, it is only lightly spiced and makes a good accompaniment to most other dishes. It goes particularly well with lamb or chicken curries.

SERVES 4

INGREDIENTS
15ml/1 tbsp corn oil
50 g/2oz/4 tbsp butter
2.5ml/½ tsp crushed coriander seeds
2.5ml/½ tsp white cumin seeds
6 dried red chillies
1 small Savoy cabbage, shredded
12 mangetouts (snow peas)
3 fresh red chillies, seeded and sliced
12 baby corn cobs
salt

FOR THE GARNISH
25g/1oz/¼ cup flaked (slivered) almonds, toasted
1 tbsp chopped fresh coriander (cilantro)

1 Heat the oil and butter in a deep round-based frying pan or a karahi and add the coriander seeds, cumin seeds and dried red chillies.

2 Add the shredded cabbage and mangetouts to the pan and stir-fry for about 5 minutes. Add the fresh red chillies, baby corn cobs and salt to taste, and fry for a further 3 minutes. Transfer to a warmed serving dish, if you wish, and garnish with the toasted flaked almonds and chopped fresh coriander. Serve hot.

VARIATION
Use 12 green beans, trimmed and halved, and 1 red (bell) pepper, cut into strips, in place of the baby corn cobs and mangetouts.

Masala Beans with Fenugreek

The term masala *refers to the blending of several spices to achieve a distinctive flavour. Many different spice combinations are blended together to produce a variety of flavours, and it is this subtle skill that makes Indian cuisine unique.*

Serves 4

Ingredients
1 onion
5ml/1 tsp ground cumin
5ml/1 tsp ground coriander
5ml/1 tsp sesame seeds
5ml/1 tsp chilli powder
2.5ml/½ tsp crushed garlic
1.5ml/¼ tsp ground turmeric
5ml/1 tsp salt
30ml/2 tbsp vegetable oil
1 tomato, quartered
225g/8oz/1½ cups green beans, blanched
1 bunch fresh fenugreek leaves, stems discarded
60ml/4 tbsp chopped fresh coriander (cilantro)
15ml/1 tbsp lemon juice

1 Roughly chop the onion. Put in a food processor or blender with the cumin and coriander, sesame seeds, chilli powder, garlic, turmeric and salt. Process for 30–45 seconds until a rough paste is formed.

2 In a wok, karahi or large pan, heat the oil over a medium heat and fry the spice paste for about 5 minutes, stirring occasionally.

3 Add the tomato quarters, blanched green beans, fresh fenugreek leaves and chopped coriander. Stir-fry for about 5 minutes, then sprinkle over the lemon juice, stir to combine and serve immediately.

Masala Okra

Okra are a very popular Indian vegetable. In this recipe they are stir-fried with a dry, spicy masala to make a delicious side dish. When buying okra, choose firm, brightly coloured, unblemished pods that are less than 10cm/4in long.

SERVES 4

INGREDIENTS
450g/1lb okra
2.5ml/½ tsp ground turmeric
5ml/1 tsp cayenne pepper
15ml/1 tbsp ground cumin
15ml/1 tbsp ground coriander
1.5ml/¼ tsp salt
1.5ml/¼ tsp sugar
15ml/1 tbsp lemon juice
15ml/1 tbsp desiccated (dry unsweetened shredded) coconut
30ml/2 tbsp chopped fresh coriander (cilantro)
45ml/3 tbsp oil
2.5ml/½ tsp cumin seeds
2.5ml/½ tsp black mustard seeds
chopped fresh tomatoes, to garnish
poppadums, to serve

1 Wash, dry and trim the okra. In a bowl, combine the turmeric, cayenne pepper, cumin, ground coriander, salt, sugar, lemon juice, coconut and coriander.

2 Heat the oil in a large frying pan. Add the cumin seeds and mustard seeds and fry for about 2 minutes, or until they begin to splutter. Add the spice mixture and continue to fry for a further 2 minutes.

3 Add the okra to the pan, cover and cook over a low heat for 10 minutes, or until tender. Garnish with chopped tomatoes and serve with poppadums.

OKRA IN YOGURT

This tangy vegetable dish can be served as an accompaniment, but also makes an excellent vegetarian meal served with dhal and chapatis. Make sure that you do not overcook the okra, as it can take on an unpleasant texture.

SERVES 4

INGREDIENTS
450g/1lb okra
30ml/2 tbsp vegetable oil
2.5ml/½ tsp onion seeds
3 fresh red or green chillies, chopped
1 onion, sliced
1.5ml/¼ tsp ground turmeric
10ml/2 tsp desiccated (dry unsweetened shredded) coconut
2.5ml/½ tsp salt
15ml/1 tbsp natural (plain) yogurt
2 tomatoes, quartered
15ml/1 tbsp chopped fresh coriander (cilantro)

1 Wash and trim the okra, cut into 1cm/½in pieces and set aside. Heat the oil in a large pan. Add the onion seeds, chillies and onion, and fry for 5 minutes.

2 Lower the heat under the pan and add the turmeric, desiccated coconut and salt. Fry for about 1 minute, stirring continuously. Add the okra to the pan. Turn the heat to medium-high and stir-fry briskly for a few minutes, or until the okra has turned lightly golden.

3 Add the yogurt, tomatoes and fresh coriander. Cook for a further 2 minutes. Transfer to a warmed serving dish and serve immediately.

COOK'S TIP
When buying okra, choose blemish-free specimens.
Wash well, rubbing each gently with your fingertips.

OKRA WITH LENTILS

This is a substantial vegetable dish, which is enhanced by the inclusion of tangy green mango. It is bursting with the aromatic flavours of fenugreek, ginger, garlic and coriander and is delightfully spicy. It is good as a main dish or accompaniment.

SERVES 4

INGREDIENTS
115g/14oz/⅔ cup yellow lentils
45ml/3 tbsp corn oil
2.5ml/½ tsp onion seeds
2 onions, sliced
2.5ml/½ tsp ground fenugreek
5ml/1 tsp grated fresh root ginger
5ml/1 tsp crushed garlic
7.5ml/1½ tsp chilli powder
1.5ml/¼ tsp ground turmeric
5ml/1 tsp ground coriander
1 green (unripe) mango, peeled and sliced
450g/1lb okra, trimmed and cut into 1cm/½in pieces
7.5ml/1½ tsp salt
2 fresh red chillies, seeded and sliced
30ml/2 tbsp chopped fresh coriander (cilantro)
1 tomato, sliced

1 Wash the lentils and place in a pan with water to cover. Bring to the boil and cook for about 25 minutes until soft but not mushy. Drain and set aside.

2 Heat the oil in a deep round-based frying pan and fry the onion seeds until they begin to pop. Add the onions and fry until golden. Lower the heat and add the ground fenugreek, ginger, garlic, chilli powder, turmeric and ground coriander.

3 Add the mango slices and the okra. Stir well and add the salt, red chillies and fresh coriander. Stir-fry for about 3 minutes or until the okra is cooked. Add the lentils and sliced tomato and cook for 3 minutes. Serve hot.

STUFFED OKRA

The Gujarati community in West India excels in the art of vegetarian cooking. Although the native Gujaratis are strict vegetarians, who do not even eat eggs, this easy-to-make dish will happily accompany most meat and poultry dishes.

SERVES 4–6

INGREDIENTS
15ml/1 tbsp amchur (dried mango powder)
2.5ml/½ tsp ground ginger
2.5ml/½ tsp ground cumin
2.5ml/½ tsp chilli powder (optional)
2.5ml/½ tsp ground turmeric
vegetable oil, for mixing and frying
225g/8oz large okra
30ml/2 tbsp cornflour (cornstarch)
salt

1 In a bowl, mix the amchur, ginger, cumin, chilli powder, if using, turmeric and salt with a few drops of vegetable oil. Cover and leave the mixture to rest for 1–2 hours or refrigerate overnight.

2 Wash and dry the okra, then trim the tips. Make a slit lengthways in the centre of each okra; do not cut all the way through.

3 Using your fingers, part the slit of each okra carefully without opening it all the way and fill each pod with as much spice mixture as possible. Put all the okra into a clean plastic bag with the cornflour and shake the bag gently, ensuring the okra are covered evenly.

4 Pour vegetable oil into a wok, karahi or large pan to a depth of 2.5cm/1in. Heat the oil and fry the stuffed okra in small batches for 5–8 minutes or until brown and slightly crisp. Serve hot.

CAULIFLOWER IN COCONUT SAUCE

Coconut is used for both sweet and savoury dishes in southern Indian cooking. Here it complements the subtle flavour of the cauliflower beautifully, while the inclusion of lemon juice gives the dish a sharp edge.

SERVES 4–6

INGREDIENTS
15ml/1 tbsp gram flour (besan)
5ml/1 tsp chilli powder
15ml/1 tbsp ground coriander
5ml/1 tsp ground cumin
5ml/1 tsp mustard powder
5ml/1 tsp ground turmeric
60ml/4 tbsp vegetable oil
6–8 curry leaves
5ml/1 tsp cumin seeds
1 cauliflower, broken into florets
175ml/6fl oz/³⁄₄ cup thick coconut milk
juice of 2 lemons
salt
lime slices, to garnish

1 In a bowl, mix the flour with a little water to make a paste. Add the chilli, coriander, cumin, mustard, turmeric and salt. Stir in 120ml/4fl oz/½ cup water.

2 Heat the oil in a wok, karahi or large pan, then fry the curry leaves and the cumin seeds. Add the spice paste and simmer for about 5 minutes. If the sauce is too thick, add a little hot water.

3 Add the cauliflower and coconut milk to the pan. Bring to the boil, reduce the heat, cover and cook until the cauliflower is tender but still crunchy. Add the lemon juice, mix throughly and serve hot, garnished with lime slices.

MIXED VEGETABLE CURRY

Curries based on a variety of vegetables are cooked throughout India, but they all differ from one another according to the spicing and the method of cooking. This particular version, made with onion seeds, is a typical example from the east and north-east of the country, where the dish is known as chorchori.

SERVES 4–6

INGREDIENTS

350g/12oz mixed vegetables such as potatoes, carrots, green beans,
  peas, cauliflower, cabbage, mangetouts (snow peas) and button
  (white) mushrooms
30ml/2 tbsp vegetable oil
2.5ml/½ tsp mustard seeds
5ml/1 tsp cumin seeds, freshly roasted
2.5ml/½ tsp onion seeds
5ml/1 tsp ground turmeric
2 garlic cloves, crushed
6–8 curry leaves
1 dried red chilli
5ml/1 tsp granulated sugar
150ml/¼ pint/⅔ cup natural (plain) yogurt mixed with
  5ml/1 tsp cornflour (cornstarch), well beaten
salt
fresh bay leaves, to garnish

COOK'S TIP
If you like, mix gram flour (besan) with the yogurt instead of the cornflour. Like the cornflour, it will prevent the yogurt from curdling but it will also lend a nutty taste to the dish.

1 Prepare all the vegetables you have chosen: string the beans; scrub and cube the potatoes; break the cauliflower into florets; peel and dice the carrots; shred the cabbage; trim the mangetouts; wash the mushrooms and leave them whole.

2 Heat a large, deep-sided pan with enough water to cook all the vegetables and bring to the boil. Add the potatoes and carrots and cook until nearly tender, then add all the other vegetables and cook until nearly tender but still firm, by which time the potatoes will be cooked. Drain well.

3 Heat the vegetable oil in a large pan and add the mustard, cumin and onion seeds. When they start to pop, add the turmeric, garlic, curry leaves and red chillies and fry gently until the garlic is golden and the chilli nearly burnt. Reduce the heat.

4 Gently stir the drained vegetables into the spices, add the sugar and season with salt to taste. Gradually stir the yogurt mixed with the cornflour into the vegetables. Heat through and serve immediately, garnished with fresh bay leaves.

VEGETABLE KORMA

The blending of spices is an ancient art in India. In this delicate, creamy dish, the aim is to produce a subtle, aromatic curry rather than an assault on the senses.

SERVES 4

INGREDIENTS
50g/2oz/¼ cup butter
2 onions, sliced
2 garlic cloves, crushed
2.5cm/1in piece fresh root ginger, grated
5ml/1 tsp ground cumin
15ml/1 tbsp ground coriander
6 cardamom pods
5cm/2in cinnamon stick
5ml/1 tsp ground turmeric
1 fresh red chilli, seeded and finely chopped
1 potato, peeled and cut into 2.5cm/1in cubes
1 small aubergine (eggplant)
115g/4oz/1½ cups mushrooms, thickly sliced
115g/4oz/1 cup green beans, cut into 2.5cm/1in lengths
60ml/4 tbsp natural (plain) yogurt
150ml/¼ pint/⅔ cup double (heavy) cream
5ml/1 tsp garam masala
salt and ground black pepper
fresh coriander (cilantro) sprigs, to garnish
poppadums, to serve

> COOK'S TIP
> *Any combination of vegetables can be used for this korma. Vegetables that work well include carrots, cauliflower, broccoli, peas and chickpeas.*

1 Melt the butter in a heavy pan. Add the sliced onions and cook for 5 minutes until soft and translucent. Add the garlic and ginger and cook for 2 minutes, then stir in the cumin, coriander, cardamom pods, cinnamon stick, turmeric and chilli. Cook, stirring continuously, for about 30 seconds.

2 Add the potato, aubergine and mushrooms to the pan and pour in 175ml/ 6fl oz/³/₄ cup water. Cover the pan, bring the mixture to the boil, then lower the heat and simmer gently for about 15 minutes. Add the green beans and cook, uncovered, for a further 5 minutes.

3 Using a slotted spoon, remove the vegetables to a warmed serving dish and keep hot. Boil the cooking liquid until it reduces a little. Season generously with salt and pepper, then stir in the yogurt, cream and garam masala. Pour the sauce over the vegetables and garnish with fresh coriander. Serve with poppadums.

Vegetables Stuffed with Spices & Nuts

It is hard to beat the Gujarati community when it comes to the creation of imaginative vegetarian dishes. In this fabulous recipe, potatoes and aubergines are stuffed with an irresistible blend of spices and peanuts. They are very good served with Indian bread or with poultry and meat curries.

SERVES 4

INGREDIENTS
12 small potatoes
8 baby aubergines (eggplant)
single (light) cream (optional), to garnish

FOR THE STUFFING
15ml/1 tbsp sesame seeds
30ml/2 tbsp ground coriander
30ml/2 tbsp ground cumin
2.5ml/½ tsp salt
1.5ml/¼ tsp chilli powder
2.5ml/½ tsp ground turmeric
10ml/2 tsp granulated sugar
1.5ml/¼ tsp garam masala
15ml/1 tbsp peanuts, roughly crushed
15ml/1 tbsp gram flour (besan)
2 garlic cloves, crushed
15ml/1 tbsp lemon juice
30ml/2 tbsp chopped fresh coriander (cilantro)

FOR THE SAUCE
30ml/2 tbsp vegetable oil
2.5ml/½ tsp black mustard seeds
400g/14oz can chopped tomatoes
30ml/2 tbsp chopped fresh coriander (cilantro)
150ml/¼ pint/⅔ cup water

1 Preheat the oven to 200°C/400°F/Gas 6. Make slits in the potatoes and baby aubergines, making sure that you do not cut right through them.

2 Mix all the ingredients for the stuffing together on a plate. Stuff the potatoes and aubergines with the spice mixture and place in a greased ovenproof dish. Set aside any leftover stuffing.

3 To make the sauce, heat the vegetable oil in a pan and fry the mustard seeds for about 2 minutes until they begin to splutter, then add the chopped tomatoes and coriander and any leftover stuffing, together with the water. Simmer for about 5 minutes until the sauce thickens, stirring occasionally.

4 Pour the sauce over the potatoes and aubergines. Cover and bake for about 25 minutes until the vegetables are soft. Garnish with single cream, if using and serve immediately.

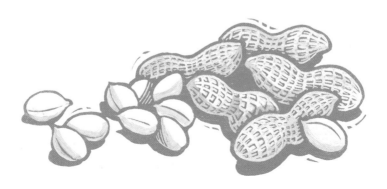

CUMIN-SCENTED VEGETABLES WITH TOASTED ALMONDS

Cabbage is a traditional vegetable in India. Although neither baby corn cobs nor mangetouts are used in Indian cooking, combining new ideas with traditional ones can create exciting and original dishes, as this recipe shows.

SERVES 4

INGREDIENTS
15ml/1 tbsp vegetable oil
50g/2oz/4 tbsp butter
2.5ml/½ tsp crushed coriander seeds
2.5ml/½ tsp white cumin seeds
6 dried red chillies
1 small Savoy cabbage, shredded
12 mangetouts (snow peas)
3 fresh red chillies, seeded and sliced
12 baby corn cobs, halved
salt

FOR THE GARNISH
25g/1oz/¼ cup flaked (sliced) almonds, toasted
15ml/1 tbsp chopped fresh coriander (cilantro)

1 Heat the oil and butter in a wok, karahi or large pan and add the crushed coriander seeds, cumin seeds and dried red chillies.

2 Add the shredded cabbage and mangetouts to the spices in the pan and stir-fry briskly for about 5 minutes, until the cabbage starts to turn crisp.

3 Add the fresh red chillies, and baby corn cobs to the pan and season with salt to taste. Stir-fry for a further 3 minutes. Garnish with the toasted almonds and fresh coriander, and serve hot.

MIXED VEGETABLES IN COCONUT SAUCE

A vegetable dish is an essential part of an Indian meal, even for a simple occasion, where one or two may be served with dhal, raita and rice. This recipe, in which the vegetables are simmered in coconut milk, is typical of southern India.

SERVES 4

INGREDIENTS
225g/8oz potatoes, cut into 5cm/2in cubes
125g/4oz/³/4 cup green beans
150g/5oz carrots, scraped and cut into 5cm/2in pieces
1 small aubergine (eggplant), about 225g/8oz, quartered lengthways
75g/3oz coconut milk powder
5ml/1 tsp salt
30ml/2 tbsp vegetable oil
6–8 fresh or 8–10 dried curry leaves
1–2 dried red chillies, chopped
5ml/1 tsp ground cumin
5ml/1 tsp ground coriander
2.5ml/¹/2 tsp ground turmeric

1 Put the potatoes, beans and carrots in a pan, add 300ml/½ pint/1¼ cups of water and bring to the boil. Reduce the heat, cover and cook for 5 minutes. Meanwhile, cut the aubergine into 5cm/2in pieces, then add to the pan.

2 Blend the coconut milk powder with 200ml/7fl oz/scant 1 cup hot water; add to the pan with the salt. Bring to a simmer, cover and cook for 6–7 minutes.

3 In a small pan, heat the oil over a medium heat and add the curry leaves and the chillies. Immediately follow with the cumin, coriander and turmeric. Stir-fry the spices for 15–20 seconds and pour the entire contents of the pan over the vegetables. Stir to distribute the spices evenly and serve.

CORN IN RICH ONION SAUCE

The Punjab region is famous for its corn, where it is used in many delicacies. Here, halved corn cobs are cooked in a thick, rich onion sauce, in a classic Punjabi dish. It is excellent served with warm naan bread.

SERVES 4

INGREDIENTS
4 corn cobs, thawed if frozen
vegetable oil, for frying
1 large onion, finely chopped
2 garlic cloves, crushed
5cm/2in piece fresh root ginger, crushed
2.5ml/½ tsp ground turmeric
2.5ml/½ tsp onion seeds
2.5ml/½ tsp cumin seeds
2.5ml/½ tsp five-spice powder
pinch of chilli powder
6–8 curry leaves
2.5ml/½ tsp granulated sugar
200ml/7fl oz/scant 1 cup natural (plain) yogurt

1 Cut each corn cob in half. Heat the oil in a wok, karahi or large pan and fry the corn until golden brown. Remove the corn and set aside.

2 Remove all but 30ml/2 tbsp oil from the pan. Grind the onion, garlic and ginger to a paste using a mortar and pestle or in a food processor. Transfer to a bowl and mix in the spices, chilli powder, curry leaves and sugar.

3 Heat the oil gently and fry the onion paste mixture for 8–10 minutes until all the spices have blended well and the oil separates from the sauce. Leave the mixture to cool slightly and fold in the yogurt. Mix to a smooth sauce. Add the corn and mix well, so that all the pieces are covered with the sauce. Reheat gently for about 10 minutes, being careful not to boil. Serve hot.

Spinach with Golden Potatoes

The combination of spinach and potato is generally known as aloo saag *or* saag aloo. *As with most Indian dishes, there are different versions using the same or similar ingredients. This recipe is from Bengal, where it is known as* palong saaker ghonto.

Serves 4–6

Ingredients
450g/1lb spinach
30ml/2 tbsp vegetable oil
5ml/1 tsp black mustard seeds
1 onion, thinly sliced
2 garlic cloves, crushed
2.5cm/1in piece fresh root ginger, finely chopped
675g/1½lb firm potatoes, cut into 2.5cm/1in chunks
5ml/1 tsp chilli powder
5ml/1 tsp salt

1 Blanch the spinach in boiling water for 3–4 minutes, then drain well and leave to cool. When cool enough to handle, squeeze out any remaining liquid using the back of a wooden spoon or with your hands.

2 Heat the oil in a large pan over a medium heat and fry the mustard seeds until they begin to splutter. Add the onion, garlic and fresh root ginger and fry for about 5 minutes, stirring continuously.

3 Stir the potatoes, chilli powder, salt and 120ml/4fl oz/½ cup water into the spices and cook for 8 minutes, stirring occasionally. Add the spinach, then cover the pan and simmer for 10–15 minutes until the potatoes are tender. Serve at once.

Variation
Enhance the flavour by adding fresh red chillies in step 2. Omit the chilli powder in step 3.

Dry-spiced Potatoes with Cauliflower

This dish, known as aloo gobi *in most Indian restaurants, has remained one of the most popular over the years. It may be served simply with a salad and some pickle, or serve it as an accompaniment to a meat or poultry main dish.*

SERVES 4

INGREDIENTS
450g/1lb potatoes
30ml/2 tbsp vegetable oil
5ml/1 tsp cumin seeds
1 fresh green chilli, finely chopped
450g/1lb cauliflower, broken into florets
5ml/1 tsp ground coriander
5ml/1 tsp ground cumin
1.5ml/¼ tsp chilli powder
2.5ml/½ tsp ground turmeric
2.5ml/½ tsp salt
chopped fresh coriander (cilantro), to garnish
tomato and onion salad and a pickle, to serve

1 Peel the potatoes and cut them into 2.5cm/1in cubes. Par-boil them in a pan of lightly salted water for about 10 minutes, drain well and set aside.

2 Heat the oil in a wok, karahi or large pan over a medium heat and fry the cumin seeds for about 2 minutes until they begin to splutter. Add the fresh green chilli and fry for a further 1 minute.

3 Add the cauliflower florets to the pan and fry, stirring, for 5 minutes. Add the potatoes, the spices and salt to the cauliflower and cook for a further 7–10 minutes, or until both vegetables are tender. Garnish with chopped fresh coriander and serve with a tomato and onion salad and a pickle.

KARAHI POTATOES WITH WHOLE SPICES

Spices work wonderfully with potatoes. Even just a light touch can bring about a complete transformation. For this recipe choose floury potatoes, as they will give a better result than a waxy variety. Serve with parathas.

SERVES 4

INGREDIENTS
45ml/3 tbsp vegetable oil
2.5ml/½ tsp white cumin seeds
3 curry leaves
5ml/1 tsp crushed dried red chillies
2.5ml/½ tsp mixed onion, mustard and fenugreek seeds
2.5ml/½ tsp fennel seeds
3 garlic cloves, roughly chopped
2.5ml/½ tsp grated fresh root ginger
2 onions, sliced
6 new potatoes, cut into 5mm/¼in slices
15ml/1 tbsp chopped fresh coriander (cilantro)
1 fresh red chilli, seeded and sliced
1 fresh green chilli, seeded and sliced

1 Heat the oil in a wok, karahi or large pan. Lower the heat slightly and add the cumin seeds, curry leaves, dried chillies, mixed onion, mustard and fenugreek seeds, the fennel seeds, chopped garlic and grated ginger. Fry for about 1 minute, stirring occasionally.

2 Add the sliced onions to the pan and fry gently for a further 5 minutes, or until the onions are golden brown. Add the sliced potatoes, fresh coriander and red and green chillies. Mix together well. Cover the pan tightly with a lid or foil, making sure the foil does not touch the food. Cook over a very low heat for about 7 minutes, or until the potatoes are tender. Serve hot.

POTATOES WITH ROASTED POPPY SEEDS

Tiny black poppy seeds are used in Indian cooking as a thickening agent, and to lend a nutty taste to sauces. It is the creamy white variety of poppy seed that is used here, rather than the ones with a blue-grey hue that are used for baking.

SERVES 4

INGREDIENTS
45ml/3 tbsp white poppy seeds
45–60ml/3–4 tbsp vegetable oil
675g/1½lb potatoes, peeled and cut into 1cm/½in cubes
2.5ml/½ tsp black mustard seeds
2.5ml/½ tsp onion seeds
2.5ml/½ tsp cumin seeds
2.5ml/½ tsp fennel seeds
1–2 dried red chillies, chopped or broken into small pieces
2.5ml/½ tsp ground turmeric
2.5ml/½ tsp salt
150ml/¼ pint/⅔ cup warm water
fresh coriander (cilantro) sprigs, to garnish
puris and natural (plain) yogurt, to serve

1 Preheat a wok, karahi or large pan over a medium heat. When the pan is hot, reduce the heat slightly and add the poppy seeds. Stir them around in the pan until they are just a shade darker. Remove from the pan and allow to cool.

2 In the pan, heat the vegetable oil over a medium heat and fry the potato cubes until light brown on all sides. Remove the potatoes with a slotted spoon and drain on kitchen paper.

3 Add the mustard seeds to the pan. As soon as they begin to pop, stir in the onion, cumin and fennel seeds, and the chillies. Let the chillies blacken.

4 Stir in the turmeric and then the fried potatoes and salt. Stir well and add the warm water. Cover the pan with the lid and reduce the heat to low. Cook for 8–10 minutes, or until the potatoes are tender.

5 Grind the cooled poppy seeds using a pestle and mortar or coffee grinder. Stir the ground seeds into the potatoes. It should form a thick paste that clings to the potatoes. If there is too much liquid, continue to stir over a medium heat until you have the right consistency. Transfer to a serving dish. Garnish with coriander and serve with puris and natural yogurt.

COOK'S TIPS
• *Do not allow the dried chillies to burn or they will become bitter. Remove them from the pan when they have blackened.*
• *When they are ground, poppy seeds release an oil, which may prevent the blade of a spice mill or coffee grinder from moving. If this happens, scrape away anything that sticks to the blades and start again.*

BOMBAY POTATO

This well-known and deliciously flavoured dish is served in most Indian restaurants in the West, and its name may originate from a dish that is sold by street vendors in Bombay. Serve with parathas or soft white bread.

SERVES 4–6

INGREDIENTS
450g/1lb new potatoes
5ml/1 tsp ground turmeric
60ml/4 tbsp vegetable oil
2 dried red chillies
6–8 curry leaves
2 onions, finely chopped
2 fresh green chillies, finely chopped
50g/2oz coarsely chopped fresh coriander (cilantro)
1.5ml/¼ tsp asafoetida
2.5ml/½ tsp each cumin, mustard, onion, fennel and nigella seeds
15–30ml/1–2 tbsp lemon juice, to taste
salt

1 Scrub the potatoes under running water and cut into small pieces. Cook in a pan of lightly salted boiling water with 2.5ml/½ tsp of the turmeric until tender. Drain well, then coarsely mash. Set aside.

2 Heat the oil in a separate pan and fry the dried chillies and curry leaves until the chillies are nearly burnt. Add the onions, green chillies, coriander, remaining turmeric, asafoetida and spice seeds, and cook until the onions are soft.

3 Gently stir the potatoes into the pan and add a few drops of water. Cook gently over a low heat for 10 minutes, mixing well to ensure an even distribution of the spices. Add lemon juice to taste. Serve hot.

POTATOES IN TAMARIND SAUCE

In this popular potato dish from the state of Karnataka, the combination of chilli and tamarind awakens the taste buds immediately. This version adapts the traditional recipe slightly, to reduce the pungency and enhance the dish's fiery appearance.

SERVES 4–6

INGREDIENTS

450g/1lb small new potatoes, washed and dried
25g/1oz whole dried red chillies
7.5ml/1½ tsp cumin seeds
4 garlic cloves
90ml/6 tbsp vegetable oil
60ml/4 tbsp thick tamarind juice
30ml/2 tbsp tomato purée (paste)
4 curry leaves
5ml/1 tsp granulated sugar
1.5ml/¼ tsp asafoetida
salt
coriander (cilantro) sprigs and lemon wedges, to garnish

1 Cook the potatoes in a large pan of boiling water until fully cooked. Drain and cool in iced water to prevent further cooking.

2 Soak the dried chillies in a bowl of warm water for 5 minutes. Drain and grind with the cumin seeds and garlic to a coarse paste either using a pestle and mortar or in a food processor.

3 Heat the vegetable oil in a karahi or heavy pan and fry the paste, tamarind juice, tomato purée, curry leaves, salt, sugar and asafoetida until the oil runs. Add the drained potatoes. Reduce the heat, cover and simmer for 5 minutes. Garnish with sprigs of fresh coriander and serve with lemon wedges.

POTATOES IN YOGURT SAUCE

The potato was first introduced to India by Dutch traders, and it has since been elevated to gourmet status. In Indian cuisine, the humble potato takes on delicious flavourings of simple whole spices, or of blends of spices ground together.

SERVES 4

INGREDIENTS
12 new potatoes, halved
300g/½ pint/1¼ cups natural (plain) yogurt, whisked
300ml/½ pint/1¼ cups water
1.5ml/¼ tsp ground turmeric
5ml/1 tsp chilli powder
5ml/1 tsp ground coriander
2.5ml/½ tsp ground cumin
5ml/1 tsp soft brown sugar
30ml/2 tbsp vegetable oil
5ml/1 tsp cumin seeds
15ml/1 tbsp chopped fresh coriander (cilantro), plus sprigs
   to garnish (optional)
2 fresh green chillies, sliced
salt
bhaturas or chapatis, to serve

1 Boil the potatoes in salted water, until just tender. Drain and set aside. Meanwhile, mix together the yogurt, water, turmeric, chilli powder, ground coriander, ground cumin, 5ml/1 tsp salt and sugar in a bowl. Set aside.

2 Heat the vegetable oil in a wok, karahi or large pan, and add the cumin seeds. Fry gently until they begin to splutter. Reduce the heat, stir in the yogurt mixture and cook for about 3 minutes over a medium heat.

3 Add the chopped fresh coriander, green chillies and cooked potatoes. Stir to mix then cook for a further 5–7 minutes, stirring occasionally. Transfer to a warmed serving dish and garnish with coriander sprigs, if using. Serve immediately with hot bhaturas or chapatis.

STUFFED BANANAS

Bananas are cooked with spices in southern India. Some recipes use lots of chillies tempered by adding coconut milk and tamarind juice. Green bananas or plantains are available from Indian stores, or use unripe eating bananas instead.

SERVES 4

INGREDIENTS
4 green bananas or plantains
30ml/2 tbsp ground coriander
15ml/1 tbsp ground cumin
5ml/1 tsp chilli powder
2.5ml/½ tsp salt
1.5ml/¼ tsp ground turmeric
5ml/1 tsp granulated sugar
15ml/1 tbsp gram flour (besan)
45ml/3 tbsp chopped fresh coriander (cilantro), plus sprigs to garnish
90ml/6 tbsp vegetable oil
1.5ml/¼ tsp cumin seeds
1.5ml/¼ tsp black mustard seeds
chapatis, to serve

1 Trim the bananas or plantains and cut each crossways into three equal pieces, leaving the skin on. Make a slit along each piece of banana, without cutting all the way through the flesh.

2 On a plate combine the ground coriander, cumin, chilli powder, salt, turmeric, sugar, gram flour, chopped fresh coriander and 15ml/1 tbsp of the vegetable oil. Use your fingers to combine well. Carefully stuff the spice mixture into the slit in each piece of banana, taking care not to break the bananas in half.

3 Heat the remaining oil in large pan, and fry the cumin and mustard seeds for 2 minutes or until they begin to splutter. Add the bananas and toss in the oil.

4 Cover and simmer for 15 minutes until the bananas are soft but not mushy. Garnish with coriander sprigs, and serve with warm chapatis.

CHILLI & MUSTARD FLAVOURED PINEAPPLE

Pineapple is cooked with coconut milk and a blend of spices in this southern Indian dish, which could be served with any meat, fish or vegetable curry. The chilli adds heat, and the mustard seeds lend a rich, nutty flavour that complements the sharpness of the pineapple, while the coconut milk provides a delectable creamy sweetness.

SERVES 4

INGREDIENTS
1 pineapple
50ml/2fl oz/1¼ cup water
150ml/¼ pint/⅔ cup canned coconut milk
2.5ml/½ tsp ground turmeric
2.5ml/½ tsp crushed dried chillies
5ml/1 tsp salt
10ml/2 tsp granulated sugar
15ml/1 tbsp groundnut (peanut) oil
2.5ml/½ tsp mustard seeds
2.5ml/½ tsp cumin seeds
1 small onion, finely chopped
1–2 dried red chillies, broken
6–8 curry leaves

COOK'S TIP
Use canned pineapple in natural juice to save time. You will need approximately 500g/1¼lb drained pineapple to serve 4 people.

1 Quarter the pineapple lengthways, so that you end up with four boat-shaped pieces. Peel them and remove the eyes and the central core. Cut into bitesize pieces.

2 Put the pineapple in a wok, karahi or large pan and add the water, with the coconut milk, turmeric and crushed dried chillies. Bring to a slow simmer over a low heat, and cook, covered, for 10–12 minutes, or until the pineapple is soft, but not mushy.

3 Add the salt and granulated sugar, and continue to cook gently, uncovered, until the sauce has thickened slightly.

4 Heat the oil in a second pan, and add the mustard seeds. As soon as they begin to pop, add the cumin seeds and the onion. Fry for 6–7 minutes, stirring regularly, until the onion is soft.

5 Add the chillies and curry leaves. Fry for a further 1–2 minutes and then pour the mixture over the pineapple. Stir well, then remove from the heat. Serve hot or cold, but not chilled.

LENTILS, PEAS & BEANS

Indian cooking makes wonderful use of the many different lentils, peas and beans available. These ingredients are highly nutritious and cheap, and can be combined with other vegetables and flavoured with spices and herbs to create tasty main courses and side dishes that are delicious served with rice or Indian bread. Most dried pulses need to be soaked overnight before cooking, and it is important to follow the cooking procedures and timings. In many dishes, lentils and split peas can be used interchangeably, so use what you have to hand and alter the cooking times as necessary.

TARKA DHAL

Tarka is a hot oil seasoning that is folded into a dish before serving. This particular dish is commonly found in Bengal, Assam and Bangladesh.

SERVES 4–6

INGREDIENTS
115g/4oz/½ cup red lentils or 50g/2oz/¼ cup chana dhal or yellow split peas, washed
5ml/1 tsp grated fresh root ginger
5ml/1 tsp crushed garlic
2.5ml/¼ tsp ground turmeric
2 fresh green chillies, chopped
7.5ml/1½ tsp salt

FOR THE TARKA
30ml/2 tbsp vegetable oil
1 onion, sliced
2.5ml/½ tsp mixed mustard and onion seeds
4 dried red chillies
1 tomato, sliced

TO GARNISH
15ml/1 tbsp chopped fresh coriander (cilantro)
1–2 fresh green chillies, seeded and sliced
15ml/1 tbsp chopped fresh mint

1 Place the lentils, chana dhal or yellow split peas in a large pan with 600ml/ 1 pint/2½ cups water and the ginger, garlic, turmeric, chillies and salt. Bring to the boil and cook for about 20 minutes, or until soft, then mash with the back of a spoon until soupy. Add a little more water if necessary.

2 To prepare the tarka, heat the oil in another pan and fry the onion with the mustard and onion seeds, dried red chillies and sliced tomato for 2 minutes.

3 Pour the tarka over the dhal and garnish with the chopped fresh coriander, fresh green chillies and chopped mint. Serve immediately.

DHAL WITH COCONUT & TARKA

This wonderful dish of red lentils with a spicy topping is deliciously aromatic.
Serve it with plenty of freshly baked naan bread for mopping up the sauce.

SERVES 4

INGREDIENTS
50g/2oz/¼ cup butter
10ml/2 tsp black mustard seeds
1 onion, finely chopped
2 garlic cloves, finely chopped
5ml/1 tsp ground turmeric
5ml/1 tsp ground cumin
2 fresh green chillies, seeded and finely chopped
225g/8oz/1 cup red lentils
300ml/½ pint/1¼ cups canned coconut milk
1 quantity tarka or coriander baghar
fresh coriander (cilantro), to garnish

1 Melt the butter in a large heavy pan. Add the mustard seeds. When they start to pop, add the onion and garlic and cook for 5–10 minutes until soft.

2 Stir the turmeric, cumin and chillies into the onion mixture and cook for 2 minutes. Stir in the lentils, 1 litre/1¾ pints/4 cups water and the coconut milk. Bring to the boil, then cover and simmer for about 40 minutes, adding more water if needed. The lentils should be soft and should have absorbed most of the liquid.

3 Prepare the tarka or coriander baghar and pour immediately over the dhal mixture. Garnish with fresh coriander leaves and serve immediately.

COOK'S TIP
This dish is equally good made with moong dhal,
the yellow-green split mung bean that is widely used
in Indian cookery.

Lentil Dhal with Roasted Garlic & Whole Spices

This spicy lentil dhal makes a sustaining and comforting meal when served with rice or Indian breads and any dry-spiced sih, particularly a cauliflour or potato curry.

SERVES 4–6

INGREDIENTS
40g/1½oz/3 tbsp butter or ghee
1 onion, chopped
2 green chillies, seeded and chopped
15ml/¹ tbsp chopped fresh root ginger
225g/8oz/1 cup yellow or red lentils, washed
45ml/3 tbsp roasted garlic purée
5ml/1 tsp ground cumin
5ml/1 tsp ground coriander
200g/7oz tomatoes, peeled and diced
a little lemon juice
salt and ground black pepper
fresh coriander (cilantro sprigs) and fried onion and garlic slices to garnish

FOR THE SPICE MIX
30ml/2 tbsp groundnut (peanut) oil
4–5 shallots, sliced
2 garlic cloves, thinly sliced
15g/1½oz/1 tbsp butter or ghee
5ml/1 tsp cumin seeds
3–4 small dried red chillies
8–10 fresh curry leaves

1 Melt the butter or ghee in a large pan and cook the onion, chillies and ginger for about 10 minutes, or until golden.

2 Stir in the lentils and 900ml/1½ pints/3¾ cups water, then bring to the boil. Reduce the heat and part cover the pan. Simmer, stirring occasionally, for about 55 minutes, until similar to a very thick soup.

3 Stir the roasted garlic purée, cumin and ground coriander into the lentil mixture and season with salt and pepper. Cook for 10–15 minutes, uncovered, stirring frequently to prevent the dhal sticking to the base of the pan. Stir in the tomatoes and adjust the seasoning, adding a little lemon juice to taste.

4 To make the whole spice mix, heat the oil in a small, heavy pan. Add the shallots and fry over a medium heat, stirring occasionally, until browned and crisp. Add the garlic and cook, stirring frequently, until the garlic colours slightly. Use a draining spoon to remove the shallot mixture from the pan and set aside.

5 Melt the butter or ghee in the same pan. Add the cumin and mustard seeds and fry until the mustard seeds pop. Stir in the chillies, curry leaves and the shallot mixture, then immediately swirl the mixture into the cooked dhal. Garnish with coriander, onions and garlic and serve immediately.

LENTILS SEASONED WITH GARLIC OIL

This recipe, known as sambhar, *varies considerably within the southern states of India. A single vegetable or a combination of two or more vegetables may be added to the lentils.* Sambhar *is traditionally served with* idlis *(steamed rice dumplings) or* dosai *(stuffed rice pancakes) but is also good with plain boiled rice.*

SERVES 4–6

INGREDIENTS
120ml/8 tbsp vegetable oil
2.5ml/½ tsp mustard seeds
2.5ml/½ tsp cumin seeds
2 dried red chillies
1.5ml/¼ tsp asafoetida
6–8 curry leaves
2 garlic cloves, crushed, plus 2 garlic cloves, sliced
30ml/2 tbsp desiccated (dry, unsweetened, shredded) coconut
225g/8oz/1 cup red lentils, picked over, washed and drained
10ml/2 tsp sambhar masala
2.5ml/½ tsp ground turmeric
450g/1lb mixed vegetables, such as okra, courgettes (zucchini),
  aubergine (eggplant) cauliflower, shallots and (bell) peppers
60ml/4 tbsp tamarind juice
4 firm tomatoes, quartered
a few fresh coriander (cilantro) leaves, chopped

> COOK'S TIP
> *Red lentils are used in this recipe, but the traditional choice would be yellow split lentils, which are known as toor dhal or tuvar dhal.*

1 Heat half the oil in a wok, karahi or large pan, and stir-fry the mustard seeds, cumin seeds, chillies, asafoetida, curry leaves, crushed garlic and coconut until the coconut begins to brown.

2 Stir the red lentils, sambhar masala and turmeric into the coconut mixtur and stir-fry for 2–3 minutes. Add 450ml/¾ pint/scant 2 cups water to the pan. Bring the mixture to the boil, then reduce the heat to low.

3 Cover the pan and leave to simmer gently for 25–30 minutes, or until the lentils are mushy. Add the mixed vegetables, tamarind juice and tomatoes. Cook until the vegetables are just tender.

4 Heat the remaining oil in a small pan over a low heat, and fry the garlic slices until golden. Stir the coriander leaves into the oil, then pour the mixture over the lentils and vegetables. Mix at the table before serving.

Lemon & Coconut Dhal

This warm spicy dish is wonderfully aromatic and can be served either as a dip with poppadums or as a main-meal accompaniment.

Serves 8

Ingredients
5cm/2 in piece fresh root ginger
1 onion
2 garlic cloves
2 small fresh red chillies, seeded
30ml/2 tbsp sunflower oil
5ml/1 tsp cumin seeds
150g/5oz/⅔ cup red lentils, washed
15ml/1 tbsp hot curry paste
200ml/7fl oz/scant 1 cup coconut cream
juice of 1 lemon
a handful of fresh coriander (cilantro) leaves
25g/1oz/¼ cup flaked (slivered) almonds
salt and ground black pepper

1 Peel and finely chop the ginger, onion and garlic. Finely chop the chillies. Heat the oil in a large shallow pan. Add the ginger, onion, garlic, chillies and cumin. Cook for 5 minutes, until softened but not coloured, stirring occasionally.

2 Stir the lentils, 250ml/8fl oz/1 cup water and the curry paste into the spices. Bring to the boil, cover and cook over a low heat for 15–20 minutes, stirring occasionally, until the lentils are just tender and not yet broken.

3 Stir all but 30ml/2 tbsp of the coconut cream into the lentils. Bring to the boil and cook, uncovered, for 15–20 minutes. Remove from the heat, then stir in the lemon juice and coriander leaves. Season to taste.

4 Heat a frying pan and toast the almonds for 1–2 minutes, stirring frequently, until golden brown. Stir three-quarters of the almonds into the dhal. Transfer to warmed serving dish and swirl in the remaining coconut cream. Scatter the reserved almonds over the top and serve warm.

CREAMY BLACK LENTILS

Black lentils or urad dhal *are available whole, split, and skinned and split. Generally speaking, whole lentils are used in the north of India and split lentils in the west and south.*

SERVES 4–6

INGREDIENTS
175g/6oz/³⁄4 cup black lentils, soaked then drained
50g/2oz/¹⁄4 cup red split lentils
120ml/4fl oz/¹⁄2 cup double (heavy) cream, plus extra to serve
120ml/4fl oz/¹⁄2 cup natural (plain) yogurt
5ml/1 tsp cornflour (cornstarch)
45ml/3 tbsp ghee or vegetable oil
1 onion, finely chopped
5cm/2in piece fresh root ginger, crushed
4 fresh green chillies, chopped
1 tomato, chopped
2.5ml/¹⁄2 tsp chilli powder
2.5ml/¹⁄2 tsp ground turmeric
2.5ml/¹⁄2 tsp ground cumin
2 garlic cloves, sliced
salt
fresh coriander (cilantro) sprigs and sliced red chilli, to garnish

1 Place the black and red lentils in a large pan, cover with water and bring to the boil. Simmer for about 30 minutes until tender. Mash and cool. In a bowl, combine the cream, yogurt and cornflour, then stir into the cooled lentils.

2 Heat 15ml/1 tbsp of the ghee or oil in a wok, karahi or large pan, and fry the onion, ginger, half the chillies and the tomato until the onion is soft. Add the ground spices and salt and fry for a further 2 minutes. Add to the lentil mixture and mix well. Reheat, transfer to a heatproof serving dish and keep warm.

3 Heat the remaining ghee or oil in a heavy frying pan over a low heat and fry the garlic slices and remaining fresh green chillies until the garlic slices are golden brown. Pour the flavoured oil over the lentils and fold in just before serving with extra cream handed separately.

Spiced Lentils with Spinach

Spinach cooked with chana dhal *or split peas makes a wholesome dish. Serve with naan bread, chapatis or rice, and a fresh salad or tangy chutney.*

SERVES 4

INGREDIENTS
175g/6oz/³⁄₄ cup chana dhal or yellow split peas
30ml/2 tbsp vegetable oil
1.5ml/¼ tsp black mustard seeds
1 onion, thinly sliced
2 garlic cloves, crushed
2.5cm/1in piece fresh root ginger, grated
1 fresh red chilli, finely chopped
275g/10oz frozen spinach, thawed
1.5ml/¼ tsp chilli powder
2.5ml/½ tsp ground coriander
2.5ml/½ tsp garam masala
2.5ml/½ tsp salt

1 Wash the chana dhal or split peas in several changes of cold water. Place in a large bowl, cover with cold water and leave to soak for 30 minutes.

2 Drain the chana dhal or split peas and put in a large pan with 175ml/6fl oz/ ³⁄₄ cup water. Bring to the boil, cover, and simmer for about 20–25 minutes, or until soft. Cook, uncovered, until the cooking liquid has evaporated.

3 Heat the oil in a wok, karahi or large pan and fry the mustard seeds for about 2 minutes until they begin to splutter. Add the onion, garlic, ginger and chilli and fry for 5–6 minutes, then add the spinach and cook for 10 minutes, or until the spinach is dry and the liquid is absorbed. Stir in the remaining spices and salt and cook for 2–3 minutes.

4 Add the chana dhal or split peas to the spinach in the pan and cook, stirring, for about 5 minutes. Serve hot.

LENTILS WITH OKRA

This is a substantial vegetable dish, which is enhanced by the inclusion of tangy green mango. It is bursting with flavour and is delightfully spicy.

SERVES 4

INGREDIENTS
115g/14oz/⅔ cup yellow lentils, washed
45ml/3 tbsp corn oil
2.5ml/½ tsp onion seeds
2 onions, sliced
2.5ml/½ tsp ground fenugreek
5ml/1 tsp grated fresh root ginger
5ml/1 tsp crushed garlic
7.5ml/1½ tsp chilli powder
1.5ml/¼ tsp ground turmeric
5ml/1 tsp ground coriander
1 green (unripe) mango, peeled and sliced
450g/1lb okra, trimmed and cut into 1cm/½in pieces
7.5ml/1½ tsp salt
2 fresh red chillies, seeded and sliced
30ml/2 tbsp chopped fresh coriander (cilantro)
1 tomato, sliced

1 Place the lentils in a pan with enough water to cover. Bring to the boil and cook for about 20 minutes until soft but not mushy. Drain and set aside.

2 Heat the oil in a deep round-based frying pan or karahi and fry the onion seeds until they begin to pop. Add the sliced onions and fry until golden brown. Lower the heat and add the ground fenugreek, ginger, garlic, chilli powder, turmeric and ground coriander.

3 Add the mango slices and the okra. Stir well and add the salt, red chillies and fresh coriander. Stir-fry for about 3 minutes or until the okra is cooked. Add the cooked lentils and sliced tomato and cook for a further 3 minutes. Serve hot.

GRILLED AUBERGINES WITH CHILLI LENTILS

This nutritious and satisfying dish is ideal as a main meal for vegetarians but may also be served as an accompaniment to a meat dish. It is very simple to make and is good served with plain boiled rice or chapatis.

SERVES 4

INGREDIENTS
2 large aubergines (eggplant), sliced
175g/6oz/¾ cup split red lentils, rinsed and drained
2 garlic cloves, crushed,
1 onion, finely chopped
1 fresh red chilli, sliced
10ml/2 tsp ground coriander
5ml/2 tsp ground cumin
600ml/1 pint/2½ cups vegetable stock
olive oil, for brushing
150g/5oz/⅔ cup Greek (strained plain) yogurt
salt and ground black pepper
cayenne pepper, to sprinkle

COOK'S TIP
The cool, creamy yogurt counteracts the heat of the chillies and helps to soothe the palate. Yogurt is a good accompaniment for any spicy dish.

1 Arrange the aubergine slices in a colander and sprinkle with salt. Leave to drain for 30 minutes, then rinse and dry on paper towels.

2 Place the red lentils in a large pan with the crushed garlic, onion, chilli, coriander and cumin. Pour in the vegetable stock. Bring to the boil, cover and simmer for about 20 minutes, or until tender. Keep warm.

3 Meanwhile, preheat a hot grill (broiler). Brush a baking sheet lightly with oil and arrange the aubergine slices on the sheet. Brush the aubergine slices with oil and sprinkle with salt and ground black pepper. Grill (broil) for 10–15 minutes, or until tender and golden brown, turning once.

4 Arrange the aubergine slices on warmed serving plates and spoon over alternate spoonfuls of spiced lentils and Greek yogurt. Sprinkle with a little cayenne pepper and serve hot.

MADRAS SAMBAL WITH GREEN BEANS

This delicious dish is regularly cooked in almost every southern Indian home and served as part of a meal. There are many different variations, and you can use any combination of vegetables that are in season.

SERVES 4

INGREDIENTS
225g/8oz toovar dhal or split red lentils
2.5ml/½ tsp ground turmeric
2 large potatoes, cut into 2.5cm/1in chunks
30ml/2 tbsp vegetable oil
2.5ml/½ tsp black mustard seeds
1.5ml/¼ tsp fenugreek seeds
4 curry leaves
1 onion, thinly sliced
115g/4oz green beans, cut into 2.5cm/1in lengths
5ml/1 tsp salt
2.5ml/½ tsp chilli powder
15ml/1 tbsp lemon juice
60ml/4 tbsp dessicated (dry unsweetened shredded) coconut
toasted coconut shavings, to garnish
fresh coriander (cilantro) chutney, to serve

COOK'S TIP
Curry leaves are widely used in Southern Indian cooking. They are available fresh and dried in Indian stores. Dried leaves are grey-green in colour and fresh leaves should be unbruised and have springy stalks.

1 Wash the toovar dhal or lentils in several changes of cold water. Place in a heavy pan with 600ml/1 pint/2½ cups water and the turmeric. Cover and simmer for 30−35 minutes or until the lentils are soft.

2 Par-boil the potatoes in a large pan of boiling water for about 10 minutes. Drain well and set aside.

3 Heat the vegetable oil in a large frying pan and fry the mustard seeds, fenugreek seeds and curry leaves for 2–3 minutes until the seeds begin to splutter. Add the sliced onion and green beans and fry for 7–8 minutes. Add the par-boiled potatoes and cook for a further 2 minutes.

4 Stir the toovar dhal or lentils into the vegetables with the salt, chilli powder and lemon juice and simmer for about 2 minutes. Stir in the desiccated coconut and simmer for about 5 minutes. Sprinkle over the toasted coconut and serve with a bowl of fresh coriander chutney.

Sweet Rice
with Hot-Sour Chickpeas

Many Indians enjoy dishes that combine sweet flavours with others that are hot or sour. Here, the basmati rice has a distinctly sweet flavour and goes wonderfully well with the hot-sour taste of the spicy chickpeas.

SERVES 6

INGREDIENTS
350g/12oz/1⅔ cups dried chickpeas, soaked overnight
60ml/4 tbsp vegetable oil
1 large onion, very finely chopped
225g/8oz tomatoes, peeled and finely chopped
15ml/1 tbsp ground coriander
15ml/1 tbsp ground cumin
5ml/1 tsp ground fenugreek
5ml/1 tsp ground cinnamon
1–2 fresh hot green chillies, seeded and finely sliced
2.5cm/1in piece fresh root ginger, grated
60ml/4 tbsp lemon juice
15ml/1 tbsp chopped fresh coriander (cilantro)
salt and ground black pepper

FOR THE RICE
40g/1½oz/3 tbsp ghee or butter
4 cardamom pods
4 cloves
350g/12oz/1¾ cups basmati rice, soaked and drained
5–10ml/1–2 tsp granulated sugar
5–6 saffron strands, soaked in warm water

1 Drain the chickpeas well and place in a large pan. Pour in water to cover, bring to the boil, then reduce the heat and simmer, covered, for 1–2 hours until tender, topping up the liquid from time to time if necessary. Drain the chickpeas, reserving the cooking liquid.

2 Heat the oil in a pan. Reserve about 30ml/2 tbsp of the chopped onion and add the rest to the pan. Fry over a medium heat for 4–5 minutes, stirring.

3 Add the tomatoes to the pan. Cook over a medium-low heat for 5–6 minutes, until they are very soft, stirring and mashing them frequently.

4 Stir the coriander, cumin, fenugreek and cinnamon into the tomatoes. Cook for 30 seconds, then add the chickpeas and 350ml/12fl oz/1½ cups of the reserved cooking liquid. Season with salt, then cover and simmer for 15–20 minutes, stirring occasionally and adding more liquid if necessary.

5 Meanwhile, prepare the rice. Melt the ghee or butter in a pan and fry the cardamom pods and cloves for a few minutes. Remove the pan from the heat, and when the fat has cooled a little, pour in 650ml/22fl oz/2¾ cups boiling water and stir in the basmati rice. Cover tightly and cook by the absorption method for 10 minutes.

6 When the rice is cooked, add the sugar and saffron liquid and stir thoroughly. Cover again. The rice will keep warm while you finish cooking the chickpeas.

7 Mix the reserved onion with the sliced chillies, ginger and lemon juice, and stir the mixture into the chickpeas. Add the chopped coriander and adjust the seasoning if necessary. Serve with the rice.

MASALA CHANNA

This is a typical Calcutta street food known as ghughni. *Plates full of* ghughni, *with the wholesome taste of chickpeas laced with spices and tamarind juice, are enjoyed with flat breads such as chapatis and parathas.*

SERVES 4

INGREDIENTS
225g/8oz/1¼ cups dried chickpeas, soaked overnight
50g/2oz tamarind pulp
45ml/3 tbsp vegetable oil
2.5ml/½ tsp cumin seeds
1 onion, finely chopped
2 garlic cloves, crushed
2.5cm/1in piece fresh root ginger, grated
1 fresh green chilli, finely chopped
5ml/1 tsp ground cumin
5ml/1 tsp ground coriander
1.5ml/¼ tsp ground turmeric
2.5ml/½ tsp salt
225g/8oz tomatoes, skinned and finely chopped
2.5ml/½ tsp garam masala
chopped chillies and chopped onion, to garnish

COOK'S TIP
The tamarind juice made from the tamarind pulp can be poured into ice-cube trays, frozen and stored for up to 12 months. Make double the quantity and freeze half for using at a later time.

1 Drain the chickpeas and place in a large pan with double the volume of cold water. Bring to the boil and boil vigorously for 10 minutes. Skim off any scum, then cover and simmer for 1–2 hours, or until tender.

2 Meanwhile, break up the tamarind pulp and soak in 120ml/4fl oz/½ cup boiling water for about 15 minutes. Use the back of a spoon to rub the tamarind through a sieve (strainer) into a bowl, discarding any stones (pits) and fibre.

3 Heat the vegetable oil in a wok, karahi or large pan and fry the cumin seeds for 2 minutes until they begin to splutter. Add the chopped onion, garlic, ginger and chilli and fry for 5 minutes.

4 Add the ground cumin, coriander, turmeric and salt to the pan and fry for 3 minutes. Add the chopped tomatoes and tamarind juice. Stir to combine, bring to the boil and simmer for 5 minutes.

5 Add the chickpeas and garam masala to the sauce, cover and simmer for about 15 minutes. Garnish with the chillies and onion.

SPICY CHICKPEAS WITH FRESH ROOT GINGER

Chickpeas are filling, nourishing and cheap. Here they are cooked with spices and served with a refreshing raita made with spring onions and mint. Serve with plain boiled rice or flatbreads such as chapatis.

SERVES 4–6

INGREDIENTS
225g/8oz/1¼ cups dried chickpeas, soaked overnight
30ml/2 tbsp vegetable oil
1 small onion, chopped
4cm/½in piece fresh root ginger, finely chopped
2 garlic cloves, finely chopped
1.5ml/¼ tsp ground turmeric
450g/1lb tomatoes, peeled, seeded and chopped
30ml/2 tbsp finely chopped fresh coriander (cilantro)
10ml/2 tsp garam masala
salt and ground black pepper
fresh coriander (cilantro) sprigs, to garnish

FOR THE RAITA
150ml/¼ pint/⅓ cup natural (plain) yogurt
2 spring onions (scallions), finely chopped
5ml/1 tsp toasted cumin seeds
30ml/2 tbsp chopped fresh mint
a pinch of cayenne pepper, or to taste

1 Drain the chickpeas and put them in a large pan with cold water to cover. Bring to the boil, and boil rapidly for 10 minutes, skimming off any scum. Lower the heat and simmer gently for 1–2 hours, or until tender. Drain well.

2 Heat a karahi or wok until hot and add the oil. Add the onion and stir-fry for 2–3 minutes, then add the ginger, garlic and turmeric. Stir-fry for a few seconds more. Add the tomatoes, chickpeas and seasoning, bring to the boil, then simmer for 10–15 minutes until the tomatoes have reduced to a thick sauce.

3 Meanwhile, make the raita. In a bowl, mix together the yogurt, spring onions, toasted cumin seeds, chopped fresh mint and cayenne pepper to taste. Set aside.

4 Just before the end of cooking, stir in the chopped fresh coriander and garam masala into the chickpeas. Serve immediately garnished with fresh coriander sprigs and accompanied by the raita.

CHANA DHAL & BOTTLE GOURD CURRY

Chana dhal, also known as Bengal gram, is a very small type of chickpea grown in India. It has a nutty taste and gives a fabulous earthy flavour to the food. Chana dhal is available from good Indian stores. Yellow split peas make a good substitute in terms of appearance and require the same cooking time, but the flavour is not quite the same. This dish is good served with a dry meat curry.

SERVES 4–6

INGREDIENTS
175g/6oz/⅔ cup chana dhal or yellow split peas, washed
60ml/4 tbsp vegetable oil
2 fresh green chillies, chopped
1 onion, chopped
2 garlic cloves, crushed
5cm/2in piece fresh root ginger, grated
6–8 curry leaves
5ml/1 tsp chilli powder
5ml/1 tsp ground turmeric
450g/1lb bottle gourd or marrow (large zucchini), courgettes (zucchini), squash
  or pumpkin, peeled, pithed and sliced
60ml/4 tbsp tamarind juice
2 tomatoes, chopped
salt
a handful of fresh coriander (cilantro) leaves, chopped

> COOK'S TIP
> *If using courgettes, add them along with the tamarind juice, tomatoes and fresh coriander in step 3. Courgettes need much less cooking time than the other vegetables suggested for this recipe.*

1 Place the chana dhal or yellow split peas in a large pan with 450ml/¾ pint/2 cups water, seasoned with salt. Bring to the boil, then simmer for about 30 minutes until tender but not mushy. Set aside without draining away any excess water.

2 Heat the vegetable oil in a large pan, add the green chillies, onion, garlic, ginger, curry leaves, chilli powder, turmeric and salt and fry until the onions have softened. Add the gourd or other vegetable pieces and stir to mix well.

3 Add the chana dhal or yellow split peas and water to the vegetables and bring to the boil. Add the tamarind juice, tomatoes and coriander. Simmer until the gourd or other vegetable is cooked. Serve hot.

CHICKPEAS WITH SPICED POTATO CAKES

This is a typical Bombay street snack that locals eat happily while walking along the beach or watching a cricket match. It is the kind of food that brings together the cosmopolitan population of the city.

MAKES 10–12

INGREDIENTS
30ml/2 tbsp vegetable oil
30ml/2 tbsp ground coriander
30ml/2 tbsp ground cumin
2.5ml/½ tsp ground turmeric
2.5ml/½ tsp salt
2.5ml/½ tsp granulated sugar
30ml/2 tbsp gram flour (besan), mixed with a little water to make a paste
450g/1lb/3 cups boiled chickpeas, drained
2 fresh green chillies, chopped
5cm/2in piece fresh root ginger, crushed
85g/3oz/1½ cups chopped fresh coriander (cilantro)
2 firm tomatoes, chopped

FOR THE POTATO CAKES
450g/1lb potatoes, boiled and mashed
4 fresh green chillies, finely chopped
50g/2oz/1 cup finely chopped fresh coriander (cilantro)
7.5ml/1½ tsp ground cumin
5ml/1 tsp amchur (dried mango powder)
vegetable oil, for shallow frying
salt
fresh mint sprigs, to garnish

1 Heat the vegetable oil in a wok, karahi or large pan. Fry the coriander, cumin, turmeric, salt, sugar and gram flour paste until the water has evaporated and the oil has separated.

2 Add the chickpeas to the spices, and stir in the chopped chillies, ginger, fresh coriander and tomatoes. Toss the ingredients well and cook gently for about 5 minutes. Transfer to a serving dish and keep warm.

3 To make the potato cakes, place the mashed potato in a large bowl and add the green chillies, chopped fresh coriander, cumin, amchur and salt. Mix together until all the ingredients are well blended.

4 Using your hands, shape the potato mixture into 10–12 cakes. Heat the oil in a shallow frying pan and fry the cakes on both sides until golden brown. Transfer to a serving dish, garnish with mint sprigs and serve with the chickpeas.

CURRIED SPINACH & CHICKPEAS

This mildly spiced dish combines the simple flavours of spinach, chickpeas, potatoes and cheese perfectly. Try serving it with a spoonful of natural (plain) yogurt and plenty of warm naan bread to make a tasty, satisfying meal.

SERVES 6

INGREDIENTS
45ml/3 tbsp vegetable oil
2 garlic cloves, crushed
1 onion, roughly chopped
30ml/2 tbsp medium curry paste
15ml/1 tbsp black mustard seeds
45g/1lb potatoes, cut into small cubes
450g/1lb frozen leaf spinach, thawed
400g/14oz can chickpeas, drained
225g/8oz paneer or haloumi cheese, cubed
15ml/1 tbsp lime juice
salt and ground black pepper
fresh coriander (cilantro) sprigs, to garnish

1 Heat the oil in a large, heavy pan and cook the garlic and onion over a medium heat for about 5 minutes until the onion begins to soften, stirring frequently. Add the curry paste and mustard seeds and cook for 1 minute.

2 Add the potatoes, to the pan and pour over 475ml/16fl oz/2 cups water. Bring to the boil and simmer, uncovered, for 20–25 minutes, until the potatoes are almost tender and most of the liquid has evaporated, stirring occasionally.

3 Meanwhile, place the thawed spinach in a strainer and press out as much liquid as possible. Using a sharp knife, chop it roughly.

4 Stir the spinach and chickpeas into the potatoes and cook for a further 5 minutes, or until the potatoes are tender. Add a little more water, if necessary (it should not be too wet). Stir frequently to prevent the mixture from sticking to the pan. Stir in the paneer or haloumi cheese and lime juice, adjust the seasoning, and serve garnished with fresh coriander.

Mung Beans with Potatoes

These green beans are one of the quicker-cooking beans that do not require soaking. They are therefore very easy to use. In this recipe they are cooked with potatoes and traditional Indian spices to create a tasty, nutritious dish.

SERVES 4

INGREDIENTS
200g/7oz/1 cup mung beans
225g/8oz potatoes, cut into 2cm/¼in chunks
30ml/2 tbsp oil
2.5ml/½ tsp cumin seeds
1 fresh green chilli, finely chopped
1 garlic clove, crushed
2.5cm/1in piece fresh root ginger, finely chopped
1.5ml/¼ tsp ground turmeric
2.5ml/½ tsp cayenne pepper
5ml/1 tsp salt
5ml/1 tsp sugar
4 curry leaves, plus extra to garnish
5 tomatoes, peeled and finely chopped
15ml/1 tbsp tomato purée (paste)
plain rice, to serve

1 Wash the beans. Place them in a pan with 750ml/1¼ pints/3 cups water. bring to the boil, cover and simmer for about 30 minutes, or until tender. In a separate pan, par-boil the potatoes, then drain well.

2 Heat the oil and fry the cumin seeds, until they splutter. Add the chilli, garlic and ginger and fry for 3–4 minutes.

3 Add the turmeric, cayenne pepper, salt and sugar to the pan and cook for 2 minutes, stirring to prevent the mixture from sticking.

4 Add the curry leaves, tomatoes and tomato purée to the spices and simmer for 5 minutes, or until the sauce thickens. Stir the tomato sauce and potatoes into the mung beans. Serve with plain boiled rice, and garnish with curry leaves.

Kidney Bean Curry

This dish, known as rajma *in Punjabi, is a fine example of the area's hearty, robust cuisine. It is a widely eaten dish all over the state, and is even sold by street vendors. Plain boiled rice makes the perfect accompaniment for this dish.*

Serves 4

Ingredients
225g/8oz/1¼ cups dried red kidney beans, soaked overnight
30ml/2 tbsp vegetable oil
2.5ml/½ tsp cumin seeds
1 onion, thinly sliced
1 fresh green chilli, finely chopped
2 garlic cloves, crushed
2.5cm/1in piece fresh root ginger, grated
30ml/2 tbsp curry paste
5ml/1 tsp ground cumin
5ml/1 tsp ground coriander
2.5ml/½ tsp chilli powder
2.5ml/½ tsp salt
400g/14oz can chopped tomatoes
30ml/2 tbsp chopped fresh coriander (cilantro)

Cook's Tip
If you do not have time to soak and cook the kidney beans, drained and well-rinsed canned beans work very well as an alternative.

1 Drain the beans and place in a large pan with double the volume of water. Boil vigorously for 10 minutes. Drain, rinse and return the beans to the pan. Add double the volume of water and bring to the boil. Reduce the heat, then cover and cook for 1–1½ hours, or until the beans are soft. (This process is essential in order to remove the toxins that are present in dried kidney beans.)

2 Meanwhile, heat the vegetable oil in a wok, karahi or large pan and fry the cumin seeds for 2 minutes until they begin to splutter.

3 Add the sliced onion, green chilli, garlic and ginger to the pan and fry for about 5 minutes. Stir in the curry paste, cumin, coriander, chilli powder and salt, and cook for a further 5 minutes.

4 Add the tomatoes to the spice mixture and simmer for about 5 minutes. Add the kidney beans and fresh coriander, reserving a little for the garnish. Cover and cook for 15 minutes adding a little more water if necessary. Serve garnished with the reserved coriander.

FISH & SHELLFISH

The waters of India's coastline abound with fish and shellfish, and the inland waterways and lakes provide a wealth of freshwater fish, too. Some of the fish indigenous to the subcontinent are not available in the West, but substitutes can be made with very good results. Each area of the country has a different approach to flavouring and spicing its fish dishes. Goa is well known for its dishes flavoured with coconut, while Kerala uses wonderful spice mixes produced locally. On the east coast, Bengal prides itself on its unique fish and shellfish dishes. Most recipes included in this chapter are easy and quick to prepare. Fish often requires very little cooking, and you can produce an impressive-looking meal that tastes really delicious in a matter of minutes.

GRILLED KING PRAWNS WITH STIR-FRIED SPICES

Traditionally, king prawns are marinated, then grilled in the tandoor to produce classic tandoori king prawns. It is possible to achieve similar results by grilling the prawns under a very hot electric or gas grill (broiler).

SERVES 4

INGREDIENTS
45ml/3 tbsp natural (plain) yogurt
5ml/1 tsp paprika
5ml/1 tsp grated fresh root ginger
16–20 peeled, cooked king prawns (jumbo shrimp), thawed if frozen
15ml/1 tbsp vegetable oil
3 onions, sliced
2.5ml/½ tsp fennel seeds, crushed
2.5cm/1in piece cinnamon stick
5ml/1 tsp crushed garlic
5ml/1 tsp chilli powder
1 yellow (bell) pepper, seeded and roughly chopped
1 red (bell) pepper, seeded and roughly chopped
salt
15ml/1 tbsp fresh coriander (cilantro) leaves, to garnish
boiled rice, to serve

VARIATION
If you are not keen on the anise flavour of fennel seeds you could use cumin or caraway seeds instead.

1 In a bowl, blend together the yogurt, paprika and ginger and season with salt to taste. Add the prawns to the mixture, stir to coat well and leave in a cool place to marinate for 30–45 minutes.

2 Meanwhile, heat the vegetable oil in a wok, karahi or large pan and fry the sliced onions with the fennel seeds and the cinnamon stick over a medium heat until the onions soften and turn golden.

3 Lower the heat and stir in the crushed garlic and chilli powder. Add the chopped yellow and red peppers to the pan and stir-fry gently for 3–5 minutes.

4 Remove the pan from the heat and transfer the onion and spice mixture to a warmed serving dish, discarding the cinnamon stick. Set aside.

5 Preheat the grill (broiler) to medium. Put the marinated prawns in a grill (broiler) pan or flameproof dish and place under the grill to darken their tops and achieve a chargrilled effect. Add the prawns to the onion and spice mixture, garnish with fresh coriander and serve with plain boiled rice.

Prawns with Garlic

Prawns have a particular affinity with garlic. To enhance the flavour of the garlic, fry it very gently without letting it brown completely. These spice-coated prawns are delicious served with a salad, or with plenty of warm naan bread.

Serves 4

Ingredients
15ml/1 tbsp vegetable oil
3 garlic cloves, roughly halved
3 tomatoes, chopped
2.5ml/½ tsp salt
5ml/1 tsp crushed dried red chillies
5ml/1 tsp lemon juice
mango chutney, to taste
1 fresh green chilli, chopped
16–20 peeled, cooked king prawns (jumbo shrimp), thawed if frozen
fresh coriander (cilantro) sprigs and chopped spring onions (scallions), to garnish

1 In a wok, karahi or large pan, heat the vegetable oil over a low heat and fry the garlic halves gently until they are tinged with golden brown.

2 Add the chopped tomatoes, salt, crushed red chillies, lemon juice, some mango chutney and the chopped fresh chilli to the garlic. Stir to combine well.

3 Add the peeled prawns to the pan, then increase the heat and stir-fry briskly, making sure the prawns are mixed well with the tomato mixture until they are thoroughly heated through.

4 Transfer the prawns in the sauce to a warmed serving dish and garnish with the coriander sprigs and chopped spring onions. Serve immediately.

Cook's Tip
When buying fresh prawns, choose specimens with a firm, crisp shell and a fresh smell. Do not buy them if they smell of ammonia.

KING PRAWN KORMA

Prawns are the most popular shellfish in Bengal. This dish is cooked in the style of
malai chingri, *which means prawns cooked in dairy or coconut cream. Because of the*
richness of the ingredients, just serve plain boiled rice with this korma.

SERVES 4

INGREDIENTS
12 peeled, cooked king prawns (jumbo shrimp), thawed if frozen
45ml/3 tbsp natural (plain) yogurt
5ml/1 tsp paprika
5ml/1 tsp garam masala
15ml/1 tbsp tomato purée (paste)
60ml/4 tbsp coconut milk
5ml/1 tsp chilli powder
15ml/1 tbsp vegetable oil
5ml/1 tsp crushed garlic
5ml/1 tsp grated fresh root ginger
2.5cm/1in piece cinnamon stick, halved
2 cardamom pods
salt
15ml/1 tbsp chopped fresh coriander (cilantro), to garnish

1 If using prawns that have been frozen, drain thoroughly in a sieve (strainer) over a bowl to ensure that all excess liquid is removed before cooking.

2 Place the yogurt, paprika, garam masala, tomato purée, coconut milk, chilli powder and 150ml/¼ pint/⅔ cup water into a large glass bowl, and season to taste with salt. Stir until the ingredients are well blended then set aside.

3 Heat the vegetable oil in a wok, karahi or large pan, add the crushed garlic, ginger, cinnamon and cardamom pods, and season to taste with salt. Fry very gently over a low heat for 1–2 minutes.

4 Pour the spice mixture into the pan and bring to the boil, stirring occasionally. Add the prawns and cook, stirring constantly, until the sauce starts to thicken. Garnish with chopped coriander and serve.

Prawn Curry

The Bay of Bengal provides Bengal and Orissa with enormous quantities of fish and shellfish. Eating plenty of fish, greens, lentils and peas is a way of life here. The food is generally cooked in mustard oil, which lends a distinctive, nutty flavour.

Serves 4

Ingredients
675g/1½lb raw tiger prawns (jumbo shrimp)
4 dried red chillies
50g/2oz/1 cup desiccated (dry unsweetened shredded) coconut
5ml/1 tsp black mustard seeds
1 large onion, chopped
45ml/3 tbsp vegetable oil
4 bay leaves
2.5cm/1in piece fresh root ginger, chopped
2 garlic cloves, crushed
15ml/1 tbsp ground coriander
5ml/1 tsp chilli powder
5ml/1 tsp salt
4 tomatoes, finely chopped

1 Peel the prawns. Run a sharp knife along the back of each prawn and remove the black vein. Leave a few prawns unpeeled, setting them aside for the garnish.

2 Dry-fry the chillies, coconut, mustard seeds and onion in a large pan for about 5 minutes, stirring continuously. Process to a coarse paste in a food processor.

3 Heat the vegetable oil in the pan and fry the bay leaves for 1 minute. Add the chopped ginger and the garlic, and fry for 2–3 minutes. Add the ground coriander, chilli powder, salt and the spice paste and fry for about 5 minutes.

4 Add the tomatoes and about 175ml/6fl oz/¾ cup water to the pan and simmer for 5–6 minutes. Add the prawns and cook for 4–5 minutes, or until they turn pink and the edges start to curl. Serve garnished with the reserved whole prawns.

Karahi Prawns & Fenugreek

The combination of both ground and. fresh fenugreek makes this a very fragrant and delicious dish. When preparing fresh fenugreek, use the leaves whole, but discard the stalks, which would add a bitter flavour to the dish.

SERVES 4–6

INGREDIENTS
60ml/4 tbsp corn oil
2 onions, sliced
2 tomatoes, sliced
7.5ml/1½ tsp crushed garlic powder
5ml/1 tsp chilli powder
5ml/1 tsp ground cumin
5ml/1 tsp ground coriander
5ml/1 tsp salt
150g/5oz paneer, cubed
5ml/1 tsp ground fenugreek
1 bunch fresh fenugreek leaves
450g/1lb cooked prawns (shrimp)
2 fresh red chillies, sliced
30ml/2 tbsp chopped fresh coriander (cilantro)
50g/2oz/⅓ cup canned black-eyed beans (peas), drained
15ml/1 tbsp lemon juice

1 Heat the oil in a deep round-based frying pan or a karahi. Lower the heat slightly and add the onions and tomatoes. Fry for about 3 minutes.

2 Add the garlic powder, chilli powder, ground cumin, ground coriander, salt, paneer and the ground and fresh fenugreek to the pan. Lower the heat and stir-fry for about 2 minutes.

3 Add the prawns, red chillies, fresh coriander and the black-eyed beans and mix well. Cook for a further 3–5 minutes, stirring occasionally, or until the prawns are heated through. Sprinkle over the lemon juice and serve immediately.

PRAWNS WITH PANEER

The classic Indian cheese, paneer, is an excellent source of protein and is widely used in place of meat. Its mild flavour makes a perfect partner for the succulent king prawns and aromatic spices in this memorable and very popular dish.

SERVES 4

INGREDIENTS
30ml/2 tbsp tomato purée (paste)
60ml/4 tbsp Greek (strained plain) yogurt
7.5ml/1½ tsp garam masala
5ml/1 tsp chilli powder
5ml/1 tsp crushed garlic
5ml/1 tsp salt
10ml/2 tsp amchur (dried mango powder)
5ml/1 tsp ground coriander
115g/4oz/½ cup butter
15ml/1 tbsp corn oil
175g/6oz paneer, cubed
12 cooked king prawns (jumbo shrimp), peeled
45ml/3 tbsp fresh green chillies, chopped
45ml/3 tbsp chopped fresh coriander (cilantro)
150ml/¼ pint/⅔ cup single (light) cream

COOK'S TIP
If you make your own paneer for this dish, make it the day before you plan to use it in a recipe; it will then be firmer and easier to handle. Fresh paneer will keep for about 1 week in the refrigerator.

1 In a small bowl, blend the tomato purée, yogurt, garam masala, chilli powder, garlic, salt, amchur and ground coriander and set aside.

2 Melt the butter with the oil in a deep round-based frying pan or karahi. Lower the heat slightly and quickly fry the paneer and prawns for about 2 minutes. Remove with a slotted spoon and drain on kitchen paper.

3 Pour the spice mixture into the fat left in the pan and stir-fry for about 1 minute. Add the paneer and prawns, and cook for 7–10 minutes, stirring occasionally, until the prawns are heated through.

4 Add the fresh green chillies and most of the chopped coriander to the prawns and paneer, and pour in the cream. Heat through for about 2 minutes, garnish with the remaining coriander and serve immediately.

PRAWNS IN HOT SAUCE

This sizzling prawn dish is cooked in a fiery hot sauce containing chilli powder and ground green chillies mixed with other spices. Serve it with a cooling cucumber raita, which will help to soften the piquant flavour.

SERVES 4

INGREDIENTS
2 onions, roughly chopped
30ml/2 tbsp tomato purée (paste)
5ml/1 tsp ground coriander
1.5ml/¼ tsp ground turmeric
5ml/1 tsp chilli powder
2 fresh green chillies
45ml/3 tbsp chopped fresh coriander (cilantro)
30ml/2 tbsp lemon juice
5ml/1 tsp salt
45ml/3 tbsp corn oil
16 cooked king prawns (jumbo shrimp)
1 fresh green chilli, chopped (optional)

1 Put the onions, tomato purée, ground coriander, turmeric, chilli powder, whole green chillies, 30ml/2 tbsp of the fresh coriander, the lemon juice and salt into the bowl of a food processor. Process for about 1 minute. If the mixture seems too thick, add a little water to loosen it.

2 Heat the oil in a deep round-based frying pan or karahi. Lower the heat slightly and add the spice mixture. Fry the mixture for 3–5 minutes or until the sauce has thickened slightly.

3 Add the prawns to the pan and stir-fry over a medium heat. As soon as the prawns are heated through, transfer to a serving dish and garnish with the rest of the fresh coriander and the chopped green chilli, if using. Serve immediately.

PARSEE PRAWN CURRY

After arriving on the west coast of India, the Parsee community migrated to different parts of the country. The majority, however, made Bombay their home. They have cleverly integrated their cooking style into the exotic tastes of Indian cuisine.

SERVES 4–6

INGREDIENTS
60ml/4 tbsp vegetable oil
1 onion, finely sliced, plus 2 onions, finely chopped
6 garlic cloves, crushed
5ml/1 tsp chilli powder
7.5ml/1½ tsp ground turmeric
50ml/2fl oz/¼ cup tamarind juice
5ml/1 tsp mint sauce
15ml/1 tbsp demerara (raw) sugar
450g/1lb raw king prawns (jumbo shrimp)
75g/3oz coriander (cilantro) leaves, chopped, plus extra leaves to garnish
salt

1 Heat the oil and fry the sliced onion until golden. In a bowl, mix the garlic, chilli powder and turmeric with a little water. Add to the pan and cook.

2 Add the chopped onions to the pan and fry gently until the onions become translucent, then stir in the tamarind juice, mint sauce, sugar and salt. Simmer for a further 3 minutes.

3 Carefully peel and devein the king prawns, then pat dry with kitchen paper. Add the prawns to the onion and spice mixture with a small amount of water and stir-fry until the prawns turn bright pink.

4 When the prawns are cooked, add the chopped coriander and stir-fry over a high heat to thicken the sauce. Garnish with extra coriander and serve.

GOAN PRAWN CURRY

Excellent fish and shellfish dishes are a feature of Goan cuisine. Numerous varieties of fish and shellfish are found along the extended coastline and inland waterways.

SERVES 4

INGREDIENTS
15g/½oz/1 tbsp ghee or butter
2 garlic cloves, crushed
450g/1lb small raw prawns (shrimp), peeled and deveined
15ml/1 tbsp groundnut (peanut) oil
4 cardamom pods
4 cloves
5cm/2in piece cinnamon stick
15ml/1 tbsp mustard seeds
1 large onion, finely chopped
½–1 fresh red chilli, seeded and sliced
4 tomatoes, peeled, seeded and chopped
175ml/6fl oz/¾ cup fish stock or water
350ml/12fl oz/1½ cups coconut milk
45ml/3 tbsp fragrant spice mix
10–20ml/2–4 tsp chilli powder
salt

1 Melt the ghee or butter in a wok, karahi or large pan, add the garlic and stir over a low heat for a few seconds. Add the prawns and stir-fry briskly to coat. Transfer to a plate and set aside.

2 In the same pan, heat the oil over a low heat and fry the cardamom pods, cloves and cinnamon stick for 2 minutes. Add the mustard seeds and fry for 1 minute. Add the onion and chilli and fry for 7–8 minutes, or until softened and lightly browned. Add the remaining ingredients and bring to a slow simmer. Cook gently for 6–8 minutes and add the prawns. Simmer for 5–8 minutes until the prawns are cooked through. Spoon into a warmed dish and serve.

GOAN-STYLE MUSSELS

This is a simple and very quick way to cook mussels in a delicious fragrant coconut sauce. Serve with plenty of naan bread or white bread rolls.

SERVES 4

INGREDIENTS
900g/2lb live mussels
115g/4oz/½ cup creamed coconut
45ml/3 tbsp oil
1 onion, finely chopped
3 garlic cloves, crushed
2.5cm/1in piece fresh root ginger, finely chopped
2.5ml/½ tsp ground turmeric
5ml/1 tsp ground cumin
5ml/2 tsp ground coriander
1.5ml/¼ tsp salt
chopped fresh coriander (cilantro), to garnish

1 Scrub the mussels in cold water and remove the beards. Discard any mussels that are already open and do not close when tapped sharply.

2 In a bowl, dissolve the creamed coconut in 470ml/15fl oz/1⅞ cups boiling water and set aside until needed.

3 Heat the oil in a large pan and fry the onion for about 5 minutes. Add the garlic and ginger and fry for 2 minutes. Stir in the turmeric, cumin, coriander and salt and fry for another 2 minutes. Add the dissolved coconut, bring to the boil and simmer for about 5 minutes.

4 Add the mussels to the pan, cover and cook for 6–8 minutes or until all the mussels are cooked and open. Discard any that have not opened. Spoon the mussels on to a warmed serving platter and pour the sauce over. Garnish with the chopped coriander and serve immediately.

MARINATED FRIED FISH

Fish and shellfish are a strong feature of the cuisine in the coastal region of southern India. Kerala, on the southernmost tip of the country, produces some of the finest fish and shellfish dishes. These are flavoured with local spices, grown in the fabulous spice plantation that is the pride and joy of the state.

SERVES 4

INGREDIENTS
1 small onion, coarsely chopped
4 garlic cloves, crushed
5cm/2in piece fresh root ginger, chopped
5ml/1 tsp ground turmeric
10ml/2 tsp chilli powder
4 red mullets or snappers
vegetable oil, for shallow frying
5ml/1 tsp cumin seeds
3 fresh green chillies, finely sliced
salt
lemon or lime wedges, to serve

1 In a food processor, process the onion, garlic, ginger, turmeric and chilli powder with salt to make a smooth paste. Make several slashes on both sides of the fish and rub them with the spice paste. Set aside in a cool place to rest for 1 hour. Excess fluid will be released as the salt dissolves, so lightly pat the fish dry with kitchen paper without removing the paste.

2 Heat the oil in a pan and fry the cumin seeds and sliced chillies for 1 minute. Add the fish, in batches if necessary, and fry on one side. When the first side is sealed, turn them over very gently. Fry until golden brown on both sides, drain and serve hot, with lemon or lime wedges for squeezing over.

COOK'S TIP
To create a deeper flavour with a fresh edge, add 15ml/1 tbsp chopped fresh coriander (cilantro) leaves to the spice paste in step 1.

FISH STEW

Cooking fish with vegetables is very much a tradition in eastern regions. This hearty dish with potatoes, peppers and tomatoes is perfect served with breads such as chapatis or parathas. You can try other combinations, such as green beans and spinach, but you do need a starchy vegetable in order to thicken the sauce.

SERVES 4

INGREDIENTS
30ml/2 tbsp vegetable oil
5ml/1 tsp cumin seeds
1 onion, chopped
1 red (bell) pepper, thinly sliced
1 garlic clove, crushed
2 fresh red chillies, finely chopped
2 bay leaves
2.5ml/½ tsp salt
5ml/1 tsp ground cumin
5ml/1 tsp ground coriander
5ml/1 tsp chilli powder
400g/14oz can chopped tomatoes
2 large potatoes, cut into 2.5cm/1in chunks
300ml/½ pint/1¼ cups fish stock
4 cod fillets
chapatis, to serve

1 Heat the oil in a wok, karahi or large pan over a medium heat and fry the cumin seeds for 30–40 seconds until they begin to splutter. Add the onion, red pepper, garlic, chillies and bay leaves and fry for 5–7 minutes more until the onions have browned.

2 Add the salt, cumin, coriander and chilli powder and cook for 1–2 minutes. Stir in the tomatoes, potatoes and fish stock. Bring to the boil and simmer for a further 10 minutes, or until the potatoes are almost tender.

3 Add the fish fillets, then cover the pan and allow to simmer for 5–6 minutes until the fish is just cooked through. Serve hot with chapatis.

FISH JALFREZI

In Bengal, fish curry and rice are eaten together on a daily basis. This is a rather unusual dish, using canned tuna cooked in the style of jalfrezi, and is ideal for a lunch or supper dish. Served with boiled basmati rice and dhal, it will also make a very satisfying family meal – just increase the quantities as required.

SERVES 4

INGREDIENTS
45ml/3 tbsp vegetable oil
1.5ml/¼ tsp cumin seeds
2.5ml/½ tsp ground cumin
2.5ml/½ tsp ground coriander
2.5ml/½ tsp chilli powder
1.5ml/¼ tsp salt
2 garlic cloves, crushed
1 onion, thinly sliced
1 red (bell) pepper, seeded and thinly sliced
1 green (bell) pepper, seeded and thinly sliced
400g/14oz can tuna, drained
1 fresh green chilli, finely chopped
2.5cm/1in piece fresh root ginger, grated
1.5ml/¼ tsp garam masala
5ml/1 tsp lemon juice
30ml/2 tbsp chopped fresh coriander (cilantro)
fresh coriander (cilantro) sprigs, to garnish
pitta bread and cucumber raita, to serve

COOK'S TIP
Place the pitta bread on a grill (broiler) rack and grill (broil) until it puffs up. It will then be much easier to split with a sharp knife, ready for filling.

1 Heat the vegetable oil in a wok, karahi or large pan over a medium heat and fry the cumin seeds for 30–40 seconds until they begin to splutter.

2 Add the ground cumin, coriander, chilli powder and salt to the pan. Cook for 2 minutes. Add the garlic, onion and peppers and increase the heat a little. Stir-fry the vegetables for 5–7 minutes until the onions have browned.

3 Stir in the tuna, fresh chilli and grated ginger and cook for 5 minutes. Add the garam masala, lemon juice and fresh coriander and continue to cook for a further 3–4 minutes. Serve in warmed pitta bread with cucumber raita, garnished with fresh coriander.

FISH IN A RICH TOMATO & ONION SAUCE

It is difficult to imagine the cuisine of eastern India without fish. Bengal is as well known for its fish and shellfish dishes as Goa on the west coast. In both regions, coconut is used extensively, and the difference in the taste, as always, lies in the spicing. This onion-rich dish is known as kalia *in Bengal, and a firm-fleshed fish is essential so that it does not disintegrate during cooking.*

SERVES 4

INGREDIENTS
675g/1½lb steaks of firm-textured fish such as tuna or monkfish, skinned
30ml/2 tbsp lemon juice
5ml/1 tsp salt
5ml/1 tsp ground turmeric
60ml/4 tbsp vegetable oil, plus extra for shallow frying
40g/1½oz/½ cup plain (all-purpose) flour
2.5ml/½ tsp ground black pepper
10ml/2 tsp granulated sugar
1 large onion, finely chopped
15ml/1 tbsp grated fresh root ginger
15ml/1 tbsp crushed garlic
5ml/1 tsp ground coriander
2.5–5ml/½–1 tsp hot chilli powder
175g/6oz canned chopped tomatoes, including the juice
30ml/2 tbsp chopped fresh coriander (cilantro) leaves, to garnish
plain boiled rice, to serve

1 Cut the fish into 7.5cm/3in pieces and place in a large bowl. Add the lemon juice and sprinkle with half the salt and half the turmeric. Mix gently with your fingertips and set aside for 15 minutes.

2 Pour enough oil into a 23cm/9in frying pan to cover the base to a depth of 1cm/½in and heat over a medium setting. Mix the flour and pepper and dust the fish in the seasoned flour. Add to the oil in a single layer and fry until browned on both sides and a light crust has formed. Drain on kitchen paper.

3 In a wok, karahi or large pan, heat 60ml/4 tbsp oil. When the oil is hot, but not smoking, add the sugar and let it caramelize. As soon as the sugar is brown, add the onion, ginger and garlic and fry for 7–8 minutes. Stir regularly.

4 Add the ground coriander, chilli powder and the remaining turmeric. Stir-fry for about 30 seconds and add the tomatoes. Cook until the tomatoes are mushy and the oil has separated from the spice paste, stirring regularly.

5 Pour 300ml/½ pint/1¼ cups warm water and the remaining salt into the pan, and bring to the boil. Carefully add the fried fish, reduce the heat to low and simmer, uncovered, for 5–6 minutes. Transfer to a warmed serving dish and garnish with the coriander leaves. Serve with plain boiled rice.

COOK'S TIP
Like all ground spices, ground turmeric will lose its potency on keeping. Buy only small quantities, and store the powder in an airtight container, in a cupboard away from strong light.

FISH FILLETS IN COCONUT

Use fresh fish fillets to make this dish if you can, as they have much more flavour than frozen ones. If you are using frozen fillets, ensure that they are completely thawed before using.

SERVES 4

INGREDIENTS
30ml/2 tbsp corn oil
5ml/1 tsp onion seeds
4 dried red chillies
3 garlic cloves, sliced
1 onion, sliced
2 tomatoes, sliced
30ml/2 tbsp desiccated (dry unsweetened shredded) coconut
5ml/1 tsp salt
5ml/1 tsp ground coriander
4 flatfish fillets, such as plaice, sole or flounder, each weighing about 75g/3oz
15ml/1 tbsp lime juice
15ml/1 tbsp chopped fresh coriander (cilantro)

1 Heat the oil in a deep round-based frying pan or karahi. Lower the heat slightly and add the onion seeds, dried red chillies, garlic slices and onion. Cook for about 4 minutes, stirring once or twice.

2 Add the sliced tomatoes, desiccated coconut, salt and ground coriander to the pan and stir to combine thoroughly.

3 Cut each fish fillet into 3 pieces. Drop the fish pieces into the sauce and turn them over gently until they are well coated. Cook for 5–7 minutes. Add 150ml/ ¼ pint/⅔ cup water, lime juice and fresh coriander, and cook for 3–5 minutes until the water has almost all evaporated. Serve immediately.

FISH CAKES

Goan fish and shellfish are skilfully prepared with spices to make cakes of all shapes and sizes, while the rest of India makes fish kebabs. Although haddock is used in this recipe, you can use other less expensive white fish, such as coley or whiting.

MAKES 20

INGREDIENTS
450g/1lb skinned haddock or cod
2 potatoes, peeled, boiled and coarsely mashed
4 spring onions (scallions), finely chopped
4 fresh green chillies, finely chopped
5cm/2in piece fresh root ginger, crushed
a few coriander (cilantro) and mint sprigs, chopped
2 eggs
breadcrumbs, for coating
vegetable oil, for shallow frying
salt and ground black pepper
lemon wedges and chilli sauce, to serve

1 Place the skinned fish in a lightly greased steamer and steam gently over a pan of boiling water until cooked. Remove the steamer from the heat but leave the fish on the steaming tray until cool.

2 When the fish is cool, crumble it coarsely into a large bowl, using a fork. Mix in the mashed potatoes, spring onions, chillies, crushed ginger, chopped fresh coriander and mint, and one of the eggs. Season to taste with plenty of salt and ground black pepper.

3 Shape the mixture into cakes. Beat the remaining egg and dip the cakes in it, then coat with the breadcrumbs. Heat the oil and fry the cakes until brown on all sides. Serve with the lemon wedges and chilli sauce.

CHICKEN DISHES

Poultry is an extremely versatile meat. You can serve it in a fiery tomato and chilli sauce or cook it in a mild, creamy sauce with almonds or coconut, cream and yogurt. It can be cooked as a tikka, accompanied with salad or perhaps a yogurt sauce. Poultry can be cooked on its own, combined with just a few spices, or mixed with vegetables, fruits, nuts or pulses. Some dishes are quite dry, while others have rich sauces that are best accompanied by rice and breads. In India, a chicken will usually be chopped into pieces with the bones intact, but some recipes in this chapter call for boned portions that have more appeal to the Western palate.

Chicken in Coconut Milk

In Bengal, this dish is known as murgi malai. *The word* murgi *means chicken and* malai *means cream, which can be either dairy or coconut. Sweet, fragrant coconut is a favourite ingredient of the region, and it grows in abundant supply in Bengal, Orissa and Assam. It can be used to add a rich, creamy quality to many dishes.*

Serves 4

INGREDIENTS
15ml/1 tbsp ground almonds
15ml/1 tbsp desiccated (dry unsweetened shredded) coconut
85ml/3fl oz/⅓ cup coconut milk
175g/6oz/⅔ cup fromage frais or ricotta cheese
7.5ml/1½ tsp ground coriander
5ml/1 tsp chilli powder
5ml/1 tsp crushed garlic
7.5ml/1½ tsp grated fresh root ginger
5ml/1 tsp salt
30ml/2 tbsp vegetable oil
450g/1lb chicken breast fillets, skinned and cubed
3 cardamom pods
1 bay leaf
1 dried red chilli, crushed
30ml/2 tbsp chopped fresh coriander (cilantro)

1 Dry-roast the almonds and coconut in a wok, karahi or large pan, until they turn a shade darker. Transfer the mixture to a large glass bowl.

2 Add the coconut milk, fromage frais or ricotta cheese, ground coriander, chilli powder, garlic, ginger and salt to the bowl. Mix together well.

3 Heat the vegetable oil in the pan, and add the chicken cubes, cardamom pods and bay leaf. Stir-fry for about 2 minutes to seal the chicken.

4 Pour the coconut mixture into the pan and stir well. Lower the heat, add the chilli and coriander, then cover and cook for 10–12 minutes, stirring occasionally. Uncover the pan, then stir and cook for 2 minutes more.

CHICKEN KORMA

Korma is not really a dish but a technique employed in Indian cooking. It simply means braising. There are different types of kormas: they can be light and aromatic or rich and creamy, and there are fiery ones too. The character of the dish is a reflection of its place of origin. This one comes from Delhi – the centre of Mogul cuisine.

SERVES 4

INGREDIENTS
25g/1oz/¼ cup blanched almonds
2 garlic cloves, crushed
2.5cm/1in piece fresh root ginger, chopped
30ml/2 tbsp vegetable oil
675g/1½lb chicken breast fillets, skinned and cubed
3 cardamom pods
1 onion, finely chopped
10ml/2 tsp ground cumin
1.5ml/¼ tsp salt
150ml/¼ pint/⅔ cup natural (plain) yogurt
175ml/6fl oz/¾ cup single (light) cream
toasted flaked (sliced) almonds and fresh coriander (cilantro) sprigs, to garnish
plain boiled rice, to serve

1 Process the blanched almonds, garlic and ginger in a food processor with 30ml/2 tbsp water to make a smooth paste.

2 Heat the oil in a wok, karahi or large pan, and cook the chicken for 10 minutes. Remove the chicken and set aside. Add the cardamom pods and fry for 2 minutes. Add the onion and fry for 5 minutes. Stir in the almond paste, cumin and salt. Cook for 5 minutes, stirring frequently.

3 Whisk the yogurt and add it to the onion mixture a tablespoonful at a time. Cook gently, until the yogurt has all been absorbed. Return the chicken to the pan. Cover and simmer for 5–6 minutes, or until the chicken is tender.

4 Stir the cream into the pan and simmer for 5 minutes. Garnish with toasted flaked almonds and fresh coriander, and serve with plain boiled rice.

Chicken Pasanda

A pasanda is a very, very mild dish cooked with subtle spices, fresh cream, yogurt and ground nuts. It is ideal for those who dislike fiery dishes and for children. Serve with plain, boiled rice, which goes well with the rich, creamy sauce.

SERVES 4

INGREDIENTS
60ml/4 tbsp Greek (strained plain) yogurt
2.5ml/½ tsp black cumin seeds
4 cardamom pods
6 black peppercorns
10ml/2 tsp garam masala
2.5cm/1in piece cinnamon stick
15ml/1 tbsp ground almonds
5ml/1 tsp crushed garlic
5ml/1 tsp grated fresh root ginger
5ml/1 tsp chilli powder
5ml/1 tsp salt
675g/1½lb chicken, skinned, boned and cubed
75ml/5 tbsp corn oil
2 onions, diced
3 fresh green chillies, chopped
30ml/2 tbsp chopped fresh coriander (cilantro), plus extra to garnish (optional)
120ml/4fl oz/½ cup single (light) cream

COOK'S TIP
Garam masala is a classic Indian spice mix that can be bought ready-made. It has a rich, warm, aromatic flavour. The basic blend includes cloves, cinnamon, cardamom, peppercorns, bay leaf, mace, cumin and coriander.

1 Combine the yogurt, cumin seeds, cardamom pods, peppercorns, garam masala, cinnamon stick, ground almonds, garlic, ginger, chilli powder and salt in a mixing bowl. Add the chicken pieces, stir until well covered and leave to marinate in a cool place for about 2 hours.

2 Heat the corn oil in a large karahi or deep round-based frying pan. Add the diced onions and fry for 2–3 minutes, stirring frequently.

3 Spoon the chicken mixture into the pan and stir well to combine with the onions. Cook over a medium heat for 12–15 minutes, or until the sauce thickens and the chicken is cooked through.

4 Add the green chillies and fresh coriander to the pan, and pour in cream. Bring to the boil and serve garnished with more coriander, if liked.

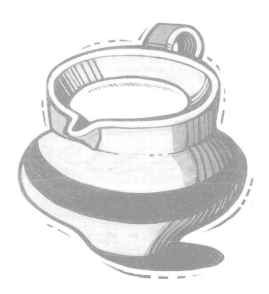

Chicken & Mushrooms in Cashew Nut Sauce

Nut pastes were introduced into northern Indian cooking by the Moguls, the travellers who provided what was probably the most important outside influence on Indian cuisine. Mughlai food, as this style of cooking has come to be known, is famed for its rich yet delicate flavours. This dish is good served with plain boiled rice and a sharp-tasting, aromatic fruit chutnry.

Serves 4

Ingredients
2 onions
30ml/2 tbsp tomato purée (paste)
50g/2oz/½ cup cashew nuts
7.5ml/1½ tsp garam masala
5ml/1 tsp crushed garlic
5ml/1 tsp chilli powder
15ml/1 tbsp lemon juice
1.5ml/¼ tsp ground turmeric
5ml/1 tsp salt
15ml/1 tbsp natural (plain) yogurt
30ml/2 tbsp vegetable oil
15ml/1 tbsp chopped fresh coriander (cilantro), plus extra to garnish
15ml/1 tbsp sultanas (golden raisins)
450g/1lb chicken breast fillets, skinned and cubed
175g/6oz button (white) mushrooms

1 Cut the onions into quarters, then place in a food processor or blender. Process for 1 minute, scraping down the sides of the bowl if necessary.

2 Add the tomato purée, cashew nuts, garam masala, crushed garlic, chilli powder, lemon juice, turmeric, salt and yogurt to the puréed onions and process for a further 1–1½ minutes.

3 In a wok, karahi or large pan, heat the oil, lower the heat to medium and pour in the onion and spice mixture from the food processor or blender Fry gently, stirring frequently, for about 2 minutes, lowering the heat if necessary.

4 Add the fresh coriander, sultanas and cubed chicken to the pan and continue to stir-fry for a further minute. Add the mushrooms, pour in 300ml/½ pint/ 1¼ cups water and bring to a gentle simmer. Cover the pan and cook over a low heat for about 10 minutes.

5 After this time, check that the chicken is cooked all the way through and the sauce is thick. Continue to cook for a little longer if necessary. Transfer to a warmed serving dish and garnish with chopped fresh coriander.

Mild Green Calcutta Curry of Chicken & Vegetables

The addition of coconut milk creates a rich, creamy sauce that is sweet with dried and fresh fruit and fragrant with coriander and mint. Serve this curry with grilled naan bread or steamed rice and a crisp salad.

Serves 4

Ingredients
4 garlic cloves, chopped
15ml/1 tbsp chopped fresh root ginger
2–3 fresh green chillies, chopped
½ bunch fresh coriander (cilantro), leaves only, roughly chopped
1 onion, chopped
juice of 1 lemon
pinch of cayenne pepper
2.5ml/½ tsp curry powder
2.5ml/½ tsp ground cumin
2–3 pinches ground cloves
large pinch ground coriander
3 boneless chicken breast fillets or thighs, skinned and cut into bitesize pieces
30ml/2 tbsp vegetable oil
2 cinnamon sticks
250ml/8fl oz/1 cup chicken stock
250ml/8fl oz/1 cup coconut milk
15–30ml/1–2 tbsp sugar
1–2 bananas
¼ pineapple, peeled and diced
handful of sultanas (golden raisins)
handful of raisins or currants
2–3 sprigs fresh mint, finely shredded
juice of ¼–½ lemon
salt

1 Put the garlic, ginger, chillies, fresh coriander, onion, lemon juice, salt, cayenne pepper, curry powder, cumin, cloves and coriander in a food processor or blender and process to make a paste.

2 Toss the chicken pieces with about 15–30ml/1–2 tbsp of the spice mixture and set aside in a cool place to marinate for several hours.

3 Heat the vegetable oil in a wok, karahi or frying pan, then add the remaining spice mixture and cook over a medium heat, stirring continuously, for about 10 minutes, or until the paste is lightly browned.

4 Add the cinnamon sticks, stock, coconut milk and sugar to the pan, stir, bring to the boil, then reduce the heat and simmer for about 10 minutes.

5 Stir the marinated chicken into the sauce and cook for about 2 minutes, or until the chicken becomes opaque.

6 Meanwhile, peel and dice the bananas. Add all the fruit to the curry, stir gently and cook for 1–2 minutes. Stir in the mint and some lemon juice. Check the seasoning and add more salt, spicing and lemon juice if necessary. Serve at once.

CHICKEN IN MASALA SAUCE

The use of green spice mixes is popular all over India. Although in southern India the mixes are generally used to cook vegetables and fish, in the north, where most people are meat-eaters, they are more often used to prepare meat and poultry dishes.

SERVES 4

INGREDIENTS
1 crisp green eating apple, peeled, cored and cubed
60ml/4 tbsp fresh coriander (cilantro) leaves
30ml/2 tbsp fresh mint leaves
150ml/¼ pint/⅔ cup natural (plain) yogurt
45ml/3 tbsp fromage frais or ricotta cheese
2 fresh green chillies, seeded and chopped
1 bunch spring onions (scallions), chopped
5ml/1 tsp salt
5ml/1 tsp granulated sugar
5ml/1 tsp crushed garlic
5ml/1 tsp grated fresh root ginger
15ml/1 tbsp vegetable oil
225g/8oz chicken breast fillets, skinned and cubed
25g/1oz/2 tbsp sultanas (golden raisins)

1 Place the apple, 45ml/3 tbsp of the coriander, the mint, yogurt, fromage frais or ricotta cheese, chillies, spring onions, salt, sugar, garlic and ginger in a food processor or blender and process for 1 minute. Scrape down the outside of the bowl and process for a few seconds more.

2 Heat the oil in a wok, karahi or large pan, pour in the yogurt mixture and cook very gently over a low heat for about 2 minutes.

3 Add the chicken pieces to the sauce and stir well to combine. Cook over a medium-low heat for 12–15 minutes, or until the chicken is fully cooked. Sprinkle the sultanas and the remaining coriander over the chicken (do not mix in, but leave as a garnish).

Kashmiri Chicken Curry

Surrounded by the snow-capped Himalayas, Kashmir is popularly known as the Switzerland of the East. The state is also renowned for its rich culinary heritage, and this aromatic dish is one of the simplest among the region's rich repertoire.

SERVES 4

INGREDIENTS
20ml/4 tsp Kashmiri masala paste
60ml/4 tbsp tomato ketchup
5ml/1 tsp Worcestershire sauce
5ml/1 tsp five-spice powder
5ml/1 tsp granulated sugar
8 chicken joints, skinned
45ml/3 tbsp vegetable oil
5cm/2in piece fresh root ginger, finely shredded
4 garlic cloves, crushed
juice of 1 lemon
15ml/1 tbsp coriander (cilantro) leaves, finely chopped
salt

1 To make the marinade, mix the masala paste, tomato ketchup, Worcestershire sauce, five-spice powder, salt and sugar in a bowl. Allow the mixture to rest in a warm place until the sugar has dissolved.

2 Rub the chicken pieces with the marinade and allow to rest in a cool place for a further 2 hours, or in the refrigerator overnight. Bring the chicken back to room temperature before cooking.

3 Heat the oil in a wok, karahi or large pan and fry half the ginger and all the garlic until golden. Add the chicken and fry until both sides are sealed. Cover and cook until the chicken is tender, and the oil has separated from the sauce.

4 Sprinkle the chicken with the lemon juice, remaining ginger and chopped coriander leaves, and mix well. Serve hot.

KARAHI CHICKEN WITH SAFFRON

This beautifully aromatic chicken dish is partly cooked in the oven. The addition of saffron gives the dish a wonderful golden tint, while the yogurt, almonds and cream help to create a delicious creamy sauce. It is good served with plain boiled rice.

SERVES 4

INGREDIENTS
50g/2oz/4 tbsp butter
30ml/2 tbsp corn oil
1–1½kg/2½–3lb chicken, skinned and cut into 8 pieces
1 onion, chopped
5ml/1 tsp garlic
2.5ml/½ tsp crushed black peppercorns
2.5ml/½ tsp crushed cardamom pods
1.5ml/¼ tsp ground cinnamon
7.5ml/1½ tsp chilli powder
150ml/¼ pint/⅔ cup natural (plain) yogurt
50g/2oz/½ cup ground almonds
15ml/1 tbsp lemon juice
5ml/1 tsp salt
5ml/1 tsp saffron threads, crushed
150ml/¼ pint/⅔ cup single (light) cream
30ml/2 tbsp chopped fresh coriander (cilantro), to garnish

> COOK'S TIP
> *Saffron threads should be crushed before using. Powdered saffron is also available but it loses its flavour more readily. Store saffron in an airtight container in a cool, dark place for up to 6 months.*

1 Preheat the oven to 180°C/350°F/Gas 4. Melt the butter with the oil in a deep round-based frying pan or karahi. Add the chicken pieces and fry for about 5 minutes until lightly browned. Remove the chicken using a slotted spoon, leaving behind as much of the fat as possible, and set aside.

2 Add the onion to the pan, and fry over a medium heat for about 5 minutes until lightly browned. Meanwhile, mix together the garlic, black peppercorns, cardamom, cinnamon, chilli powder, yogurt, ground almonds, lemon juice, salt and saffron threads in a mixing bowl.

3 Pour the yogurt mixture into the pan and stir-fry for about 1 minute. Add the chicken pieces, and continue to stir-fry for a further 2 minutes. Add 150ml/ ¼ pint/⅔ cup water and bring to a gentle simmer.

4 Transfer the contents of the pan to a casserole dish and cover with a lid, or, if using a karahi, cover with foil. Transfer to the oven and cook for about 30 minutes, until the chicken is cooked through.

5 Once cooked, transfer the chicken to a frying pan and stir in the cream. Reheat gently over a very low heat for about 2 minutes. Garnish with fresh coriander.

Karahi Chicken with Coriander & Mint

Both coriander and mint are herbs with a robust, aromatic flavour that compete well with the strong influences of spring onions, ginger and chilli in this dish. Serve with plain boiled rice or rice cooked with a few whole spices and perhaps an Indian bread such as naan bread or parathas.

Serves 4

INGREDIENTS
450g/1lb chicken breast fillets, skinned and cut into strips
30ml/2 tbsp vegetable oil
2 small bunches spring onions (scallions), roughly chopped
5ml/1 tsp grated fresh root ginger
5ml/1 tsp crushed dried red chilli
30ml/2 tbsp lemon juice
30ml/2 tbsp chopped fresh coriander (cilantro), plus sprigs to garnish
30ml/2 tbsp chopped fresh mint, plus sprigs to garnish
3 tomatoes, seeded and roughly chopped
5ml/1 tsp salt

1 Put the chicken into a large pan, pour over 300ml/½ pint/1¼ cups water, bring to the boil. Lower the heat and simmer for 10 minutes, or until the water has evaporated and the chicken is cooked. Remove from the heat and set aside.

2 Heat the oil in another large pan, add the chopped spring onions and stir-fry for about 2 minutes until soft. Add the chicken and stir-fry over a medium heat for about 3 minutes, or until the chicken is browned.

3 Add the ginger, chilli, lemon juice, chopped coriander and mint, the tomatoes and salt, and stir gently to blend the flavours. Transfer to a warmed serving platter and serve garnished with fresh coriander and mint sprigs.

Karahi Chicken with Fresh Fenugreek

This dish inspired a style of cooking known as karahi cuisine in northern India, where fenugreek is a typical and very popular flavouring. Although fresh leaves are obtainable, dried fenugreek leaves can be used for convenience.

SERVES 4

INGREDIENTS
225g/8oz chicken thigh meat, skinned and cut into strips
225g/8oz chicken breast fillets, skinned and cut into strips
2.5ml/½ tsp crushed garlic
5ml/1 tsp chilli powder
2.5ml/½ tsp salt
10ml/2 tsp tomato purée (paste)
30ml/2 tbsp vegetable oil
1 bunch fresh fenugreek leaves or 15ml/1 tbsp dried fenugreek
15ml/1 tbsp chopped fresh coriander (cilantro)

1 Bring a large pan of water to the boil, add the chicken strips and cook for 5–7 minutes. Drain and set aside.

2 Place the garlic, chilli powder and salt in a small bowl with the tomato purée and stir well to combine.

3 Heat the vegetable oil in a wok, karahi or large pan. Lower the heat and add the tomato purée mixture. Add the cooked chicken pieces and stir-fry for 5–7 minutes. Lower the heat again.

4 Add the fenugreek and the chopped fresh coriander to the pan. Continue to stir-fry for 5–7 minutes, then pour in 300ml/½ pint/1¼ cups water, cover and cook for a further 5 minutes. Serve hot.

CHICKEN WITH GREEN MANGO

Green or unripe mango is meant only for cooking purposes. These fruits are smaller than eating mangoes, and they have a sharper taste. They can be bought from Indian stores and markets. The flavour of this dish is surprisingly tart.

SERVES 4

INGREDIENTS

1 green (unripe) mango or cooking apple
450g/1lb chicken breast fillets, skinned and cubed
1.5ml/¼ tsp onion seeds
5ml/1 tsp grated fresh root ginger
2.5ml/½ tsp crushed garlic
5ml/1 tsp chilli powder
1.5ml/¼ tsp ground turmeric
5ml/1 tsp salt
5ml/1 tsp ground coriander
30ml/2 tbsp vegetable oil
2 onions, sliced
4 curry leaves
2 tomatoes, quartered
2 fresh green chillies, chopped
30ml/2 tbsp chopped fresh coriander (cilantro)

> COOK'S TIP
> *If you cannot find green or unripe mangoes, cooking apples can make an easy alternative, although the flavour will obviously not be wholly authentic. If using apple, coat the slices with lemon juice in step 1 to prevent discoloration.*

1 To prepare the mango, peel the skin and slice the flesh thickly. Discard the stone from the middle. Place the mango slices in a bowl, cover and set aside.

2 Put the cubed chicken into a large mixing bowl and add the onion seeds, ginger, garlic, chilli powder, turmeric, salt and ground coriander. Mix the spices with the chicken, then stir in half the mango slices.

3 Heat the oil in a wok, karahi or large pan over a medium heat, and fry the sliced onions until golden brown. Add the curry leaves to the pan, and stir very gently to release their flavour.

4 Gradually add the chicken to the pan, stirring all the time. Stir-fry briskly over a medium heat until the chicken becomes opaque.

5 Pour 300ml/½ pint/1¼ cups water into the pan, stir in the tomatoes and chillies, lower the heat and cook for 12–15 minutes, stirring frequently, until the chicken is cooked through and the water has been completely absorbed. Stir in the chopped coriander and serve immediately.

CHICKEN SAAG

The word saag *means greens and, traditionally, spinach is the usual choice for adding to meat and poultry, although other greens also work well. Chicken Saag is one of the best-known dishes to have originated in the state of Punjab. It is very good served with warmed naan bread.*

SERVES 4

INGREDIENTS
225g/8oz fresh spinach leaves, washed
2.5cm/1in piece fresh root ginger, grated
2 garlic cloves, crushed
1 fresh green chilli, roughly chopped
30ml/2 tbsp vegetable oil
2 bay leaves
1.5ml/¼ tsp black peppercorns
1 onion, finely chopped
4 tomatoes, skinned and finely chopped
10ml/2 tsp curry powder
5ml/1 tsp salt
5ml/1 tsp chilli powder, plus extra to garnish
45ml/3 tbsp natural (plain) yogurt, plus extra to garnish
8 chicken thighs, skinned

COOK'S TIP
Suitable green vegetables to use in place of the spinach include: Swiss chard, curly kale, spring greens and even the green parts of leeks. The overall flavour will be altered depending on the vegetable you choose.

1 Put the spinach in a pan, with just the water that clings to the leaves after washing. Cover tightly and cook for 5 minutes. Put the spinach, ginger, garlic and chilli with 50ml/2fl oz/¼ cup water into a food processor and process to a purée.

2 Heat the vegetable oil, add the bay leaves and peppercorns and fry for 2 minutes. Add the onion and fry for 6–8 minutes more.

3 Add the chopped tomatoes to the pan and simmer for about 5 minutes. Stir in the curry powder, salt and chilli powder and stir well to mix. Cook for a further 2 minutes. Add the spinach purée and 150ml/¼ pint/⅔ cup water to the pan, and simmer for 5 minutes.

4 Gradually stir the yogurt into the spinach mixture, about 15ml/1 tbsp at a time and, once it has all been incorporated, simmer for about 5 minutes.

5 Add the chicken to the pan and stir to combine. Cover and cook for 25–30 minutes, or until the chicken is tender. Drizzle over some natural yogurt and dust lightly with chilli powder.

CHICKEN IN A TOMATO SAUCE

If you like tomatoes, you will love this chicken dish. It makes a semi-dry curry and is delicious served with a lentil dish and plain boiled rice.

SERVES 4

INGREDIENTS
60ml/4 tbsp corn oil
6 curry leaves
2.5ml/½ tsp mixed onion and mustard seeds
8 tomatoes, sliced
5ml/1 tsp ground coriander
5ml/1 tsp chilli powder
5ml/1 tsp salt
5ml/1 tsp ground cumin
5ml/1 tsp crushed garlic
675g/1½lb chicken, skinned, boned and cubed
15ml/1 tbsp sesame seeds, toasted
15ml/1 tbsp chopped fresh coriander (cilantro)

1 Heat the corn oil in a karahi or deep round-based frying pan until the oil is just smoking. Add the curry leaves and onion and mustard seeds and stir well. Stir-fry for 30 seconds, then lower the heat and add the sliced tomatoes. Stir to combine.

2 Mix together the coriander, chilli powder, salt, cumin and garlic in a small bowl. Tip the spice mixture over the tomatoes in the pan.

3 Add the chicken to the pan. Stir-fry for about 5 minutes until the chicken is lightly browned. Pour in 150ml/¼ pint/⅔ cup water and continue cooking, stirring occasionally, until the sauce thickens and the chicken is opaque and cooked through. Sprinkle the toasted sesame seeds and the chopped fresh coriander over the top of the dish and serve.

CHICKEN WITH LENTILS

This is rather an unusual combination of flavours, with the amchur giving a delicious tangy flavour to this spicy dish. Serve with parathas if you wish.

SERVES 4–6

INGREDIENTS
75g/3oz]½ cup chana dhal
60ml/4 tbsp corn oil
2 leeks, chopped
6 large dried red chillies
4 curry leaves
5ml/1 tsp mustard seeds
10ml/2 tsp amchur (dried mango powder)
2 tomatoes, chopped
2.5ml/½ tsp chilli powder
5ml/1 tsp ground coriander
5ml/1 tsp salt
450g/1lb chicken, skinned, boned and cubed
15ml/1 tbsp chopped fresh coriander (cilantro)

1 Wash the chana dhal carefully and remove any stones. Place in a pan with enough water to cover, bring to the boil and cook for about 10 minutes until soft but not mushy. Drain and set aside in a bowl.

2 Heat the oil in a karahi or deep round-based frying pan. Lower the heat slightly and add the leeks, dried red chillies, curry leaves and mustard seeds. Stir-fry gently for 2–3 minutes. Add the amchur, tomatoes, chilli powder, ground coriander, salt and cubed chicken to the pan, and stir-fry for 7–10 minutes.

3 Stir the cooked lentils into the vegetables and cook for a further 2 minutes, or until the chicken is cooked through. Garnish with fresh coriander and serve.

Jeera Chicken

This is an aromatic dish with the delicious, distinctive taste of cumin. Serve simply with a crisp salad and a cucumber raita or yogurt mixed with herbs.

SERVES 4

INGREDIENTS
45ml/3 tbsp cumin seeds
45ml/3 tbsp vegetable oil
2.5ml/½ tsp black peppercorns
4 cardamom pods
2 green chillies, seeded and finely chopped
2 garlic cloves, crushed
2.5cm/1in piece fresh root ginger, grated
5ml/1 tsp ground coriander
10ml/2 tsp ground cumin
2.5ml/½ tsp salt
8 chicken pieces, such as thighs and drumsticks, skinned
5ml/1 tsp garam masala
fresh coriander (cilantro) and chilli powder, to garnish

1 Toast 15ml/1 tbsp of the cumin seeds in a dry frying pan, stirring continuously, until they darken slightly and give off a nutty aroma. Be careful not to burn them as this will impare the flavour. Set aside.

2 Heat the vegetable oil in a large pan and fry the remaining cumin seeds, black peppercorns and cardamom pods for 2–3 minutes.

3 Add the chillies, garlic and ginger to the pan and fry for 2 minutes. Add the ground coriander, cumin and salt and cook for 2–3 minutes more.

4 Add the chicken pieces to the spices in the pan, then cover the pan and simmer gently for 20–25 minutes, or until the chicken is cooked through.

5 Add the garam masala and reserved cumin seeds to the chicken, stir to combine and cook for a further 5 minutes. Garnish with fresh coriander and sprinkle with a little chilli powder.

CHICKEN DHANSAK

Dhansak curries originated in the Parsee community and are traditionally made with a combination of lentils and meat with flavoursome spicing.

SERVES 4

INGREDIENTS
115g/4oz/½ cup green lentils
475ml/16fl oz/2 cups chicken stock
45ml/3 tbsp oil
5ml/1 tsp cumin seeds
2 curry leaves
1 onion, finely chopped
2.5cm/1in piece freshly chopped root ginger
1 fresh green chilli, finely chopped
5ml/1 tsp ground cumin
5ml/1 tsp ground coriander
1.5ml/¼ tsp salt
1.5ml/¼ tsp cayenne pepper
400g/14oz can chopped tomatoes
8 chicken pieces, skinned
60ml/4 tbsp chopped fresh coriander (cilantro), plus sprigs to garnish
5ml/1 tsp garam masala
plain and yellow rice, to serve

1 Rinse the lentils well. Put into a large heavy pan with the stock. Bring to the boil, cover and simmer for 15–20 minutes. Set aside without draining.

2 Heat the oil in a large pan and fry the cumin seeds and curry leaves for 2 minutes. Add the onion, ginger and chilli and fry for about 5 minutes. Stir in the cumin, coriander, salt and cayenne pepper with 30ml/2 tbsp water. Add the chopped tomatoes and the skinned chicken pieces to the pan and stir to combine. Cover and cook gently for 10–15 minutes.

3 Add the lentils and their stock, the coriander and garam masala to the pan, and cook for about 10 minutes or until the chicken is tender. Garnish with coriander sprigs and serve with plain and yellow rice.

Chicken Dopiaza

This classic dish is rich with onions and spices. The origin of the word dopiaza *is rather unclear. In the Hindi language* Do *means two and* piaz *is onion. Hence the popular belief that the word refers to the use of twice the amount or two different types of onions. However, dopiaza is essentially a Mogul dish, and history has it that it was named after Emperor Akbar's courtier, Mullah Dopiaza.*

Serves 4

Ingredients
45ml/3 tbsp vegetable oil
8 small onions, peeled and halved halved
2 bay leaves
8 cardamom pods
4 cloves
3 dried red chillies
8 black peppercorns
2 onions, finely chopped
2 garlic cloves, crushed
2.5cm/1in piece fresh root ginger, finely chopped
5ml/1 tsp ground coriander
5ml/1 tsp ground cumin
2.5ml/½ tsp ground turmeric
5ml/1 tsp chilli powder
2.5ml/½ tsp salt
4 tomatoes, skinned and finely chopped
8 chicken pieces, skinned
plain boiled rice or chapatis, to serve

1 Heat 30ml/2 tbsp vegetable oil in a wok, karahi or large pan and fry the halved small onions until soft. Remove from the pan and set aside.

2 Add the remaining oil to the pan and fry the bay leaves, cardamom pods, cloves, dried chillies and peppercorns for 2 minutes. Add the chopped onions, garlic and ginger and fry for 5 minutes. Add the ground coriander, cumin, turmeric, chilli powder and salt and cook for 2 minutes.

3 Add the tomatoes and 120ml/4fl oz/½ cup water to the pan and simmer for 5 minutes until the sauce begins to thicken. Add the chicken pieces, stir to combine and cook for about 15 minutes more.

4 Add the reserved small onions to the pan, stir well, then cover and cook for a further 10 minutes, or until the chicken is tender. Serve with plenty of plain boiled rice or chapatis.

COOK'S TIPS
• To peel the small onions more easily, place them in a bowl and pour over boiling water. Leave to soak for about 2 minutes, then peel. Soaking in water soften the skins, making it easier to remove them.
• Soaking tomatoes in boiling water also helps when peeling off their skins. However, they need to be soaked for about 30 seconds only.

CHICKEN IN TAMARIND SAUCE

Tamarind paste gives the dish a sweet-and-sour flavour. Poussins are the ideal size for use in this dish and can be used in place of chicken.

SERVES 4–6

INGREDIENTS
60ml/4 tbsp tomato ketchup
15ml/1tbsp tamarind paste
7.5ml/1½ tsp chilli powder
7.5ml/1½ tsp salt
15ml/1 tbsp sugar
7.5ml/1½ tsp grated fresh root ginger
7.5ml/1½ tsp crushed garlic
30ml/2 tbsp desiccated (dry unsweetened shredded) coconut
30ml/2 tbsp sesame seeds
5ml/1 tsp poppy seeds
5ml/1 tsp ground cumin
7.5ml/1½ tsp ground coriander
2 × 450g/1lb chickens, skinned and each cut into 6–8 pieces
75ml/5 tbsp corn oil
8 curry leaves
2.5ml/½ tsp onion seeds
3 large dried red chillies
2.5ml/½ tsp fenugreek seeds
10–12 cherry tomatoes
45ml/3 tbsp chopped fresh coriander (cilantro)
2 fresh green chillies, chopped

1 Put the tomato ketchup and tamarind paste into a large mixing bowl. Add 60ml/4 tbsp water and blend together with a fork.

2 Add the chilli powder, salt, sugar, ginger, garlic, desiccated coconut, sesame and poppy seeds, ground cumin and ground coriander to the mixture. Stir.

3 Add the chicken pieces to the bowl and stir until they are well coated with the spice mixture. Cover and set aside in a cool place.

4 Heat the corn oil in a deep round-based frying pan, wok or a karahi. Add the curry leaves, onion seeds, dried red chillies and fenugreek seeds and fry over a high heat for about 1 minute.

5 Lower the heat to medium and add the chicken pieces, along with their sauce, 2 or 3 pieces at a time, mixing as you go. When all the chicken pieces are in the pan, stir them around well using a slotted spoon. Simmer gently for about 15 minutes, or until all the chicken is cooked through.

6 Add the cherry tomatoes, fresh coriander and green chillies to the pan and stir to mix well. Cook until the tomatoes are heated through then serve.

CUMIN-SCENTED CHICKEN

Pungent cumin is wonderfully aromatic without any harshness. Its rather warm and assertive nature gives this dish a distinctive flavour and aroma. Cumin is also reputed to have curative properties.

SERVES 4

INGREDIENTS
45ml/3 tbsp cumin seeds
45ml/3 tbsp vegetable oil
2.5ml/½ tsp black peppercorns
4 cardamom pods
2 fresh green chillies, finely chopped
2 garlic cloves, crushed
2.5cm/1in piece fresh root ginger, grated
5ml/1 tsp ground coriander
10ml/2 tsp ground cumin
2.5ml/½ tsp salt
8 chicken pieces, such as thighs and drumsticks, skinned
5ml/1 tsp garam masala
chilli powder (optional) and cucumber raita, garnished with fresh coriander
   (cilantro), to serve

1 Preheat a wok or round-based frying pan and toast 15ml/1 tbsp of the cumin seeds for 1–2 minutes until they release their aroma. Set aside.

2 Heat the oil in a wok or large pan and fry the remaining cumin seeds, black peppercorns and cardamom pods for about 2 minutes.

3 Add the green chillies, garlic and grated fresh root ginger to the pan and fry for 2 minutes. Then add the ground coriander and cumin with the salt, and cook over a medium heat, stirring, for a further 1–2 minutes.

4 Add the chicken to the spices and stir thoroughly until well mixed. Cover and cook gently for 20–25 minutes.

5 Add the garam masala and toasted cumin seeds to the chicken. Cook for 5 minutes more. Sprinkle with chilli powder, if liked, and serve with a cucumber raita.

MUGHLAI-STYLE CHICKEN

This dish, from Andhra Pradesh, has the subtle flavouring of the nizami cooking style, which has a distinct Mogul influence. It has a heady aroma of saffron and a captivating silky almond and cream sauce.

SERVES 4

INGREDIENTS
4 chicken breast fillets, rubbed with a little garam masala
2 eggs, beaten with salt and pepper
90ml/6 tbsp ghee or vegetable oil
1 large onion, finely chopped
5cm/2in piece fresh root ginger, finely crushed
4 garlic cloves, finely crushed
4 cloves
4 cardamom pods
5cm/2in piece cinnamon stick
2 bay leaves
15–20 saffron threads
150ml/¼ pint/⅔ cup natural (plain) yogurt, beaten with
   5ml/1 tsp cornflour (cornstarch)
75ml/5 tbsp/⅓ cup double (heavy) cream
50g/2oz ground almonds
salt

1 Brush the chicken fillets with the beaten eggs. In a wok, karahi or large pan, heat the ghee or vegetable oil and fry the chicken until cooked through and browned on both sides. Remove the chicken from the pan and keep warm.

2 In the same pan, fry the chopped onion, ginger, garlic, cloves, cardamom pods, cinnamon and bay leaves. When the onion turns golden, remove the pan from the heat, allow the contents to cool a little and mix in the saffron and yogurt.

3 Return the chicken to the pan, along with any juices, and cook gently until the chicken is tender. Adjust the seasoning if necessary.

4 Just before serving, fold in the double cream and ground almonds. Make sure the curry is piping hot before serving.

CHICKEN MADRAS

Madras, one of India's largest cities, is the capital of Tamil Nadu. The city is generally regarded as the heartland of southern Indian cuisine. It is surrounded by long stretches of beautiful beaches, shared between the Bay of Bengal to the east and the Indian Ocean to the south. The food is mainly vegetarian, but the small Muslim and Christian communities have a wonderful range of meat- and poultry-based dishes.

SERVES 4

INGREDIENTS
450g/1lb chicken breast fillets, skinned
45ml/3 tbsp tomato purée (paste)
large pinch of ground fenugreek
1.5ml/¼ tsp ground fennel seeds
5ml/1 tsp grated fresh root ginger
7.5ml/1½ tsp ground coriander
5ml/1 tsp crushed garlic
5ml/1 tsp chilli powder
1.5ml/¼ tsp ground turmeric
30ml/2 tbsp lemon juice
5ml/1 tsp salt
45ml/3 tbsp vegetable oil
2 onions, diced
2–4 curry leaves
2 fresh green chillies, seeded and chopped
15ml/1 tbsp chopped fresh coriander (cilantro), plus sprigs to garnish
naan bread, to serve

> COOK'S TIP
> *Fenugreek is one of the most powerful Indian spices and it has a lingering flavour. Take care not to use too much, as it can cause the dish to become bitter.*

1 Cut the chicken breast fillets into cubes. Mix the tomato purée in a bowl with the fenugreek, fennel, ginger, ground coriander, garlic, chilli powder, turmeric, lemon juice, salt and 300ml/½ pint/1¼ cups water.

2 Heat the vegetable oil in a wok, karahi or large pan and fry the diced onions with the curry leaves until the onions are golden. Add the cubed chicken and stir for 1 minute to seal, stirring frequently.

3 Pour the tomato sauce and spice mixture into the pan. Cook for 2 minutes, stirring to ensure the ingredients are well mixed.

4 Lower the heat slightly and cook the chicken for 8–10 minutes, then add the chopped green chillies and fresh coriander. Garnish with coriander sprigs and serve with warm naan bread.

GOAN CHICKEN CURRY

Lines of swaying palm trees and the raised borders of a vast patchwork of paddy fields are just two of the features that constitute the beautiful landscape of Goa. Not surprisingly, coconut, in all of its forms, is widely used to enrich Goan cuisine. This creamy, aromatic dish is delicious served with plain boiled rice and lentil dishes. Offer a tangy mint or coconut chutney as well.

SERVES 4

INGREDIENTS
75g/3oz/1½ cups desiccated (dry unsweetened shredded) coconut
30ml/2 tbsp vegetable oil
2.5ml/½ tsp cumin seeds
4 black peppercorns
15ml/1 tbsp fennel seeds
15ml/1 tbsp coriander seeds
2 onions, finely chopped
2.5ml/½ tsp salt
8 small chicken pieces, such as thighs and drumsticks, skinned
fresh coriander (cilantro) sprigs and lemon wedges, to garnish

COOK'S TIP
To save time, make the spiced coconut mixture the day before and chill it in the refrigerator, then continue from step 6 when required.

1 Put the desiccated coconut in a bowl with 45ml/3 tbsp water. Set aside and leave to soak for at least 15 minutes.

2 Heat 15ml/1 tbsp of the oil in a wok, karahi or large pan and fry the cumin seeds, peppercorns, fennel and coriander seeds over a low heat for 3–4 minutes until they begin to splutter.

3 Add the finely chopped onions to the pan and fry for about 5 minutes, stirring occasionally, until the onion has softened and turned opaque.

4 Stir in the desiccated coconut, along with the soaking water and salt, and continue to fry for 5 minutes, stirring occasionally to prevent the mixture from sticking to the base of the pan.

5 Put the coconut mixture into a food processor or blender and process to form a coarse paste. Spoon into a bowl and set aside until required.

6 Heat the remaining oil and fry the chicken for 10 minutes. Add the coconut paste and stir gently to combine. Cook over a low heat for 15–20 minutes, or until the coconut mixture is golden brown and the chicken is tender.

7 Transfer the curry to a warmed serving plate, and garnish with sprigs of fresh coriander and lemon wedges for squeezing over.

CHICKEN JALFREZI

Jalfrezi was created by Indian chefs during the British Raj. Leftover cold meat, generally from the Sunday roast, which the British could not do without, was stir-fried with spices. The dish originated in Calcutta, where the East India Company was established as an important trading post by the British.

SERVES 4

INGREDIENTS
30ml/2 tbsp vegetable oil
5ml/1 tsp cumin seeds
1 onion, finely chopped
1 green (bell) pepper, finely chopped
1 red (bell) pepper, finely chopped
1 garlic clove, crushed
2cm/³⁄₄in piece fresh root ginger, chopped
15ml/1 tbsp curry paste
1.5ml/¹⁄₄ tsp chilli powder
5ml/1 tsp ground coriander
5ml/1 tsp ground cumin
2.5ml/¹⁄₂ tsp salt
675g/1¹⁄₂lb chicken breast fillets, skinned and cubed
400g/14oz can chopped tomatoes
30ml/2 tbsp chopped fresh coriander (cilantro), plus sprigs to garnish
plain boiled rice or naan bread, to serve

1 Heat the oil in a wok, karahi or large pan, and fry the cumin seeds for 30–40 seconds until they begin to splutter. Add the onion, peppers, garlic and ginger and fry for 6–8 minutes.

2 Add the curry paste to the other ingredients in the pan and stir-fry for about 2 minutes. Stir in the chilli powder, ground coriander, cumin and salt, and add 15ml/1 tbsp water. Stir-fry for a further 2 minutes.

3 Add the chicken to the pan and stir-fry for 5 minutes. Add the tomatoes and coriander. Cook, covered, for 15 minutes, or until the chicken is tender. Garnish with sprigs of fresh coriander. Serve with plain boiled rice or naan.

CHICKEN TIKKA

The word tikka *refers to the use of boneless, skinless cubes of chicken breast. Strictly speaking, the term should not be applied to other types of meat, even if they are prepared and cooked in a similar way. Chicken tikka is traditionally cooked in a tandoor (clay oven). Serve with shredded lettuce, onion rings, lime wedges and fresh coriander.*

SERVES 6

INGREDIENTS
450g/1lb chicken breast fillets, skinned and cubed
5ml/1 tsp grated fresh root ginger
5ml/1 tsp crushed garlic
5ml/1 tsp chilli powder
1.5ml/¼ tsp ground turmeric
5ml/1 tsp salt
150ml/¼ pint/⅔ cup natural (plain) yogurt
60ml/4 tbsp lemon juice
15ml/1 tbsp chopped fresh coriander (cilantro)
15ml/1 tbsp vegetable oil

1 In a large bowl, mix the chicken cubes, ginger, garlic, chilli powder, turmeric, salt, yogurt, lemon juice and coriander. Leave to marinate in a cool place for at least 2 hours, or in the refrigerator overnight.

2 Preheat the grill (broiler) to medium. Place the chicken in a grill (broiling) pan, or in a flameproof dish lined with foil, and baste with the oil. Grill (broil) the chicken for 15–20 minutes until cooked, turning and basting two or three times.

CHICKEN TIKKA MASALA

Chicken tikka is a traditional dish from northern India, whereas masala is pure invention of the West. The word refers to the sauce in which the cooked tikka is simmered. However, it is not dissimilar to another traditional Indian dish known as butter chicken, in which tandoori chicken is simmered in a creamy sauce.

SERVES 4

INGREDIENTS
675g/1½lb chicken breast fillets, skinned
90ml/6 tbsp tikka paste
60ml/4 tbsp natural (plain) yogurt
30ml/2 tbsp vegetable oil
1 onion, chopped
1 garlic clove, crushed
1 fresh green chilli, seeded and chopped
2.5cm/1in piece fresh root ginger, grated
15ml/1 tbsp tomato purée (paste)
15ml/1 tbsp ground almonds
45ml/3 tbsp ghee or butter, melted
50ml/2fl oz/¼ cup double (heavy) cream
15ml/1 tbsp lemon juice
fresh coriander (cilantro) sprigs, natural (plain) yogurt and cumin seeds, to garnish
warm naan bread, to serve

> COOK'S TIP
> *To prevent the wooden skewers from burning while under the grill (broiler), soak them in cold water for at least 30 minutes before use.*

1 Cut the chicken breast fillets into 2.5cm/1in cubes. Put half of the tikka paste and all the yogurt into a bowl, then stir in the cubed chicken. Cover with clear film (plastic wrap) and leave to marinate for 20 minutes.

2 For the tikka sauce, heat the oil and fry the onion, garlic, chilli and ginger for 5 minutes. Add the remaining tikka paste and fry for 2 minutes. Add the tomato purée, almonds and 250ml/8fl oz/1 cup water, and simmer for 15 minutes.

3 Preheat the grill (broiler). Thread the chicken on to wooden kebab skewers, then brush the chicken pieces with the melted ghee or butter and grill (broil) under a medium heat for about 15 minutes. Turn occasionally and brush the chicken pieces with more butter.

4 Put the tikka sauce in a food processor or blender and process until smooth. Return the sauce to the pan and stir in the cream and lemon juice.

5 Remove the chicken from the grill, slide the cubes off the wooden skewers and add them to the pan. Simmer gently for about 5 minutes. Garnish with fresh coriander, yogurt and toasted cumin seeds, and serve with warm naan bread.

CHICKEN TIKKA
WITH MINT YOGURT SAUCE

A delightfully refreshing yogurt sauce with mint and spring onions complements the lightly spiced, succulent chicken pieces in this delicious dish. This dish is very good served with Indian flatbreads and crisp shredded lettuce.

SERVES 4

INGREDIENTS
4 chicken breast fillets, skinned
150g/5oz/⅔ cup natural (plain) yogurt
5ml/2 tsp chilli powder
10ml/2 tsp paprika
15ml/1 tbsp tomato purée (paste)
15ml/1 tbsp lemon juice
2.5ml/½ tsp garlic salt
onion rings and lemon wedges, to serve (optional)

FOR THE SAUCE
150g/5oz/⅔ cup natural (plain) yogurt
1 spring onion (scallion), finely chopped
1 fresh green chilli, finely chopped
10ml/2 tsp mint sauce
2.5ml/½ tsp caster (superfine) sugar
salt and ground black pepper

> VARIATION
> *If you prefer, add 30ml/2 tbsp chopped fresh mint to the sauce in place of the mint sauce. It will give very similar results.*

1 Cut the chicken into fairly large chunks and place in a large bowl. Add the yogurt, chilli powder, paprika, tomato purée, lemon juice and garlic salt, and toss the chicken to mix and coat evenly. Cover the bowl and refrigerate for several hours or preferably overnight.

2 Meanwhile, make the sauce. Mix together the yogurt, spring onion, chilli, mint sauce and sugar in a small bowl and chill until required.

3 Preheat a grill (broiler) to medium-hot. Arrange the chicken pieces on a rack, or thread on to previously soaked wooden skewers, and cook for 8–10 minutes, turning occasionally, until thoroughly cooked.

4 Remove the chicken from the skewers and serve with the sauce for dipping, and onion rings and lemon wedges if you like.

TANDOORI CHICKEN

Punjab, in northern India, is the home of tandoori food. The tandoor, or clay oven, that is so widely used there, originated in Egypt and found its way into India with the Moguls. It is probably the most versatile oven in the world, as it is capable of roasting, grilling (broiling) and baking foods all at the same time.

SERVES 4–6

INGREDIENTS
1.3kg/3lb oven-ready chicken
250ml/8fl oz/1 cup natural (plain) yogurt, beaten
60ml/4 tbsp tandoori masala paste
75g/3oz/2 tbsp ghee or vegetable oil
salt
lemon slices and onion rings, to garnish
lettuce, to serve

COOK'S TIP
If the chicken is left to marinate overnight in the refrigerator, remember to remove it a hour or two before you want to start cooking to allow it to return to room temperature first.

1 Using a small, sharp knife or scissors, remove the skin from the chicken and trim off any excess fat. Using a fork, prick the flesh randomly all over.

2 Cut the chicken in half down the centre and through the breast. Cut each piece in half again. Make a few deep gashes diagonally into the flesh.

3 In a bowl, mix the yogurt with the masala paste and season with salt. Spread the chicken with the yogurt mixture, working some into the gashes. Leave to marinate in a cool place for at least 2 hours, or in the refrigerator overnight.

4 Preheat the oven to 240°C/475°F/Gas 9. Place the chicken quarters on a wire rack in a deep baking sheet. Spread the chicken with any excess marinade, reserving a little for basting halfway through the cooking time.

5 Melt the ghee or vegetable oil and pour over the chicken pieces to seal the surface. This helps to keep the centre moist during roasting. Roast the chicken for about 10 minutes, then remove from the oven, leaving the oven on.

6 Baste the chicken with the remaining marinade. Return to the oven and switch off the heat. Leave the chicken in the oven for 15–20 minutes without opening the door. Serve on a bed of lettuce and garnish with the lemon slices and onion rings.

SPICY GRILLED CHICKEN

This dish is inspired by the tandoori style of cooking, in which the meat and poultry are marinated before being grilled or roasted in a clay oven. Serve it with rice and a salad, or mixed with a mushroom dish of your choice.

SERVES 6

INGREDIENTS
12 chicken thighs
90ml/6 tbsp lemon juice
5ml/1 tsp grated fresh root ginger
5ml/1 tsp crushed garlic
5ml/1 tsp crushed dried red chillies
5ml/1 tsp salt
5ml/1 tsp soft light brown sugar
30ml/2 tbsp clear honey
30ml/2 tbsp chopped fresh coriander (cilantro), plus sprigs to garnish
1 fresh green chilli, finely chopped
30ml/2 tbsp vegetable oil
saffron rice and a mixed salad, to serve (optional)

COOK'S TIP
If you prefer, cook the chicken on a barbecue for a wonderful smoky flavour. Baste with the oil only when the chicken is almost cooked.

1 Prick the chicken thighs all over with a fork, rinse under cold running water, pat dry with kitchen paper and set aside.

2 In a large bowl, combine the lemon juice, ginger, garlic, red chillies, salt, soft brown sugar and honey. Add the chicken thighs to the bowl and stir to coat well. Cover and leave to marinate for 45 minutes.

3 Preheat the grill (broiler) to medium. Add the fresh coriander and chopped green chilli to the chicken and mix well, then transfer the chicken to a flameproof dish. Pour any remaining marinade over the chicken and baste with the vegetable oil, using a pastry brush.

4 Place the dish under the grill and cook the chicken for 15–20 minutes, turning and basting occasionally, until cooked through and evenly browned.

5 Transfer the chicken to a warmed serving dish and garnish with the fresh coriander sprigs. Serve with saffron rice and a salad, if you like.

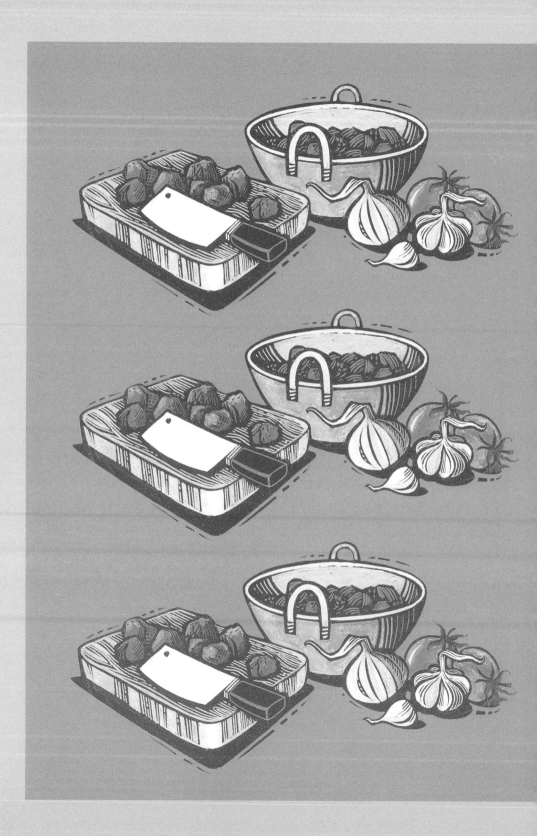

MEAT DISHES

Religion is an important aspect when considering Indian meat dishes. Hindus do not eat beef, while Muslims do not eat pork. Many traditional Indian meat dishes are made with mutton and goat. However, as these meats are not readily available in the West, lamb has been substituted for some of the recipes in this chapter. Kashmir is renowned for its tender lamb, however. Many Indian dishes combine meat and vegetables together, creating one-pot meals with a wonderful depth of flavour.

Shammi Kabab

Kababs came to India from the Middle East where the word is spelt kebab. There is a delectable range of kababs in Indian cuisine, most of which can be served either as appetizers or side dishes. A raita or a chutney is the perfect accompaniment.

Serves 5–6

Ingredients

2 onions, finely chopped
250g/9oz lean lamb, boned and cubed
50g/2oz chana dhal or yellow split peas
5ml/1 tsp cumin seeds
5ml/1 tsp garam masala
4–6 fresh green chillies
5cm/2in piece fresh root ginger, grated
a few fresh coriander (cilantro) and mint leaves, chopped,
    plus coriander (cilantro) sprigs to garnish
juice of 1 lemon
15ml/1 tbsp gram flour (besan)
2 eggs, beaten
vegetable oil, for shallow frying
salt

1 Put the onions, lamb, chana dhal or split peas, cumin seeds, garam masala, chillies and ginger and 175ml/6fl oz/¾ cup water into a large pan with salt, and bring to the boil. Simmer, covered, until the meat and dhal are cooked. Uncover and cook for a few more minutes, to reduce the excess liquid. Set aside to cool.

2 Transfer the cooled meat and dhal mixture to a food processor or blender and process to a rough paste. Put the paste into a large mixing bowl and add the chopped coriander and mint leaves, lemon juice and gram flour. Knead well with your hands to make sure the ingredients are well mixed.

3 Divide the mixture into 10–12 even-size portions and use your hands to roll each into a ball, then flatten slightly. Chill for 1 hour. Heat the vegetable oil in a frying pan. Dip the kababs in the beaten egg and shallow fry each side until golden brown. Pat dry on kitchen paper and serve hot.

MINCED LAMB WITH PEAS

This dish, known as kheema mattar, *is a favourite all over India, although it originated in the north. Generally, in India minced mutton is used, as lamb is not very easy to obtain. Minced turkey or chicken would work equally well.*

SERVES 4

INGREDIENTS
45ml/3 tbsp vegetable oil
1 onion, finely chopped
2 garlic cloves, crushed
2.5cm/1in piece fresh root ginger, grated
2 fresh green chillies, finely chopped
675g/1½lb minced (ground) lamb
5ml/1 tsp ground cumin
5ml/1 tsp ground coriander
5ml/1 tsp chilli powder
5ml/1 tsp salt
175g/6oz/1½ cups frozen peas, thawed
30ml/2 tbsp lemon juice
warm naan bread and natural (plain) yogurt, to serve

1 Heat the oil and fry the onion for about 5 minutes over a medium heat until browned. Add the garlic, ginger and chillies and fry for 2–3 minutes.

2 Add the minced lamb to the pan and stir-fry briskly for 5 minutes over a high heat. Stir in the cumin, coriander, chilli powder and salt with 300ml/½ pint/ 1¼ cups water. Cover the pan and simmer for about 25 minutes.

3 Stir the peas and lemon juice into the lamb. Cook for 10 minutes, uncovered. Serve with warm naan bread and yogurt.

COOK'S TIP
To reduce the fat content of this dish, dry-fry the lamb in a non-stick frying pan until the natural fat is released. Drain the fat, then continue as above.

LAMB KOFTA CURRY

These small meatballs reveal a Middle Eastern influence on the Indian cuisine. The Middle Eastern technique for making meatballs is still used, combined with the skilful blending of Indian spices. They make a delicious main course served with plain rice.

SERVES 4

INGREDIENTS
675g/1½lb minced (ground) lamb
1 fresh green chilli, roughly chopped
1 garlic clove, chopped
2.5cm/1in piece fresh root ginger, chopped
1.5ml/¼ tsp garam masala
1.5ml/¼ tsp salt
45ml/3 tbsp chopped fresh coriander (cilantro)

FOR THE SAUCE
30ml/2 tbsp vegetable oil
2.5ml/½ tsp cumin seeds
1 onion, chopped
1 garlic clove, chopped
2.5cm/1in piece fresh root ginger, grated
5ml/1 tsp ground cumin
5ml/1 tsp ground coriander
2.5ml/½ tsp salt
2.5ml/½ tsp chilli powder
15ml/1 tbsp tomato purée (paste)
400g/14oz can chopped tomatoes
fresh coriander (cilantro) sprigs, to garnish

COOK'S TIP
The meatballs can be prepared the day before and stored in the refrigerator until needed. This makes them ideal for a midweek supper.

1 Put the lamb, chilli, garlic and ginger, the garam masala, salt and coriander into a food processor and process until the mixture binds together.

2 Shape the mixture into 16 even-sized balls, using your hands. Cover with clear film (plastic wrap) and chill for about 10 minutes.

3 To make the sauce, heat the vegetable oil in a pan and fry the cumin seeds until they splutter. Add the onion, garlic and ginger and fry for 5 minutes. Stir in the ground cumin, coriander, salt, chilli powder, tomato purée and chopped tomatoes and simmer for 5 minutes.

4 Add the meatballs to the tomato sauce. Bring to the boil, cover and simmer for 25–30 minutes, or until the meatballs are cooked through. Garnish with sprigs of fresh coriander and serve hot.

Kashmiri Lamb Chops

These chops are cooked in a unique way, boiled in milk, and then fried. Despite the large number of spices used in this recipe, the actual dish has a mild flavour, and it is delicious served with fried rice and lentils.

SERVES 4

INGREDIENTS

8–12 lamb chops, each weighing about 50–75g/2–3oz
1 cinnamon stick
1 bay leaf
2.5ml/½ tsp fennel seeds
2.5ml/½ tsp black peppercorns
3 cardamom pods
5ml/1 tsp salt
600ml/1 pint/2½ cups milk
150ml/¼ pint/⅔ cup evaporated milk
150ml/¼ pint/⅔ cup natural (plain) yogurt
30ml/2 tbsp plain (all-purpose) flour
5ml/1 tsp chilli powder
5ml/1 tsp grated fresh root ginger
2.5ml/½ tsp garam masala
2.5ml/½ tsp crushed garlic
pinch of salt
300ml/½ pint/1¼ cups corn oil
mint sprigs and lime quarters, to garnish

> COOK'S TIP
> *These delicious lamb chops, with their tasty, crunchy yogurt coating, make ideal finger food to serve at a buffet or drinks party.*

1 Using a sharp knife, trim the lamb chops and place in a large pan with the cinnamon stick, bay leaf, fennel seeds, peppercorns, cardamom pods, salt and milk. Bring to the boil over a high heat.

2 Lower the heat and cook the lamb for 12–15 minutes, or until the milk has reduced to about half its original volume. Stir in the evaporated milk and lower the heat further. Simmer very gently until the chops are cooked through and the milk has evaporated.

3 While the chops are cooking, blend together the yogurt, flour, chilli powder, ginger, garam masala, garlic and a pinch of salt in a mixing bowl.

4 Remove the chops from the pan and discard the whole spices. Add the chops to the spicy yogurt mixture and stir to coat well.

5 Heat the corn oil in a deep round-based frying pan or karahi. Lower the heat slightly and carefully add the chops. Fry until golden brown on both sides, turning once or twice as they cook.

6 Remove the chops with a slotted spoon and transfer to a warmed serving dish. Garnish with mint sprigs and lime quarters for squeezing over and serve.

LAMB KORMA

Although southern Indian food is generally free of foreign influences, the city of Hyderabad in Andhra Pradesh has a rich heritage of Mogul cuisine.

SERVES 4–6

INGREDIENTS
15ml/1 tbsp white sesame seeds
15ml/1 tbsp white poppy seeds
50g/2oz/½ cup blanched almonds
2 fresh green chillies, seeded
6 garlic cloves, sliced
5cm/2in piece fresh root ginger, sliced
1 onion, finely chopped
45ml/3 tbsp ghee or vegetable oil
6 cardamom pods
5cm/2in piece cinnamon stick
4 cloves
900g/2lb lean lamb, boned and cubed
5ml/1 tsp ground cumin
5ml/1 tsp ground coriander
300ml/½ pint/1¼ cups cream mixed with 2.5ml/½ tsp cornflour (cornstarch)
salt
toasted sesame seeds, to garnish

1 Preheat a large pan over a medium heat, and add the sesame and poppy seeds, almonds, chillies, garlic, ginger and onion. Stir until they begin to change colour. Allow the mixture to cool, then grind to a fine paste using a mortar and pestle.

2 Heat the ghee or oil in the pan over a low heat. Fry the cardamoms, cinnamon and cloves until the cloves swell. Add the lamb, cumin and coriander and the prepared paste, and season. Increase the heat and stir well. Reduce the heat, then cover and cook for about 30 minutes, or until the lamb is almost done.

3 Remove from the heat, allow to cool a little and gradually fold in the cream, reserving 5ml/1 tsp to garnish. To serve, gently reheat the lamb, uncovered. Garnish with the sesame seeds and the reserved cream.

LAMB WITH APRICOTS

This recipe comes from the wonderful fruit-laden valley of Kashmir. The cuisine of Kashmir is renowned for its imaginative use of exotic fruits and nuts.

SERVES 4–6

INGREDIENTS
900g/2lb stewing lamb
30ml/2 tbsp vegetable oil
2.5cm/1in piece cinnamon stick
4 cardamom pods
1 onion, chopped
15ml/1 tbsp curry paste
5ml/1 tsp ground cumin
5ml/1 tsp ground coriander
1.5ml/¼ tsp salt
175g/6oz/¾ cup ready-to-eat dried apricots
350ml/12fl oz/1½ cups lamb stock
fresh coriander (cilantro), to garnish
pulao rice and apricot chutney, to serve

1 Cut away and discard any visible fat from the stewing lamb, then cut the meat into 2.5cm/1in cubes.

2 Heat the oil in a wok, karahi or large pan and fry the cinnamon stick and cardamom pods for 2 minutes. Add the chopped onion and fry gently for 6–8 minutes until soft but not browned.

3 Add the curry paste to the pan, stir and fry for about 2 minutes. Stir in the ground cumin and coriander and the salt and fry for 2–3 minutes.

4 Add the cubed lamb and dried apricots to the pan and pour over the lamb stock. Stir to combine, then cover with the lid and cook over a medium heat for 1–1½ hours, or until the lamb is tender and the apricots plump and soft.

5 Transfer the lamb to a warmed serving dish and garnish with fresh coriander. Serve with pulao rice and a tangy apricot chutney.

LAMB TIKKA

This is a traditional tikka recipe, made using lamb instead of chicken, in which the meat is marinated in yogurt and spices. The lamb can be cut into cubes, but here it is cut into strips to halve the cooking time required.

SERVES 4

INGREDIENTS
450g/1lb lamb, cut into strips
175ml/6fl oz/³⁄₄ cup natural (plain) yogurt
5ml/1 tsp ground cumin
5ml/1 tsp ground coriander
5ml/1 tsp chilli powder
5ml/1 tsp crushed garlic
5ml/1 tsp salt
5ml/1 tsp garam masala
30ml/2 tbsp chopped fresh coriander (cilantro)
30ml/2 tbsp lemon juice
30ml/2 tbsp corn oil
15ml/1 tbsp tomato purée (paste)
1 large green (bell) pepper, seeded and sliced
3 large fresh red chillies

1 Put the lamb strips, yogurt, ground cumin, ground coriander, chilli powder, garlic, salt, garam masala, fresh coriander and lemon juice into a large mixing bowl and stir thoroughly. Set aside for at least 1 hour to marinate.

2 Heat the corn oil in a deep round-based frying pan or karahi. Lower the heat slightly and add the tomato purée. Add the lamb strips to the pan, a few at a time, leaving any excess marinade behind in the bowl. Cook the lamb, stirring frequently, for 7–10 minutes or until it is well browned.

3 Add the green pepper slices and the whole red chillies. Heat through, checking that the lamb is completely cooked, and serve immediately.

HOT CHILLI MEAT

Curry leaves and chillies are two of the hallmark ingredients used in the southern states of India. This recipe has its origins in the state of Andhra Pradesh, where the hottest chillies, known as Guntur, *are grown in abundance.*

SERVES 4–6

INGREDIENTS
30ml/2 tbsp vegetable oil
1 large onion, finely sliced
5cm/2in piece fresh root ginger, grated
4 garlic cloves, crushed
12 curry leaves
45ml/3 tbsp extra hot curry paste, or 60ml/4 tbsp hot curry powder
15ml/1 tbsp chilli powder
5ml/1 tsp five-spice powder
5ml/1 tsp ground turmeric
900g/2lb lean lamb or beef, cubed
175ml/6fl oz/³⁄4 cup thick coconut milk
salt
red onion, finely sliced, to garnish
Indian bread and fruit raita, to serve

1 Heat the vegetable oil in a wok, karahi or large, pan, and fry the onion, ginger, garlic and curry leaves until the onion is soft. Add the curry paste or powder, chilli and five-spice powder and turmeric and season with salt.

2 Add the meat to the spices in the pan and stir well over a medium heat to seal and evenly brown the meat pieces. Keep stirring until the oil separates. Cover the pan and cook for about 20 minutes.

3 Stir coconut milk into the pan and simmer, covered, until the meat is cooked. Towards the end of cooking, uncover the pan to reduce the excess liquid. Garnish with red onion and serve with any Indian bread and fruit raita.

LAMB PARSEE

*This dish is similar to biryani, but here the lamb is marinated with the yogurt,
a technique that is a Parsee speciality. Serve with dhal or spiced mushrooms.*

SERVES 6

INGREDIENTS
900g/2lb lamb fillet, cut into 2.5cm/1in cubes
60ml/4 tbsp ghee or butter
2 onions, sliced
450g/1lb potatoes, cut into large chunks
chicken stock or water (see method)
450g/1lb/2⅓ cups basmati rice, soaked
generous pinch of saffron threads, dissolved in 30ml/2 tbsp warm milk
fresh coriander (cilantro) sprigs, to garnish

FOR THE MARINADE
475ml/16fl oz/2 cups natural (plain) yogurt
3–4 garlic cloves, crushed
10ml/2 tsp cayenne pepper
20ml/4 tsp garam masala
10ml/2 tsp ground cumin
5ml/1 tsp ground coriander

1 Make the marinade by combining all the ingredients in a large bowl. Add
the meat to the marinade, stir to coat, then cover and leave to marinate for
3–4 hours in a cool place or overnight in the refrigerator.

2 Melt 30ml/2 tbsp of the ghee or butter in a large pan and fry the onions for
about 6 minutes until lightly golden. Transfer to a plate.

3 Melt a further 25ml/1½ tbsp of the ghee or butter in the pan. Fry the marinated
lamb cubes in batches until evenly brown, transferring each batch in turn to a
separate plate. When all the lamb has been browned, return it to the pan and scrape
in the remaining marinade.

4 Add the potatoes to the pan and stir in about three-quarters of the fried onions.
Pour in just enough chicken stock or water to cover the mixture.

5 Bring the stew to the boil, then cover and simmer over a very low heat for 40–50 minutes until the lamb is tender and the potatoes are cooked. Preheat the oven to 160°C/325°F/Gas 3.

6 Drain the rice. Cook it in a pan of boiling stock or water for 5 minutes. Meanwhile, spoon the lamb mixture into a casserole. Drain the rice and mound it on top of the lamb, then, using the handle of a wooden spoon, make a hole down the centre. Top with the remaining fried onions, pour the saffron milk over the top and dot with the remaining ghee or butter.

7 Cover the pan with a double layer of foil and a lid. Cook in the oven for 30–35 minutes or until the rice is tender. Garnish with coriander and serve.

KARAHI LAMB

Lamb dishes are a speciality in the state of Kashmir, the only region of India where the climate is ideal for rearing lamb. In this version, the sautéed dried apricots, which are subtly flavoured with cinnamon and cardamom, add an irresistible finishing touch.

SERVES 4

INGREDIENTS
15ml/1 tbsp tomato purée (paste)
175ml/6fl oz/³⁄₄ cup natural (plain) yogurt
5ml/1 tsp garam masala
1.5ml/¹⁄₄ tsp cumin seeds
5ml/1 tsp salt
5ml/1 tsp crushed garlic
5ml/1 tsp grated fresh root ginger
5ml/1 tsp chilli powder
450g/1lb lean spring lamb, cut into strips
30ml/2 tbsp vegetable oil
2 onions, finely sliced
25g/1oz ghee, butter or margarine
2.5cm/1in piece cinnamon stick
2 cardamom pods
5 ready-to-eat dried apricots, quartered
15ml/1 tbsp chopped fresh coriander (cilantro)

> VARIATION
> *If you would prefer this curry to have a slightly hotter taste, increase the garam masala and chilli powder to 7.5ml/1½ tsp each.*

1 In a bowl, mix together the tomato purée, yogurt, garam masala, cumin seeds, salt, garlic, ginger and chilli powder. Add the lamb strips, stir to coat in the marinade and leave to marinate for at least 1 hour.

2 Heat 10ml/2 tsp of the vegetable oil in a wok, karahi or large pan and fry the sliced onions until crisp and golden brown.

3 Remove the onions from the pan using a slotted spoon. Allow them to cool, then grind them by processing briefly in a food processor or blender, or with a mortar and pestle. Reheat the oil and return the onions to the pan.

4 Add the lamb and stir-fry for about 2 minutes. Cover the pan, lower the heat and cook, stirring occasionally, for 15 minutes, or until the meat is cooked through. If required, add up to 150ml/¼ pint/⅔ cup water during the cooking. Remove from the heat and set aside.

5 Heat the ghee, butter or margarine with the remaining oil and add the cinnamon stick and cardamom pods. Stir in the apricots and cook over a low heat for 2 minutes. Pour this sauce over the lamb, then garnish with the chopped coriander leaves and serve immediately.

FRAGRANT LAMB CURRY

This dish, known as rezala, *comes from Bengal where there is a tradition of Muslim cooking. This is a legacy left by the Muslim rulers during the Mogul era.*

SERVES 4

INGREDIENTS
1 large onion, roughly chopped
10ml/2 tsp grated fresh root ginger
10ml/2 tsp crushed garlic
4–5 garlic cloves
2.5ml/½ tsp black peppercorns
6 cardamom pods
5cm/2in piece cinnamon stick, halved
8 lamb cutlets (US rib chops)
60ml/4 tbsp vegetable oil
1 large onion, finely sliced
175ml/6fl oz/¾ natural (plain) yogurt
50g/2oz/¼ cup butter
2.5ml/1 tsp salt
2.5ml/½ tsp ground cumin
2.5ml/½ tsp hot chilli powder
2.5ml/½ tsp freshly grated nutmeg
2.5ml/½ tsp granulated sugar
15ml/1 tbsp lime juice
pinch of saffron, steeped in 15ml/1 tbsp hot water for 10–15 minutes
15ml/1 tbsp rose water
naan bread or boiled basmati rice, to serve

1 Place the chopped onion in a food processor or blender. Add a little water if necessary to form a purée. Put the onion purée in a glass bowl and add the grated ginger, crushed garlic, cloves, peppercorns, cardamom pods and cinnamon. Mix thoroughly to combine.

2 Put the lamb cutlets in a large shallow glass dish and add the onion mixture. Mix thoroughly, cover the bowl and leave the lamb to marinate for 3–4 hours or overnight in the refrigerator. Bring back to room temperature before cooking.

3 In a wok, karahi or large pan, heat the vegetable oil over a medium-high heat and fry the sliced onion for 6–7 minutes, until golden brown. Remove the onion slices with a slotted spoon, squeezing out as much oil as possible on the side of the pan. Drain the onions on kitchen paper.

4 In the remaining oil, fry the marinated lamb cutlets for 4–5 minutes, stirring frequently. Reduce the heat to low, cover and cook for 5–7 minutes.

5 Meanwhile, mix the yogurt and butter together in a small pan and place over a low heat. Cook for 5–6 minutes, stirring constantly, then stir into the lamb cutlets along with the salt. Add the cumin and chilli powder and cover the pan. Cook for 45–50 minutes until the chops are tender.

6 Add the nutmeg and sugar to the pan, cook for 1–2 minutes and add the lime juice, saffron and rose water. Stir and mix well, simmer for 2–3 minutes then remove from the heat. Transfer to a warmed serving dish and garnish with the fried onion. Serve with naan bread or boiled basmati rice.

LAHORE-STYLE LAMB

Named after the city in northern Pakistan, this hearty dish has a wonderfully aromatic flavour imparted by the winter spices such as cloves, black peppercorns and cinnamon. Serve with a hot puffy naan bread.

SERVES 4

INGREDIENTS
60ml/4 tbsp vegetable oil
1 bay leaf
2 cloves
4 black peppercorns
1 onion, sliced
450g/1lb lean lamb, boned and cubed
1.5ml/¼ tsp ground turmeric
7.5ml/1½ tsp chilli powder
5ml/1 tsp crushed coriander seeds
2.5cm/1in piece cinnamon stick
5ml/1 tsp crushed garlic
7.5ml/1½ tsp salt
1.5 litres/2½ pints/6¼ cups water
50g/2oz/⅓ cup chana dhal or yellow split peas
2 tomatoes, quartered
2 fresh green chillies, chopped
15ml/1 tbsp chopped fresh coriander (cilantro)

1 Heat the vegetable oil in a wok, karahi or large pan. Lower the heat slightly and add the bay leaf, cloves, peppercorns and onion. Fry for about 5 minutes, stirring frequently, or until the onion is golden brown.

2 Add the cubed lamb, turmeric, chilli powder, coriander seeds, cinnamon stick, garlic and most of the salt, and stir-fry for about 5 minutes over a medium heat.

3 Pour in 900ml/1½ pints/3¾ cups water into the pan and cover with a lid or foil, making sure the foil does not come into contact with the food. Simmer gently for 35–40 minutes, or until the lamb is tender.

4 Put the chana dhal or split peas into a large pan with 600ml/1 pint/2½ cups water and a good pinch of salt and boil for 12–15 minutes, or until the water has almost evaporated and the lentils or peas are soft enough to be mashed. If they are too thick, add up to 150ml/¼ pint/⅔ cup more water.

5 When the lamb is tender, remove the lid or foil and stir-fry the mixture over a high heat using a wooden spoon, until some of the oil separates out and begins to appear on the sides of the pan.

6 Add the cooked chana dhal or split peas to the lamb and mix together until well combined. Stir in the quartered tomatoes, green chillies and chopped fresh coriander, and serve immediately.

VARIATION
If you prefer, use boned and cubed chicken in place of the lamb. At step 3, reduce the amount of water to 300ml/½ pint/1¼ cups and cook uncovered, stirring occasionally, for 10–15 minutes, or until the water has evaporated and the chicken is tender and cooked through completely.

ROGAN JOSH

This is one of the most popular lamb dishes to have originated in Kashmir. Traditionally, fatty meat on the bone is cooked slowly until most of the fat is separated from the meat. The fat that escapes from the meat in this way is known as rogan, *and* josh *refers to the rich red colour. The Kashmiris achieve this colour by using a combination of mild and bright red Kashmiri chillies and the juice extracted from a brightly coloured local flower.*

SERVES 4–6

INGREDIENTS
45ml/3 tbsp lemon juice
250ml/8fl oz/1 cup natural (plain) yogurt
5ml/1 tsp salt
2 garlic cloves, crushed
2.5cm/1in piece fresh root ginger, finely grated
900g/2lb lean lamb fillet, cubed
60ml/4 tbsp vegetable oil
2.5ml/½ tsp cumin seeds
2 bay leaves
4 cardamom pods
1 onion, finely chopped
10ml/2 tsp ground coriander
10ml/2 tsp ground cumin
5ml/1 tsp chilli powder
400g/14oz can chopped tomatoes
30ml/2 tbsp tomato purée (paste)
toasted cumin seeds and bay leaves, to garnish
plain boiled rice, to serve

1 In a large bowl, mix together the lemon juice, yogurt, salt, one crushed garlic clove and the ginger. Add the lamb and stir to coat the meat in the mixture. Marinate in the refrigerator overnight.

2 Heat the vegetable oil in a wok, karahi or large pan and fry the cumin seeds for about 2 minutes until they start to splutter. Add the bay leaves and cardamom pods and fry for a further 2 minutes.

3 Add the onion and remaining garlic to the pan and fry for 5 minutes. Add the coriander, cumin and chilli powder and fry for 2 minutes more.

4 Add the marinated lamb to the pan and cook for 5 minutes, stirring occasionally to prevent the mixture from sticking to the base of the pan.

5 Add the tomatoes, tomato purée and 150ml/¼ pint/⅔ cup water to the lamb. Cover and simmer for 1–1½ hours, or until the lamb is very tender. Garnish with toasted cumin seeds and bay leaves, and serve immediately with rice.

DHANSAK

The Parsees fled their native Persia about thirteen centuries ago, to avoid religious persecution, and landed in the state of Gujarat. They adopted Gujarati as their language, but developed a Parsee version, which is slightly different from the local form. In native Gujarati, dhan means wealth, but in Parsee Gujarati, it means rice and sak means vegetables. A serving of dhansak is not complete without caramelized basmati rice, the traditional accompaniment.

SERVES 4–6

INGREDIENTS
90ml/6 tbsp vegetable oil
5 fresh green chillies, chopped
2.5cm/1in piece fresh root ginger, grated
4 garlic cloves, 3 crushed and 1 sliced
2 bay leaves
5cm/2in piece cinnamon stick
900g/2lb lean lamb, cut into large pieces
175g/6oz/³/4 cup red whole lentils, washed and drained
50g/2oz/¹/4 cup each chana dhal or yellow split peas, husked moong dhal
    and red lentils, washed and drained
2 potatoes, cubed and soaked in water
1 aubergine (eggplant), cubed and soaked in water
4 onions, finely sliced, deep-fried and drained
50g/2oz fresh spinach, trimmed, washed and chopped,
    or 50g/2oz frozen spinach, thawed
25g/1oz fenugreek leaves, fresh or dried
115g/4oz carrots, or pumpkin if in season
115g/4oz fresh coriander (cilantro), chopped
50g/2oz fresh mint, chopped, or 15ml/1 tbsp mint sauce
30ml/2 tbsp dhansak masala
30ml/2 tbsp sambhar masala
10ml/2 tsp soft brown sugar
60ml/4 tbsp tamarind juice
salt

1 Heat 45ml/3 tbsp of the oil in a wok, karahi or large pan, and gently fry the fresh chillies, ginger, crushed garlic, bay leaves and cinnamon stick for 2 minutes. Add the lamb pieces and 600ml/1 pint/2½ cups water. Bring to the boil then simmer, covered, until the lamb is half-cooked.

2 Drain the meat stock into another pan and set the lamb aside. Add the lentils or other pulses to the stock and cook gently for 25–30 minutes until they are tender. Mash the lentils with the back of a spoon.

3 Drain the potatoes and aubergine and add to the lentils. Reserve a little of the deep-fried onions and stir the remainder into the pan, along with the spinach, fenugreek and carrot or pumpkin.

4 Add some hot water to the pan if the mixture seems too thick. Cook until the vegetables are tender, then mash slightly with a spoon.

5 Heat 15ml/1 tbsp of the vegetable oil in a large frying pan. Reserve a few coriander and mint leaves or sauce to use as a garnish, and gently fry the remaining leaves with the dhansak and sambhar masala, salt and sugar. Add the lamb to the herbs and spices and fry gently for 5 minutes.

6 Add the lamb to the lentils and stir. Cover, reduce the heat and cook until the lamb is tender, adding more water if necessary. Mix in the tamarind juice.

7 Heat the remaining vegetable oil in a small pan and fry the sliced garlic clove until golden brown. Sprinkle the fried garlic slices over the dhansak. Garnish with the remaining deep-fried onion and the reserved fresh coriander and mint leaves or sauce. Serve the dish hot, with caramelized basmati rice if you like.

VARIATION
Fresh pumpkin is the traditional vegetable used for dhansak. It also helps to tenderize the meat, and will add a fabulous rich golden colour to the dish.

Aromatic Lamb Curry with Cardomom-spiced Rice

This wonderfully fragrant lamb biriani, with the meat and rice cooked together in the same pot, makes a delicious meal that can be enjoyed on its own.

Serves 4

Ingredients
1 large onion, quartered
2 garlic cloves
1 small green chilli, halved and seeded
5cm/2in piece fresh root ginger
15ml/1 tbsp ghee
675g/1½lb boned shoulder or leg of lamb, cut into chunks
15ml/1 tbsp ground coriander
10ml/2 tsp ground cumin
1 cinnamon stick, broken into 3 pieces
150ml/¼ pint/⅔ cup natural (plain) yogurt
75g/3oz/⅓ cup ready-to-eat dried apricots, cut into chunks
salt and ground black pepper

For the rice
250g/9oz/1¼ cups basmati rice
6 cardomom pods, split open
25g/1oz/2 tbsp butter, cut into small pieces
45ml/ 3 tbsp toasted cashew nuts or flaked (sliced) almonds

For the garnish
1 onion, sliced and fried until golden
a few sprigs of fresh coriander (cilantro)

1 Soak a large clay pot or chicken brick in cold water for 20 minutes, then drain. Place the onion, garlic, chilli and ginger in a food processor or blender and process with 15ml/1 tbsp water, to a smooth paste.

2 Heat the ghee and vegetable oil in a heavy frying pan. Fry the lamb chunks in batches over a high heat until golden. Remove from the pan and set aside.

3 Add the onion paste to the remaining oil left in the frying pan, stir in the ground coriander and cumin, add the cinnamon stick pieces and fry for 1–2 minutes, stirring constantly with a wooden spoon.

4 Return the meat to the frying pan, then gradually add the yogurt, a spoonful at a time, stirring well between each addition with a wooden spoon. Season the meat well with plenty of salt and pepper and stir in 150ml/¼ pint/⅔ cup water.

5 Transfer the contents of the frying pan to the prepared clay pot, cover with the lid and place in an unheated oven. Set the oven to 180°C/350°F/Gas 4 and cook the meat for 45 minutes.

6 Meanwhile, prepare the basmati rice. Place the rice in a bowl, cover with cold water and leave to soak for 20 minutes. Drain the rice and place it in a large pan of boiling salted water, bring back to the boil and cook for 10 minutes. Drain well and stir in the split cardomom pods.

7 Remove the clay pot from the oven and stir in the chopped ready-to-eat apricots. Pile the cooked rice on top of the lamb and dot with the butter. Drizzle over 60ml/4 tbsp water, then sprinkle the cashew nuts or flaked almonds on top. Cover the pot and reduce the oven temperature to 150°C/300°F/Gas 2 and cook the meat and rice for 30 minutes.

8 Remove the lid from the pot and fluff up the rice with a fork. Spoon into warmed individual bowls, then sprinkle over the fried onion slices and garnish with the sprigs of fresh coriander.

MUGHLAI-STYLE LEG OF LAMB

In India, there are different names for this way of cooking a leg of lamb, two of which are shahi raan *and* peshawari raan. *Roasting a whole leg of lamb was first popularized by the Mongolian warrior Genghis Khan (1162–1227).*

SERVES 4–6

INGREDIENTS
4 large onions, chopped
4 garlic cloves
5cm/2in piece fresh root ginger, chopped
45ml/3 tbsp ground almonds
10ml/2 tsp ground cumin
10ml/2 tsp ground coriander
10ml/2 tsp ground turmeric
10ml/2 tsp garam masala
4–6 fresh green chillies
juice of 1 lemon
300ml/½ pint/1¼ cups natural (plain) yogurt, beaten
1.8kg/4lb leg of lamb
8–10 cloves
salt
15ml/1 tbsp blanched flaked (sliced) almonds, to garnish
4–6 firm tomatoes, halved and grilled (broiled), to serve

COOK'S TIP
If time permits, allow the joint to stand at room temperature for a couple of hours before roasting as this will give much better results.

1 Place the onions, garlic, ginger, almonds, cumin, coriander, turmeric, garam masala, green chillies and lemon juice in a food processor or blender, with a little salt, and process to a smooth paste. Gradually add the yogurt and blend. Grease a large, deep roasting pan and preheat the oven to 190°C/375°F/Gas 5.

2 Remove most of the fat and skin from the lamb. Using a sharp knife, make deep pockets above the bone at each side of the thick end of the leg. Make deep diagonal gashes on both sides of the lamb.

3 Push the cloves firmly into the meat, spaced evenly on all sides. Push some of the spice mixture into the pockets and gashes and spread the remainder evenly all over the meat with the back of a spoon.

4 Place the meat in the greased roasting pan and loosely cover the whole pan with foil. Roast for 2–2½ hours, or until the meat is cooked, removing the foil for the last 10 minutes of cooking time.

5 Remove the lamb from the oven and leave it to rest for about 10 minutes. Garnish with the almond flakes, and serve, carved into slices, with the grilled tomatoes.

BEEF WITH GREEN BEANS

Adding vegetables to meat and poultry dishes has been a long-standing practice in Indian cooking. Although red pepper is not normally used, it does provide visual appeal as well as enhanced flavour. As an alternative, you could use fresh red chillies.

SERVES 4

INGREDIENTS
275g/10oz fine green beans, cut into 2.5cm/1in pieces
45–60ml/3–4 tbsp vegetable oil
1 onion, sliced
5ml/1 tsp grated fresh root ginger
5ml/1 tsp crushed garlic
5ml/1 tsp chilli powder
6.5ml/1¼ tsp ground turmeric
2 tomatoes, chopped
450g/1lb beef, cubed
1 red (bell) pepper, sliced (optional)
15ml/1 tbsp chopped fresh coriander (cilantro)
2 fresh green chillies, chopped
salt

1 Cook the beans in a pan of salted water for about 5 minutes, then drain and set aside. Heat the oil in a large pan over a medium heat and fry the sliced onion for about 7 minutes until it turns golden brown. Add the ginger, garlic, chilli powder, turmeric and tomatoes and cook for about 3 minutes.

2 Add the beef to the pan and stir-fry for a further 3 minutes. Pour in 1.2 litres/ 2 pints/5 cups water, bring to the boil and lower the heat. Cover and cook for 45–60 minutes, or until most of the water has evaporated and the meat is tender.

3 Add the green beans to the pan and mix everything together well. Finally, add the red pepper, if using, with the chopped fresh coriander and green chillies and cook, stirring, for a further 7–10 minutes. Serve the curry hot.

MADRAS BEEF CURRY

Although Madras is renowned for the best vegetarian food in the country, meat-based recipes such as this one are also extremely popular. This particular recipe is a contribution by the area's small Muslim community.

SERVES 4

INGREDIENTS
60ml/4 tbsp vegetable oil
1 large onion, finely sliced
3–4 cloves
4 cardamom pods
2 whole star anise
4 fresh green chillies, chopped
2 fresh or dried red chillies, chopped
45ml/3 tbsp Madras masala paste
5ml/1 tsp ground turmeric
450g/1lb lean beef, cubed
60ml/4 tbsp tamarind juice
granulated sugar, to taste
salt
a few fresh coriander (cilantro) leaves, chopped, to garnish

1 Heat the vegetable oil in a wok, karahi or large pan over a medium heat and fry the onion slices for 8–9 minutes until they turn golden brown. Lower the heat, then add the cloves, cardamom pods, star anise, green and red chillies, the masala paste and the turmeric. Fry for 2–3 minutes.

2 Add the beef to the pan and mix well. Cover and cook over a low heat until the beef is tender. Cook uncovered on a higher heat for the last few minutes to reduce any excess liquid.

3 Fold the tamarind juice, sugar and salt into the curry. Heat through and garnish with the chopped coriander leaves. Serve immediately.

Beef Vindaloo

Vindaloo is Goa's most famous export, but its origins are in fact Portuguese. In the 16th century, when Portuguese traders embarked on their long voyage to India, they carried pork, preserved in vinegar, garlic and black pepper. The word vin *comes from* vinegar *and* aloo *is derived from* alho, *the Portuguese word for garlic.*

SERVES 4

INGREDIENTS
15ml/1 tbsp cumin seeds
4 dried red chillies
5ml/1 tsp black peppercorns
5 cardamom pods, seeds only
5ml/1 tsp fenugreek seeds
5ml/1 tsp black mustard seeds
2.5ml/½ tsp salt
2.5ml/½ tsp demerara (raw) sugar
60ml/4 tbsp white wine vinegar
60ml/4 tbsp vegetable oil
1 large onion, finely chopped
900g/2lb stewing beef, cut into 2.5cm/1in cubes
2.5cm/1in piece fresh root ginger, shredded
1 garlic clove, crushed
10ml/2 tsp ground coriander
2.5ml/½ tsp ground turmeric
plain and yellow rice, to serve

COOK'S TIP
To make plain and yellow rice, infuse (steep) a pinch of saffron threads or dissolve a little turmeric in 15ml/1 tbsp hot water in a small bowl. Stir into half the cooked rice until it is uniformly yellow. Carefully mix the yellow rice into the plain rice.

Use a mortar and pestle to grind the cumin seeds, chillies, peppercorns, cardamom seeds, fenugreek seeds and mustard seeds to a fine powder. Add the salt, sugar and white wine vinegar and mix to a thin paste.

2 Heat 30ml/2 tbsp of the oil and fry the chopped onion over a medium heat for 8–10 minutes. Put the onion and the spice mixture into a food processor or blender and process to a coarse paste.

3 Heat the remaining oil in the pan and fry the meat cubes over a medium heat for about 10 minutes, or until lightly browned. Remove the beef cubes with a slotted spoon and set aside.

4 Add the shredded ginger and crushed garlic to the pan and fry for 2 minutes. Stir in the coriander and turmeric and fry for 2 minutes more. Then add the spice and onion paste and fry for about 5 minutes.

5 Return the meat to the pan, together with 300ml/½ pint/1¼ cups water. Cover and simmer for 1–1½ hours, or until the meat is tender. Serve with the rice.

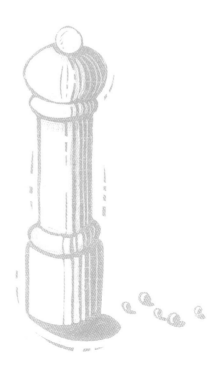

BEEF BALCHAO

Beef dishes are not very common in India, but Goa, on the west coast of the country, has a cuisine that has been influenced by three religions: Hinduism, Islam and Christianity. Goa was colonized by the Portuguese for nearly four centuries and during this time a Jesuit father, Francis Xavier, brought about a calming influence between the religions. Tolerance between the religions has become a tradition that has not faded in the region with the passing of time.

SERVES 4

INGREDIENTS
60ml/4 tbsp vegetable oil
15ml/1 tbsp grated fresh root ginger
15ml/1 tbsp crushed garlic
2.5cm/1in piece cinnamon stick, broken up
2–4 dried red chillies, chopped or torn
4 cloves
10ml/2 tsp cumin seeds
10 black peppercorns
675g/1½lb cubed beef, visible fat removed
5ml/1 tsp ground turmeric
25ml/1½ tbsp tomato purée (paste)
2.5ml/½ tsp chilli powder (optional)
1 large onion, finely sliced
5ml/1 tsp salt
5ml/1 tsp granulated sugar
10ml/2 tbsp cider vinegar

1 Heat 30ml/2 tbsp of the vegetable oil in a wok, karahi or large pan, and add the ginger and garlic. Fry for about 30 seconds.

2 Grind the broken cinnamon, chillies, cloves, cumin seeds and peppercorns to a fine powder, using a spice mill or coffee grinder. Add the spice mix to the pan and fry for a further 30 seconds, stirring continuously.

3 Add the beef and turmeric to the pan and increase the heat slightly. Fry for 5–6 minutes or until the meat starts to release its juices, stirring regularly.

4 Add 200ml/7fl oz/scant 1 cup water, tomato purée, chilli powder, if using, and bring to the boil. Cover the pan and simmer gently for 35–40 minutes.

5 Heat the remaining vegetable oil and fry the onion for 8–9 minutes until browned, stirring regularly. Add the fried onion to the beef along with the salt, sugar and cider vinegar. Stir to combine, cover and simmer gently for 30–35 minutes or until the beef is tender. Remove from the heat and serve.

COOK'S TIP
This dish will keep well in the refrigerator for up to 7 days. Before reheating, bring it back to room temperature. Add a little warm water during reheating, if it seems too dry..

RICE DISHES

Throughout the world, this delicious grain is cooked in many different ways. It can be boiled simply or cooked with other flavourings, vegetables and ingredients. In any Indian market you will see many different kinds of rice but the rice of choice in the West when cooking Indian food is basmati. This variety of long grain rice grows on the foothills of the Himalayas. The grains are long and slender, with an unusual but delicate nutty aroma and taste. This chapter contains a whole range of rice dishes, from simple side dishes to wonderful pulaos and biryanis that can be served as main courses.

SAFFRON RICE

Whole cardamom pods and cloves give this rice a subtle, sweetly spicy flavour and the saffron gives it a beautiful golden colour. Kashmir, in the northern region of India, is one of the world's major producers of saffron.

SERVES 6

INGREDIENTS
450g/1lb/2⅓ cups basmati rice, soaked for 20–30 minutes
3 cardamom pods
2 cloves
5ml/1 tsp salt
45ml/3 tbsp semi-skimmed (low-fat) milk
2.5ml/½ tsp saffron threads, crushed

1 Drain the basmati rice and place in a large pan. Pour in 750ml/1¼ pints/3 cups water. Add the cardamoms, cloves and salt. Stir, then bring to the boil. Lower the heat, then cover tightly and simmer for 5 minutes.

2 Meanwhile, place the milk in a small pan. Add the crushed saffron threads and heat through gently. Add the saffron milk to the rice and stir. Cover again and continue cooking over a low heat for 5–6 minutes until the rice is tender.

3 Remove the pan from the heat without lifting the lid. Leave the rice to stand for about 5 minutes, then fork through just before serving.

COOK'S TIP
The saffron milk can be heated in the microwave, which will allow the saffron to infuse. Combine the milk and saffron threads in a bowl and warm them for 1 minute on low.

CARAMELIZED BASMATI RICE

This is the traditional accompaniment to a dhansak *curry. The rice complements the texture of the lentils. The sugar is caramelized in hot oil before the rice is added and cooked along with a few whole spices for extra flavour.*

SERVES 4

INGREDIENTS
225g/8oz/generous 1 cup basmati rice, washed and soaked for 20–30 minutes
45ml/3 tbsp vegetable oil
20ml/4 tsp granulated sugar
4–5 cardamom pods, bruised
2.5cm/1in piece cinnamon stick
4 cloves
1 bay leaf, crumpled
2.5ml/½ tsp salt

1 Tip the soaked basmati rice in a strainer and leave to drain. In a large pan, heat the vegetable oil over a medium heat. When the oil is hot, add the granulated sugar and heat until it is caramelized.

2 Reduce the heat to low and add the cardamom pods, cinnamon stick, cloves and bay leaf to the pan. Allow to sizzle for about 15–20 seconds, then add the rice and salt. Fry gently, stirring, for 2–3 minutes.

3 Pour 475ml/16fl oz/2 cups hot water into the pan and bring to the boil. Boil steadily for about 2 minutes, then reduce the heat to very low. Cover the pan tightly with a lid and cook for 8 minutes.

4 Remove the rice from the heat and let it stand, with the lid still on, for about 6 minutes. Remove the lid and gently fluff up the rice with a fork and transfer to a warmed dish to serve.

CLASSIC PULAO

The secret of a perfect pulao is to wash the rice thoroughly, then soak it briefly. Soaking before cooking softens and moistens the grains, enabling the rice to absorb moisture during cooking, and resulting in fluffier rice.

SERVES 4

INGREDIENTS
600ml/1 pint/2½ cups hot chicken stock
generous pinch of saffron threads
50g/2oz/¼ cup butter
1 onion, chopped
1 garlic clove, crushed
2.5cm/1in piece cinnamon stick
6 cardamom pods
1 bay leaf
250g/9oz/1⅓ cups basmati rice, soaked for 20–30 minutes
50g/2oz/⅓ cup sultanas (golden raisins)
15ml/1 tbsp vegetable oil
50g/2oz/½ cup cashew nuts
naan bread and a tomato and onion salad, to serve

1 Pour the hot chicken stock into a jug (pitcher). Stir in the saffron threads and set aside. Heat the butter in a pan and fry the onion and garlic for 5 minutes. Stir in the cinnamon, cardamom pods and bay leaf and cook for 2 minutes.

2 Drain the rice and add to the pan, then cook, stirring, for 2 minutes. Pour in the saffron stock and add the sultanas. Bring to the boil, stir, then lower the heat, cover and cook gently for 10 minutes or until the rice is tender and the liquid has all been absorbed.

3 Meanwhile, heat the oil in a wok, karahi or large pan and fry the cashew nuts until browned. Drain the nuts on kitchen paper, then sprinkle them over the rice. Serve with naan bread and a tomato and onion salad.

VEGETABLE PILAU

The exquisite flavour of basmati rice, combined with the heady aroma of spices and delicious vegetables and cashew nuts, makes a sumptuous side dish. It is the perfect accompaniment to most Indian meat dishes.

SERVES 4–6

INGREDIENTS
30ml/2 tbsp oil
2.5ml/½ tsp cumin seeds
2 bay leaves
4 cardamom pods
4 cloves
1 onion, finely chopped
1 carrot, finely chopped
225g/8oz/generous 1 cup basmati rice, soaked for 30 minutes
50g/2oz/½ cup peas, thawed if frozen
50g/2oz/⅓ cup corn, thawed if frozen
25g/1oz/¼ cup cashew nuts, lightly fried
1.5ml/¼ tsp ground coriander
1.5ml/¼ tsp ground cumin
salt

1 Heat the oil in a large frying pan and fry the cumin seeds for 2 minutes. Add the bay leaves, cardamom pods and cloves and fry for 2 minutes. Add the chopped onion to the pan and fry for 5 minutes, or until lightly browned. Stir in the carrot and cook for 3–4 minutes.

2 Drain the soaked basmati rice, then add to the pan with the peas, corn and fried cashew nuts. Fry for 4–5 minutes, stirring frequently.

3 Pour 475ml/16fl oz/2 cups cold water into the pan, then add the remaining spices and salt to taste. Bring to the boil, cover, then simmer for 15 minutes until all the water is absorbed. Leave to stand, covered, for 10 minutes, then serve.

NUT PULAO

Known as pilau in Persia, pilaff in Turkey and pulao in India, these rice dishes are always made with the best-quality long grain rice and basmati is the natural choice. There are many different versions of this recipe, and this one, with walnuts and cashew nuts, makes an ideal dish for vegetarians when served with a raita.

SERVES 4

INGREDIENTS
15–30ml/1–2 tbsp vegetable oil
1 onion, chopped
1 garlic clove, crushed
1 large carrot, coarsely grated
225g/8oz/generous 1 cup basmati rice, soaked for 20–30 minutes
5ml/1 tsp cumin seeds
10ml/2 tsp ground coriander
10ml/2 tsp black mustard seeds (optional)
4 cardamom pods
450ml/¾ pint/scant 2 cups vegetable stock
1 bay leaf
75g/3oz/¾ cup mixed unsalted walnuts and cashew nuts
salt and ground black pepper
fresh coriander (cilantro) sprigs, to garnish

1 Heat the vegetable oil in a wok, karahi or large pan. Fry the onion, garlic and carrot for 3–4 minutes. Drain the rice and add to the pan with the cumin, coriander, mustard seeds, if using, and cardamom pods. Cook for 2 minutes, stirring.

2 Pour the vegetable stock into the pan and stir. Add the bay leaf and season well. Bring to the boil, lower the heat, cover and simmer for 10–12 minutes.

3 Remove the pan from the heat. Leave to stand for 5 minutes with the lid on, then check the rice. If it is cooked, there will be small steam holes on the surface of the rice. Discard the bay leaf and the cardamom pods.

4 Stir the walnuts and cashew nuts into the rice and check the seasoning. Spoon on to a warmed platter, garnish with the fresh coriander and serve.

FRUITY PULAO

This gently flavoured rice dish would complement any curry with a creamy sauce such as a korma or would provide a welcome contrast to a fiery main dish. Ring the changes and add chopped dried apricots or dates instead of the sultanas, and use pistachio or cashew nuts in place of the almonds.

SERVES 4–6

INGREDIENTS
450g/1lb/2⅓ cups basmati rice
75g/3oz/6 tbsp unsalted (sweet) butter
15ml/1 tbsp corn oil
1 bay leaf
6 black peppercorns
4 cardamom pods
5ml/1 tsp salt
75g/3oz/½ cup sultanas (golden raisins)
50g/2oz/½ cup flaked (slivered) almonds

1 Wash the rice twice in cold water, drain and set aside in a strainer. Heat the butter and corn oil in a pan. Lower the heat and add the bay leaf, peppercorns and cardamom pods, then fry for about 30 seconds.

2 Add the rice, salt, sultanas and flaked almonds to the pan. Stir-fry for about 1 minute, then pour in 1 litre/1¾ pints/4 cups water. Bring to the boil, then cover with a tight-fitting lid and lower the heat. Cook for 15–20 minutes.

3 Turn off the heat and leave the rice to stand, still covered, for about 5 minutes. Fluff up the grains of rice with a fork before serving.

COOK'S TIP
The word basmati *means "the fragrant one" in Hindi. There are various grades of basmati, but it is impossible for the shopper to differentiate between them except by trying the brands to discover the variety with the best fragrance and flavour.*

PULAO IN AROMATIC LAMB STOCK

This rich and highly aromatic dish, known as yakhni pulao, *is typical of northern Indian cooking. Traditionally, lamb is cooked on the bone, which adds extra flavour to the stock, so if you bone the lamb yourself add the bones to the stock.*

SERVES 4–6

INGREDIENTS
900g/2lb lean lamb, cubed
4 cardamom pods
2 black cardamom pods
10 whole peppercorns
4 cloves
1 onion, sliced
450g/1lb/2⅓ cups basmati rice, washed and drained
8–10 saffron threads
2 garlic cloves, crushed
5cm/2in piece fresh root ginger, crushed
5cm/2in piece cinnamon stick
salt
175g/6oz/generous 1 cup sultanas (golden raisins) and almonds, sautéed, to garnish

1 Place the cubed lamb in a large pan with 600ml/1 pint/2½ cups water and the cardamom pods, peppercorns, cloves and sliced onion. Add salt to taste, and cook until the meat is tender. Remove the meat with a slotted spoon and keep warm. Strain the stock and return it to the pan.

2 Add the drained rice, saffron threads, garlic, ginger and cinnamon stick to the stock in the pan and bring to the boil.

3 Quickly add the lamb to the pan and stir well. Bring the stock back to the boil, reduce the heat and cover. Cook for 15–20 minutes.

4 Remove the pan from the heat and stand for 5 minutes. Transfer to a warmed serving platter, garnish with the sultanas and almonds and serve.

Tricolour Pulao

Most Indian restaurants in the West serve this pulao, which has at least three different coloured grains. The effect is easily achieved with food colouring, as this recipe reveals. You can leave the third colour pure white, if you prefer.

SERVES 4–6

INGREDIENTS
450g/1lb/2⅓ cups basmati rice
75g/3oz/6 tbsp ghee or unsalted (sweet) butter
4 cloves
2 dried bay leaves
4 cardamom pods
5ml/1 tsp salt
a few drops each of yellow, green and red food colouring

1 Wash the rice twice under cold running water, then leave to soak in a bowl for 20–30 minutes. Drain the rice through a strainer and set aside.

2 Melt the ghee or butter in a wok, karahi or large pan over a low heat, and add the cloves, bay leaves, cardamom pods and salt. Add the rice. Fry for 1 minute, stirring constantly to prevent the rice grains sticking to the base of the pan.

3 Pour 1 litre/1¾ pints/4 cups water into the pan and bring to the boil. As soon as it has boiled, cover and reduce the heat to low. Cook for 10–12 minutes.

4 Just before you are ready to serve the rice, pour a few drops of each type of food colouring at different sides of the pan. Leave to stand for 5 minutes, then gently mix into the rice, using a fork. Serve the pulao immediately.

COOK'S TIP
If you do not like using artificial food colours, use natural food colouring such as turmeric blended in hot water, beetroot juice and spinach juice.

Tomato & Spinach Pulao

This is a tasty and nourishing dish for vegetarians and meat eaters alike. Serve it with a vegetable curry, or with a meat, poultry or fish curry. Add a cooling fruit raita for a wonderful contrast of colour and flavour.

SERVES 4

INGREDIENTS

30ml/2 tbsp vegetable oil
15ml/1 tbsp ghee or unsalted (sweet) butter
1 onion, chopped
2 garlic cloves, crushed
3 tomatoes, peeled, seeded and chopped
225g/8oz/generous 1 cup brown basmati rice, soaked
10ml/2 tsp dhana jeera powder or 5ml/1 tsp each ground coriander
  and ground cumin
2 carrots, coarsely grated
900ml/1½ pints/3¾ cups vegetable stock
275g/10oz young spinach leaves
50g/2oz/½ cup unsalted cashew nuts, toasted
salt and ground black pepper
naan bread, to serve

1 Heat the oil and ghee or butter in a wok, karahi or large pan, and fry the onion and garlic for 4–5 minutes until soft. Add the tomatoes and cook for 3–4 minutes, stirring, until thickened.

2 Drain the rice, add it to the tomatoes and cook for a further 1–2 minutes, stirring well, until the rice is well coated in the sauce.

3 Stir the dhana jeera powder or coriander and cumin into the rice, then add the carrots. Season with salt and pepper. Pour in the stock and stir to mix.

4 Bring the mixture to the boil, then cover tightly and simmer over a very gentle heat for 20–25 minutes, until the rice is tender. Lay the spinach on the surface of the rice, cover again, and cook for a further 2–3 minutes, until the spinach has wilted. Fold the spinach into the rice and check the seasoning. Sprinkle with toasted cashews and serve with naan bread.

TOMATO RICE

This delicious rice dish can be served as a meal on its own, perhaps with a raita and some poppadums. Alternatively it would make the ideal accompaniment to a meat, poultry or fish curry that does not include vegetables.

SERVES 4

INGREDIENTS
30ml/2 tbsp corn oil
2.5ml/½ tsp onion seeds
1 onion, sliced
2 tomatoes, sliced
1 orange or yellow (bell) pepper, sliced
5ml/1 tsp grated fresh root ginger
5ml/1 tsp crushed garlic
5ml/1 tsp chilli powder
30ml/2 tbsp chopped fresh coriander (cilantro)
1 potato, diced
7.5ml/1½ tsp salt
50g/2oz/⅓ cup frozen peas
400g/14oz/2 cups basmati rice, washed

1 Heat the corn oil in a large pan and fry the onion seeds for about 30 seconds. Add the sliced onion and fry for about 5 minutes.

2 Add the sliced tomatoes, orange or yellow pepper, ginger, garlic, chilli powder, fresh coriander, potatoes, salt and peas to the pan and stir-fry for 5 minutes.

3 Add the rice to the vegetables and stir-fry for about 1 minute. Pour in 700ml/ 24fl oz/3 cups water and bring to the boil, then lower the heat to medium. Cover and cook for 12–15 minutes. Leave the rice to stand for 5 minutes, then serve.

VARIATION
This dish is very good made with other vegetables. Try substituting the orange or yellow peppers with a handful of sliced mushrooms, 1 courgette (zucchini) cut into strips or 150g/4oz halved green beans.

CHICKEN PULAO

Like biryanis, pulaos cooked with meat and poultry make a convenient one-pot meal. A vegetable curry makes a good accompaniment, although for a simpler meal you could serve the pulao just with a raita, combining natural yogurt with any raw vegetable, such as white cabbage, grated carrots or cauliflower florets.

SERVES 4

INGREDIENTS
400g/14oz/2 cups basmati rice
75g/3oz/6 tbsp ghee or unsalted (sweet) butter
1 onion, sliced
1.5ml/¼ tsp mixed onion and mustard seeds
3 curry leaves
5ml/1 tsp grated fresh root ginger
5ml/1 tsp crushed garlic
5ml/1 tsp ground coriander
5ml/1 tsp chilli powder
7.5ml/1½ tsp salt
2 tomatoes, sliced
1 potato, cubed
50g/2oz/½ cup frozen peas, thawed
175g/6oz chicken breast fillets, skinned and cubed
60ml/4 tbsp chopped fresh coriander (cilantro)
2 fresh green chillies, chopped

1 Wash the rice thoroughly under cold running water, then leave to soak for about 30 minutes. Drain well and set aside in a strainer.

2 Melt the ghee or butter in a large pan, add the sliced onion and fry until golden. Add the mixed onion and mustard seeds, the curry leaves, root ginger, garlic, ground coriander, chilli powder and salt. Stir-fry over a low heat for about 2 minutes until the spices give off a delicious aroma.

3 Add the sliced tomatoes, cubed potato, peas and chicken to the pan and stir to mix well. Add the rice and stir gently to combine with the other ingredients.

4 Add the chopped fresh coriander and green chillies to the pan, then stir-fry for about 1 minute. Pour 700ml/1¼ pints/3 cups water into the pan, bring to the boil, then lower the heat. Cover and cook for 20 minutes.

5 Remove the pan from the heat and leave the pulao to stand for 6–8 minutes. Just before serving fluff up the grains with a fork and transfer to a serving dish.

COOK'S TIPS
- *Basmati rice should be picked over carefully before being cooked as it might contain small stones and other foreign matter.*
- *Washing the rice in cold water before boiling leads to a lighter, fluffier result.*
- *Once you have washed the rice, leave it to drain for at least 20 minutes so that it becomes quite dry again before you cook it.*

RICE WITH LENTILS

This dish is light yet satisfying, and extremely wholesome. Rice is cooked with whole and ground spices, which impart a gentle flavouring, along with lentils, potatoes and onions. It could be served as a vegetarian main dish or to accompany a meat curry.

SERVES 4

INGREDIENTS
115g/4oz/⅔ cup basmati rice
150g/5oz/⅔ cup red split lentils
1 large potato
1 large onion
30ml/2 tbsp oil
4 whole cloves
1.5ml/¼ tsp cumin seeds
1.5ml/¼ tsp ground turmeric
10ml/2 tsp salt

1 Wash the rice and lentils in several changes of cold water. Place in a bowl and pour in water to cover. Leave to soak for at least 15 minutes, then drain.

2 Meanwhile, peel the potato and rinse well, then cut into 2.5cm/1in chunks. Peel the onion and slice it very thinly.

3 Heat the oil in a large heavy pan and fry the cloves and cumin seeds for about 2 minutes until the seeds begin to splutter.

4 Add the onion and potatoes to the pan and fry for 5 minutes until slightly browned. Add the drained rice and lentils with the ground turmeric and salt and fry for about 3 minutes, stirring continuously.

5 Pour 475ml/16fl oz/2 cups water into the pan. Bring to the boil, cover tightly with a lid and simmer for 15–20 minutes, until all the water has been absorbed and the potatoes are tender. Leave the rice to stand, covered, for about 10 minutes. Fluff up the grains of rice with a fork and serve.

PRAWN BIRYANI

The recipe for biryani originated with mutton, but its popularity has tempted Indian chefs to create versions using other ingredients. As with all biryanis, this one using prawns is a meal in itself. Raita is the classic accompaniment to any biryani.

SERVES 4–6

INGREDIENTS

2 large onions, finely sliced and deep-fried
300ml/½ pint/1¼ cups natural (plain) yogurt
30ml/2 tbsp tomato purée (paste)
60ml/4 tbsp green masala paste
30ml/2 tbsp lemon juice
5ml/1 tsp black cumin seeds
5cm/2in piece cinnamon stick, or 1.5ml/¼ tsp ground cinnamon
4 cardamom pods
450g/1lb raw king prawns (jumbo shrimp), peeled and deveined
225g/8oz/3 cups small whole button (white) mushrooms
225g/8oz/2 cups frozen peas, thawed
450g/1lb/2⅓ cups basmati rice, soaked for 5 minutes in boiled water and drained
1 sachet saffron powder, mixed in 90ml/6 tbsp milk
30ml/2 tbsp ghee or unsalted (sweet) butter
salt

1 In a bowl, combine the onions, yogurt, tomato purée, masala paste, lemon juice, cumin, cinnamon, cardamom pods and salt. Add the prawns, mushrooms and peas. Stir and leave to stand for 2 hours. Preheat the oven to 190°C/375°F/Gas 5.

2 Grease the base of a heavy pan and add the prawn mixture. Cover with the rice and smooth the surface gently until you have an even layer. Pour 300ml/½ pint/ 1¼ cups water over the surface of the rice. Press holes in the rice with a spoon handle and pour into each a little saffron milk. Dot ghee or butter on the surface.

3 Place a circular piece of foil on top of the rice. Cover and cook in the oven for 45–50 minutes. Stand for 8 minutes, then stir briefly and serve.

CHICKEN BIRYANI

Biryani is a wonderful rice dish that is equally at home on the family dining table or as an impressive dinner-party centrepiece. Serve this aromatic chicken version with some grilled (broiled) or fried poppadums.

SERVES 4

INGREDIENTS
10 cardamom pods
275g/10oz/1½ cups basmati rice, soaked for 20–30 minutes then drained
2.5ml/½ tsp salt
2–3 whole cloves
5cm/2in piece cinnamon stick
45ml/3 tbsp vegetable oil
3 onions, sliced
4 chicken breast fillets, each weighing about 175g/6oz, skinned and cubed
1.5ml/¼ tsp ground cloves
1.5ml/¼ tsp hot chilli powder
5ml/1 tsp ground cumin
5ml/1 tsp ground coriander
2.5ml/½ tsp ground black pepper
3 garlic cloves, chopped
5ml/1 tsp finely chopped fresh root ginger
juice of 1 lemon
4 tomatoes, sliced
30ml/2 tbsp chopped fresh coriander (cilantro)
150ml/¼ pint/⅔ cup natural (plain) yogurt, plus extra to serve
4–5 saffron threads, soaked in 10ml/2 tsp warm milk
toasted flaked (sliced) almonds and fresh coriander (cilantro) sprigs, to garnish

1 Preheat the oven to 190°C/375°F/Gas 5. Carefully remove the seeds from half the cardamom pods and grind them finely, using a mortar and pestle. Set aside the ground seeds.

2 Bring a pan of water to the boil and add the rice, salt, whole cardamom pods, cloves and cinnamon stick. Boil for 2 minutes, then drain, leaving the whole spices in the rice. Keep the rice hot in a covered pan.

3 Heat the vegetable oil in a wok, karahi or large pan, and fry the sliced onions for 8 minutes, until softened and browned. Add the chicken and the ground spices, including the ground cardamom seeds. Mix well, then add the garlic, ginger and lemon juice. Stir-fry for about 5 minutes.

4 Transfer the chicken mixture to a casserole and arrange the tomatoes on top. Sprinkle on the chopped fresh coriander, spoon the yogurt evenly on top and cover with the drained rice.

5 Drizzle the saffron milk over the rice and pour over 150ml/¼ pint/⅔ cup water. Cover, then bake in the oven for 1 hour. Transfer the rice to a warmed serving platter and discard the whole spices. Garnish with toasted flaked almonds and sprigs of coriander, and serve immediately.

BEEF BIRYANI

This biryani is a speciality of the Indian Muslim community. The recipe may seem long, but biryani is one of the easiest and most relaxing ways of cooking, especially when you are entertaining. Once the dish is assembled and placed in the oven, it looks after itself and you can happily get on with other things.

SERVES 4

INGREDIENTS
2 large onions
2 garlic cloves, chopped
2.5cm/1in piece fresh root ginger, peeled and roughly chopped
½–1 fresh green chilli, seeded and chopped
small bunch of fresh coriander (cilantro)
60ml/4 tbsp flaked (sliced) almonds
15ml/1 tbsp ghee or butter, plus 25g/1oz/2 tbsp butter for the rice
45ml/3 tbsp vegetable oil
30ml/2 tbsp sultanas (golden raisins)
500g/1¼lb braising or stewing steak, cubed
5ml/1 tsp ground coriander
15ml/1 tbsp ground cumin
2.5ml/½ tsp ground turmeric
2.5ml/½ tsp ground fenugreek
generous pinch of ground cinnamon
175ml/6fl oz/¾ cup natural (plain) yogurt, whisked
275g/10oz/1½ cups basmati rice
about 1.2 litres/2 pints/5 cups hot chicken stock or water
salt and ground black pepper
2 hard-boiled eggs, quartered, to garnish
chapatis, to serve

1 Roughly chop one onion and place it in a food processor or blender. Add the garlic, ginger, chilli, fresh coriander and half the flaked almonds. Pour in 30–45ml/2–3 tbsp water and process to a smooth paste. Transfer the paste to a small bowl and set aside until required.

2 Finely slice the remaining onion into rings or half rings. Heat half the ghee or butter with half the oil in a heavy flameproof casserole and fry the onion rings for 10–15 minutes until golden brown. Transfer to a plate with a slotted spoon. Fry the remaining flaked almonds briefly until golden and set aside with the onion rings, then quickly fry the sultanas, stirring, until they swell. Transfer to the plate.

3 Heat the remaining ghee or butter in the casserole with a further 15ml/ 1 tbsp of the oil. Fry the cubed meat, in batches, until evenly browned on all sides. Transfer the meat to a plate and set aside.

4 Wipe the casserole clean with kitchen paper, heat the remaining oil and pour in the prepared spice paste. Cook over a medium heat for 2–3 minutes, stirring constantly, until the mixture begins to brown slightly. Stir in all the additional spices, season with salt and ground black pepper and cook for 1 minute more.

5 Lower the heat, then stir in the yogurt, a little at a time. When all of it has been incorporated into the spice mixture, return the meat to the casserole. Stir to coat, cover tightly and simmer over a gentle heat for 40–45 minutes until the meat is tender. Meanwhile, soak the rice in a bowl of cold water for 15–20 minutes.

6 Preheat the oven to 160°C/325°F/Gas 3. Drain the rice, place in a pan and add the hot chicken stock or water, together with a little salt. Bring back to the boil, cover and cook for 5 minutes.

7 Drain the rice, and pile it in a mound on top of the meat in the casserole. Using the handle of a spoon, make a hole through the rice and meat mixture, to the base of the pan. Place the fried onions, almonds and sultanas over the top and dot with knobs (pats) of butter. Cover the casserole tightly with a double layer of foil and secure with a lid.

8 Cook the biryani in the preheated oven for 30–40 minutes. To serve, spoon the mixture on to a warmed serving platter and garnish with the quartered hard-boiled eggs. Serve with chapatis.

BREADS

Naan bread and chapatis are well known in the West, and they certainly have their place in Indian cuisine. However, there are many other types of bread that can be made to serve with curries and other Indian dishes. None of the breads featured here are difficult to prepare, and the unleavened varieties take very little time at all. Some breads are baked and others are fried, making them most suitable for special occasions. Indians often serve bread with their meals, rather than rice. In the West, however, breads are often served as an extra, and they always make a welcome addition to the table.

CHAPATIS

This simple unleavened bread is made from a ground wholemeal flour known as atta, *which is finer than the Western equivalent. This special chapati flour is usually available from Indian grocers. Chapatis are the everyday bread of the Indian home and are used to pick up food in place of cutlery.*

MAKES 8–10

INGREDIENTS
225g/8oz/2 cups chapati flour or ground wholemeal (whole-wheat) flour
2.5ml/½ tsp salt

1 Place the flour and salt in a mixing bowl. Make a well in the centre and gradually stir in 175ml/6fl oz/¾ cup water, mixing well with your fingers. Form a supple dough and knead for 7–10 minutes. Cover the dough with clear film (plastic wrap) and set aside for 15–20 minutes to rest.

2 Divide the dough into 8–10 equal portions. Roll out each piece into a thin round on a well-floured surface.

3 Place a tava (chapati griddle) or heavy frying pan over a high heat. When smoke rises from it, lower the heat to medium and carefully lay a single round of dough in the centre of the pan.

4 When the chapati begins to bubble, turn it over. Press it down using a clean dishtowel or a flat spoon and turn once again. Remove the cooked chapati from the pan and keep warm in a piece of foil lined with kitchen paper. Cook the remaining chapatis in the same way and serve immediately.

COOK'S TIP
If you cannot find chapati flour, substitute an equal quantity of wholemeal flour and plain flour.

PARATHAS

These delicious flaky breads are rich in saturated fat, so reserve them for serving on special occasions. Making a paratha is somewhat similar to the technique used when making flaky pastry. The difference lies in the handling of the dough; this can be handled freely, unlike that for a flaky pastry.

MAKES 12–15

INGREDIENTS
350g/12oz/3 cups chapati flour or ground wholemeal (whole-wheat), plus
  50g/2oz/½ cup for dusting
50g/2oz/½ cup plain (all-purpose) flour
30ml/2 tbsp ghee or unsalted (sweet) butter, plus 10ml/2 tsp, melted
salt

1 Sift the flours and salt into a bowl. Make a well in the centre and add 10ml/2 tsp of unmelted ghee or butter. Fold into the flour to make a crumbly texture.

2 Gradually mix in in enough cold water to make a soft, pliable dough. Knead the dough until smooth and elastic, then cover and leave to rest for 30 minutes.

3 Divide the dough into 12–15 equal portions and keep covered. Roll out each portion on a lightly floured surface to make a round, about 10cm/4in in diameter. Brush the surface with a little of the melted ghee or butter and sprinkle with chapati flour.

4 Make a cut from the centre of each round, then lift a cut edge and roll the dough into a cone shape. Flatten it again into a ball, then roll the dough in a round, about 18cm/7in wide in diameter.

5 Heat a griddle over a high heat until it smokes. Reduce the heat and cook one paratha at a time, placing a little of the remaining ghee along the edges. Cook on each side until golden brown. Serve hot.

Naan Bread

This bread was introduced to India by the Moguls who originally came from Persia. In Persian, the word naan *means bread. Traditionally, naan is not rolled, but patted and stretched until the teardrop shape is achieved. You can, of course, roll it out to a circle, then gently pull the lower end to achieve the traditional shape.*

MAKES ABOUT 6

INGREDIENTS
5ml/1 tsp caster (superfine) sugar
5ml/1 tsp dried yeast
225g/8oz/2 cups plain (all-purpose) flour, plus extra for dusting
5ml/1 tsp ghee, melted
5ml/1 tsp salt
50g/2oz/¼ cup unsalted (sweet) butter, melted
5ml/1 tsp poppy seeds

VARIATIONS
- *Onion seeds, cumin seeds, crushed coriander seeds or chopped fresh coriander (cilantro) may be used as a topping in place of the poppy seeds.*
- *To make cardamom-flavoured naan, lightly crush the seeds from 4–5 green cardamom pods and add the flour before adding the ghee and water.*

1 Put the sugar and yeast in a small bowl and pour in 150ml/¼ pint/⅔ cup warm water. Mix well until the yeast is completely dissolved. Set aside for about 10 minutes, or until the mixture froths.

2 Place the flour in a large bowl, make a well in the centre and add the ghee, salt and the yeast mixture. Mix well, using your hands, adding a little more water if the dough is too dry.

3 Turn the dough out on to a lightly floured surface and knead for about 5 minutes, or until smooth. Return the dough to the bowl, cover and leave in a warm place for about 1½ hours, or until doubled in size.

4 Turn the dough on to a lightly floured surface and knead again for about 2 minutes. Break off small pieces of the dough with your hands, and roll into rounds, about 13cm/5in in diameter and 1cm/½in thick.

5 Place the naan breads on a sheet of greased foil under a very hot, preheated grill (broiler) for 7–10 minutes, turning twice and brushing with melted butter and sprinkling with poppy seeds during cooking.

6 Serve the naan immediately, if possible. Alternatively keep warm by wrapping in foil until ready to serve.

SPICED NAAN BREAD

Indian naan bread is traditionally baked in a fiercely hot tandoori oven. However, good results can be achieved at home by using alternative cooking methods. In this recipe, the naan bread is cooked using a combination of a hot oven and grill.

MAKES 6

INGREDIENTS
450 g/1lb/4 cups plain (all-purpose) flour
5ml/1 tsp baking powder
2.5ml/½ tsp salt
1 sachet easy-blend dried yeast
5ml/1 tsp caster (superfine) sugar
5ml/1 tsp fennel seeds
10ml/2 tsp black onion seeds
5ml/1 tsp cumin seeds
150ml/¼ pint/⅔ cup hand-hot milk
30ml/2 tbsp oil, plus extra for greasing and brushing
150ml/¼ pint/⅔ cup natural (plain) yogurt
1 egg, beaten

> VARIATION
> Vary the spices used by adding chopped chilli to the mixture, or sprinkling the surface of the bread with poppy seeds before baking.

1 Sift the flour, baking powder and salt into a large mixing bowl. Stir in the yeast, sugar, fennel seeds, black onion seeds and cumin seeds. Make a well in the centre. Stir the hand-hot milk into the flour mixture, then add the oil, yogurt and beaten egg. Mix to form a ball of dough.

2 Turn the dough out on to a lightly floured surface, then knead for about 10 minutes until smooth. Return to the clean, lightly oiled bowl and roll the dough to coat it with oil. Cover the bowl with clear film (plastic wrap) and set aside until the dough has doubled in size.

3 Put a heavy baking sheet in the oven and preheat the oven to 240°C/475°F/ Gas 9. Also preheat the grill (broiler). Lightly knead the dough again and divide it into 6 equal pieces.

4 Keep 5 pieces covered while working with the sixth. Quickly roll the piece of dough out to a tear-drop shape, brush lightly with oil and slap the naan on to the hot baking sheet. Repeat with the remaining dough.

5 Bake the naan in the oven for 3 minutes until puffed up, then place the baking sheet under the grill for about 30 seconds, or until the naan are lightly browned. Serve hot or warm.

PURIS

These delicious little deep-fried breads, shaped into discs, make it temptingly easy to overindulge. In most areas, they are made of wholemeal flour, but in the east and north-east of India, they are made from plain refined flour, and are known as loochis.

MAKES 12

INGREDIENTS
115g/4oz/1 cup unbleached plain (all-purpose) flour
115g/4oz/1 cup wholemeal (whole-wheat) flour
2.5ml/½ tsp salt
2.5ml/½ tsp chilli powder (optional)
30ml/2 tbsp vegetable oil
oil, for frying

> ### VARIATION
> *To make spinach pooris, thaw 50g/2oz frozen spinach, drain, and add to the dough with a little grated fresh root ginger and 2.5ml/½ tsp ground cumin. You may need to use a little less water.*

1 Sift the flours, salt and chilli powder, if using, into a large mixing bowl. Add the vegetable oil, then add 100–120/3½–4fl oz/scant ⅓–½ cup water and mix to a dough. Turn out on to a lightly floured surface and knead for 8–10 minutes until smooth.

2 Place the dough in an oiled bowl and cover with oiled clear film (plastic wrap). Leave to stand for about 30 minutes.

3 Turn the dough out on to a floured surface again. Divide it into 12 equal pieces. Keeping the rest of the dough covered while you work, roll each piece into a 13cm/5in round. Stack the rounds of dough, layered between clear film, to keep them moist.

4 Pour the oil for frying to a depth of 2.5cm/1in into a deep frying pan and heat it to 180°C/350°F. Using a metal fish slice (spatula), lift one puri and gently slide it into the oil; it will sink but will then return to the surface and begin to sizzle.

5 Gently press the puri into the oil. It will puff up. Turn the puri over after a few seconds and allow it to cook for a further 20–30 seconds.

6 Using a slotted spoon, remove the puri from the pan and pat dry with kitchen paper. Place the cooked puri on a large baking sheet, in a single layer, and keep warm in a low oven while you cook the remaining puris. Serve warm.

BHATURAS

These leavened, deep-fried breads are from Punjab, where the local people enjoy them with a bowl of spicy chickpea curry. The combination has become a classic over the years and is known as choley bhature. *Bhaturas must be eaten when freshly cooked and hot, and cannot be reheated.*

MAKES 10

INGREDIENTS
15g/½oz fresh yeast
5ml/1 tsp granulated sugar
200g/7oz/1¾ cups plain (all-purpose) flour, plus extra for dusting/kneading
50g/2oz/½ cup semolina
2.5ml/½ tsp salt
15g/½oz/1 tbsp ghee or butter
30ml/2 tbsp natural (plain) yogurt
oil, for frying

COOK'S TIP
Ghee is availabe from Indian stores and some supermarkets. However, it is easy to make at home. Melt unsalted (sweet) butter over a low heat. Simmer very gently until the residue becomes light golden, then leave to cool. Strain through muslin (cheesecloth) before using.

1 Mix the yeast with the sugar and 120ml/4fl oz/½ cup lukewarm water in a jug (pitcher). Sift the flour into a large bowl and stir in the semolina and salt. Rub in the ghee or butter.

2 Add the yeast mixture and yogurt to the flour and semolina and mix to a soft dough. Turn out on to a lightly floured surface and knead for about 10 minutes until smooth and elastic.

3 Place the dough in an oiled bowl, cover with oiled clear film (plastic wrap) and leave to rise, in a warm place, for about 1 hour, or until doubled in size.

4 Turn the dough out on to a lightly floured surface and knock back (punch down). Divide into 10 equal pieces and shape each into a ball. Flatten into discs with the palm of your hand. Roll out into 13cm/5in rounds.

5 Heat the oil for frying to a depth of 1cm/½in in a deep frying pan and slide one bhatura into the oil. Fry for about 1 minute, turning over after 30 seconds, then drain well on kitchen paper. Keep each bhatura warm in a low oven while frying the remaining bhaturas. Serve immediately, while piping hot.

MISSI ROTIS

These flatbreads are another speciality from Punjab, for which gram flour, known as besan, is used instead of the usual chapati flour, and mixed with wholemeal flour. In Punjab, Missi Rotis *are very popular with the refreshing yogurt drink, lassi.*

MAKES 4

INGREDIENTS
115g/4oz/1 cup gram flour (besan)
115g/4oz/1 cup wholemeal (whole-wheat) flour
1 fresh green chilli, seeded and chopped
½ onion, finely chopped
15ml/1 tbsp chopped fresh coriander (cilantro)
2.5ml/½ tsp ground turmeric
2.5ml/½ tsp salt
15ml/1 tbsp vegetable oil or melted butter
30–45ml/2–3 tbsp melted unsalted (sweet) butter or ghee

1 In a large bowl, combine the flours, chilli, onion, coriander, turmeric and salt. Stir in the oil or melted butter.

2 Mix 120–150ml/4–5fl oz/½–⅔ cup lukewarm water into the flour to make a pliable, soft dough. Turn the dough out on to a lightly floured surface and knead until smooth. Then place in a lightly oiled bowl, cover with oiled clear film (plastic wrap) and leave to rest for 30 minutes.

3 Turn the dough out on to a lightly floured surface. Divide into 4 equal pieces and shape into balls in the palms of your hands. Roll out each ball into a thick round about 15–18cm/6–7in in diameter.

4 Heat a griddle or heavy frying pan over a medium heat for a few minutes until hot. Brush both sides of one roti with some melted butter or ghee. Place in the pan and cook for 2 minutes, turning once. Brush the cooked roti lightly with melted butter or ghee again, slide it on to a plate and keep warm in a low oven while cooking the remaining rotis in the same way. Serve warm.

TANDOORI ROTIS

Rotis are the most common food eaten in central and northern India. For generations, the roti has been made with just wholemeal flour, salt and water, although the art of making rotis is generally more refined these days.

MAKES 6

INGREDIENTS
350g/12oz/3 cups chapati flour or ground wholemeal
   (whole-wheat) flour
5ml/1 tsp salt
30–45ml/2–3 tbsp melted ghee or unsalted (sweet) butter,
   for brushing

1 Sift the flour and salt into a large mixing bowl. Add 250ml/8fl oz/1 cup water and mix to a soft, pliable dough.

2 Turn the dough out on to a lightly floured surface and knead for 3–4 minutes until smooth. Place the dough in a lightly oiled bowl, cover with lightly oiled clear film (plastic wrap) and leave to rest for 1 hour.

3 Turn the dough out on to a lightly floured surface. Divide the dough into six equal pieces and shape each one into a ball. Press each ball into a larger round with the palm of your hand, cover again with lightly oiled clear film and leave to rest for about 10 minutes.

4 Meanwhile, preheat the oven to 230°C/450°F/Gas 8. Place three baking sheets in the oven to heat. Roll the rotis into 15cm/6in rounds, place two on each baking sheet and bake for 8–10 minutes. Brush the rotis with melted ghee or butter and serve warm.

COOK'S TIP
The rotis are ready to remove from the oven when light, golden-brown bubbles appear on the surface.

RED LENTIL PANCAKES

This is a type of dosa, *which is essentially a pancake from southern India. It is eaten in a similar fashion to northern Indian flatbreads. Northern Indian breads are made of wholemeal or refined flour; in the south they are made of ground lentils and rice. The rice and lentils need to be soaked overnight, and the batter must be left to ferment for 24 hours, so don't forget to leave plenty of preparation time.*

MAKES 6

INGREDIENTS
150g/5oz/³⁄4 cup long grain or basmati rice
50g/2oz/¼ cup red lentils
5ml/1 tsp salt
2.5ml/½ tsp ground turmeric
2.5ml/½ tsp ground black pepper
30ml/2 tbsp chopped fresh coriander (cilantro)
oil, for frying and drizzling

VARIATION
To make coconut lentil dosas, add 60ml/4 tbsp grated fresh coconut to the pancake batter along with the salt, ground turmeric, pepper and fresh coriander just before cooking.

1 Place the rice and lentils in a large mixing bowl, pour over 250ml/8fl oz/1 cup warm water, and set aside to soak for at least 8 hours or preferably overnight.

2 Drain off the soaking water from the rice and lentils and reserve. Place the rice and lentils in a food processor or blender and process until smooth. Blend in the reserved soaking water to make a smooth batter.

3 Scrape the rice-and-lentil mixture into a bowl, cover with clear film (plastic wrap) and leave to ferment in a warm place for about 24 hours.

4 Stir the salt, turmeric, pepper and fresh coriander into the batter. Heat a heavy frying pan over a medium heat for a few minutes until hot. Smear with oil and add about 30–45ml/ 2–3 tbsp batter.

5 Using the rounded base of a soup spoon, gently spread the batter out, using a circular motion, to make a pancake that is 15cm/6in in diameter.

6 Cook the rotis for 1½–2 minutes, or until set. Drizzle a little oil over the pancake and around the edges. Turn over and cook for about 1 minute more, or until golden brown.

7 Keep the cooked pancakes warm in a low oven or on a heatproof plate placed over a pan of simmering water and cook the remaining pancake batter in the same way. Serve warm.

PICKLES, CHUTNEYS & CONDIMENTS

Just a small spoonful of pickle or a little chutney can turn an ordinary meal into a feast. Pickles, chutneys and other accompaniments provide the final touch to many Indian meals. A raita is delicious and offers a soothing, refreshing taste to counter the fiery quality of chillies. Some dishes are quickly made using raw vegetables and herbs; others are cooked, then left to mature before use. Many of the recipes in this chapter are also suitable for serving with poppadums at the start of a meal. Once you have got the feel for making pickles and chutneys, you will be able to develop your own ideas.

SWEET & SOUR PINEAPPLE

This is a traditional Bengali dish known as tok. *The dominant flavour is ginger, and the pieces of golden pineapple, dotted with plump, juicy raisins have plenty of visual appeal with a taste to match. It is equally delicious when made with mangoes instead of pineapple. Serve as a side dish or a digestive.*

SERVES 4

INGREDIENTS
800g/1¾lb canned pineapple rings or chunks in natural juice
15ml/1 tbsp vegetable oil
2.5ml/½ tsp black mustard seeds
2.5ml/½ tsp cumin seeds
2.5ml/½ tsp onion seeds
10ml/2 tsp grated fresh root ginger
5ml/1 tsp crushed dried chillies
50g/2oz/⅓ cup seedless raisins
125g/4oz/⅔ cup granulated sugar
7.5ml/1½ tsp salt

1 Drain the pineapple and reserve the juice. Chop the pineapple rings or chunks finely (you should have approximately 500g/1¼lb).

2 Heat the vegetable oil in a wok, karahi or large pan over a medium heat and immediately add the mustard seeds. As soon as they pop, add the cumin seeds, then the onion seeds. Add the ginger and chillies and stir-fry the spices briskly for 30 seconds until they release their flavours.

3 Add the chopped pineapple, raisins, sugar and salt to the pan, then add 300ml/ ½ pint/1¼ cups of the juice (making up with a little cold water if necessary).

4 Bring the mixture to the boil, reduce the heat to medium and cook, uncovered, for 20–25 minutes. Allow to cool before serving.

MANGO CHUTNEY

Chutneys are always made of fruit, vegetables or herbs, but ingredients vary between regions. Mango and tomato chutneys are made all over India, while herb chutneys are eaten in the north and west. This chutney is spiced with fresh red chilli and root ginger, and flavoured with cardamom and coriander seeds.

MAKES 450G/1LB/2 CUPS

INGREDIENTS
3 firm green (unripe) mangoes, cut into chunks
150ml/¼ pint/⅔ cup cider vinegar
130g/4½oz/⅔ cup light muscovado (brown) sugar
1 small fresh red chilli, split
2.5cm/1in piece fresh root ginger, grated
1 garlic clove, crushed
5 cardamom pods, bruised
2.5ml/½ tsp coriander seeds, crushed
1 bay leaf
2.5ml/½ tsp salt

1 Put the mango chunks into a pan, add the cider vinegar and cover. Cook over a low heat for 10 minutes, then stir in the remaining ingredients. Bring to the boil slowly, stirring constantly.

2 Lower the heat and simmer gently for 30 minutes, until the mixture is syrupy. Leave to cool, then ladle into a hot sterilized jar and cover. Leave to rest for 1 week before serving.

COOK'S TIP
Some varieties of mangoes remain solidly green even when ripe, so make sure the ones you buy really are unripe. Choose unblemished specimens.

Apricot Chutney

This is an incredibly easy chutney to make and tastes delicious. Simply dice the apricots, grate the ginger, then cook all the ingredients together very slowly.

MAKES ABOUT 450G/1LB/2 CUPS

INGREDIENTS
450g/1lb/2 cups dried apricots, finely diced
5ml/1 tsp garam masala
275g/10oz/1¼ cups soft light brown sugar
450ml/¾ pint/scant 2 cups malt vinegar
5ml/1 tsp grated fresh root ginger
5ml/1 tsp salt
75g/3oz/½ cup sultanas (golden raisins)

1 Place all the ingredients in a large heavy pan with 450ml/¾ pint/scant 2 cups of water. Stir well to mix. Bring to the boil, then simmer for 30–35 minutes, stirring occasionally to prevent the fruit sticking to the base of the pan.

2 When the chutney becomes syrupy, remove from the heat. Leave to cool, then ladle into a hot sterilized jar and cover. Chill after opening.

TOMATO CHUTNEY

This chutney, which is bursting with flavours, is incredibly quick to prepare as it uses canned chopped tomatoes.

MAKES 450–500G/16–18OZ/2–2¼ CUPS

INGREDIENTS
90ml/6 tbsp vegetable oil
5cm/2in piece cinnamon stick
4 cloves
5ml/1 tsp freshly toasted cumin seeds
5ml/1 tsp nigella seeds
4 bay leaves
5ml/1 tsp mustard seeds, crushed
4 garlic cloves, crushed
5cm/2in piece fresh root ginger, grated
5ml/1 tsp chilli powder
5ml/1 tsp ground turmeric
60ml/4 tbsp soft light brown sugar
800g/³⁄4lb canned chopped tomatoes, drained, juice reserved

1 Heat the vegetable oil in a pan, then add the cinnamon stick, cloves, cumin seeds, nigella seeds, bay leaves and mustard seeds and fry briefly. Add the crushed garlic and fry, stirring continuously, until golden.

2 Add the fresh root ginger, chilli powder, ground turmeric, sugar and reserved tomato juice to the pan. Stir to combine, then simmer until reduced, then add the chopped tomatoes and cook for 15–20 minutes.

3 Leave the chutney to cool completely, then carefully ladle into a hot sterilized jar and cover tightly with a lid.

TOMATO & CORIANDER CHUTNEY

Indian chutneys of this type are eaten when freshly made and are not meant to be kept. The combination of fresh chilli and cayenne pepper makes this relish quite hot.

SERVES 4–6

INGREDIENTS

2 tomatoes
1 red onion
1 fresh green chilli, seeded and finely chopped
60ml/4 tbsp chopped fresh coriander (cilantro)
juice of 1 lime
2.5ml/½ tsp salt
2.5ml/½ tsp paprika
2.5ml/½ tsp cayenne pepper
2.5ml/½ tsp cumin seeds, toasted and ground

1 Using a sharp knife, dice the tomatoes and onion finely. Place them in a bowl. (You could peel the tomatoes first if you wish.)

2 Add the chilli, coriander, lime juice, salt, paprika, cayenne pepper and ground cumin seeds to the bowl. Mix well and serve as soon as possible.

MINT & COCONUT CHUTNEY

The ingredients of this chutney all have a cooling effect, making it an ideal choice for serving with a fiery main dish. Make sure it is well chilled beforehand.

MAKES ABOUT 350ML/12FL OZ/1 ½ CUPS

INGREDIENTS
50g/2oz fresh mint leaves
90ml/6 tbsp desiccated (dry unsweetened shredded) coconut
15ml/1 tbsp sesame seeds
1.5ml/¼ tsp salt
175ml/6fl oz/¾ cup natural (plain) yogurt

1 Wash the fresh mint leaves in cold water and pat dry on kitchen paper. Finely chop the leaves, using a sharp kitchen knife.

2 Put all the ingredients into a food processor or blender and process until smooth. Transfer to a sterilized jar, cover and chill until needed.

COOK'S TIP
This chutney can be stored in the refrigerator for up to 5 days. Simply stir before use.

Coconut Chutney with Onion & Chilli

Serve this refreshing chutney as an accompaniment to spicy main dishes or with raita, other chutneys and poppadums at the start of a meal.

SERVES 4–6

INGREDIENTS
200g/7oz fresh coconut, grated
3–4 fresh green chillies, seeded and chopped
20g/³⁄4oz/scant ¹⁄2 cup fresh coriander (cilantro), chopped
30ml/2 tbsp chopped fresh mint
30–45ml/2–3 tbsp lime juice
about 2.5ml/¹⁄2 tsp salt
about 2.5ml/¹⁄2 tsp caster (superfine) sugar
15–30ml/1–2 tbsp coconut milk (optional)
30ml/2 tbsp groundnut (peanut) oil
5ml/1 tsp onion seeds
1 small onion, very finely chopped
fresh coriander (cilantro) sprigs, to garnish

1 Place the grated coconut, chillies, coriander and mint in a food processor or blender. Add 30ml/2 tbsp of the lime juice, then process until thoroughly chopped. Scrape the mixture into a bowl and add more lime juice to taste. Season with salt and sugar. If the mixture is dry, stir in 15–30ml/1–2 tbsp coconut milk.

2 Heat the groundnut oil in a small pan and fry the onion seeds until they begin to pop, then reduce the heat and add the onion. Fry, stirring frequently, for 4–5 minutes until the onion is golden.

3 Stir the onion mixture into the coconut mixture and leave to cool. Garnish with fresh coriander sprigs before serving.

Tomato & Fresh Chilli Chutney

This chutney is a vibrant red colour and has a flavour to match. If you prefer a milder chutney, seed the chillies before chopping the flesh.

MAKES ABOUT 475ML/16FL OZ/2 CUPS

INGREDIENTS
1 red (bell) pepper
4 tomatoes, chopped
2 fresh green chillies, chopped
1 garlic clove, crushed
1.5ml/¼ tsp salt
2.5ml/½ tsp granulated sugar
5ml/1 tsp chilli powder
45ml/3 tbsp tomato purée (paste)
15ml/1 tbsp chopped fresh coriander (cilantro)

1 Halve the red pepper and remove the core and seeds. Roughly chop the red pepper halves and place in a food processor.

2 Add the rest of the ingredients to the food processor with 30ml/2 tbsp water and process until smooth. Transfer the chutney to a sterilized jar, cover and chill in the refrigerator until needed.

CORIANDER CHUTNEY

This chutney calls for a lot of fresh coriander so buy it from an Indian food store where it is sold in lovely fresh bunches. Asafoetida comes from a huge fennel-like plant. It has a pungent, garlicky smell and should be used sparingly. If it is not to your taste, simply leave it out of the chutney.

MAKES 400G/14OZ/1¾ CUPS

INGREDIENTS
30ml/2 tbsp vegetable oil
1 dried red chilli, crumbled
1.5ml/¼ tsp each cumin, fennel and onion seeds
1.5ml/¼ tsp asafoetida
4 curry leaves
115g/4oz/1⅓ cups desiccated (dry unsweetened shredded) coconut
10ml/2 tsp granulated sugar
3 fresh green chillies, chopped
175–225g/6–8oz/3–4 cups coriander (cilantro) leaves
60ml/4 tbsp mint sauce
juice of 3 lemons
salt

1 Heat the vegetable oil and fry the crumbled dried red chilli, cumin, fennel and onion seeds, asafoetida, curry leaves, coconut and sugar until the coconut turns golden brown. Season with salt.

2 Allow the spice mixture to cool, then use a mortar and pestle to grind the mixture with the chillies, coriander and mint sauce. Stir in the lemon juice. Transfer to a sterilized jar, cover and chill before serving.

BOMBAY DUCK PICKLE

Despite its name, Bombay duck is actually a salted, dried fish that is characterized by a strong smell and distinctive flavour. How this fish acquired the name Bombay duck in the Western world is still unknown. It can be served hot or cold, and is usually eaten with Indian breads as an accompaniment to vegetable dishes.

SERVES 4–6

INGREDIENTS
6–8 pieces Bombay duck (boil), soaked in water for 5 minutes
60ml/4 tbsp vegetable oil
2 fresh red chillies, chopped
15ml/1 tbsp granulated sugar
450g/1lb cherry tomatoes, halved
115g/4oz deep-fried onions

1 Pat the fish dry with kitchen paper. Heat the oil in a frying pan and fry the fish pieces for about 30–45 seconds on both sides until crisp. Be careful not to burn them as they will taste bitter. Drain well, leave to cool, then break into small pieces.

2 Cook the remaining ingredients until the tomatoes become pulpy and the onions are blended into a sauce. Fold in the Bombay duck and mix well. Leave to cool, then serve, or ladle into a hot sterilized jar and seal.

VARIATION
As an alternative to Bombay duck, use skinned mackerel fillets, without frying them. You will need only 30ml/2 tbsp vegetable oil to make the sauce.

Hot Lime Pickle

This tangy pickle is very hot and a little goes a long way, so don't be alarmed at the number of limes used in this recipe.

Makes 450g/1lb/2 cups

Ingredients
25 limes, cut into wedges
225g/8oz/1 cup salt
50g/2oz/¼ cup ground fenugreek
50g/2oz/¼ cup mustard powder
150g/5oz/¾ cup chilli powder
15ml/1 tbsp ground turmeric
600ml/1 pint/2½ cups mustard oil
5ml/1 tsp asafoetida
25g/1oz/2 tbsp yellow mustard seeds, crushed

1 Place the limes in a large sterilized jar or glass bowl. Add the salt and toss with the limes. Cover and leave in a warm place for 1–2 weeks, until they become soft and dull brown in colour.

2 Mix the fenugreek, mustard, chilli and turmeric and add to the limes. Cover and leave to rest in a warm place for 2–3 days. Heat the oil and fry the asafoetida and mustard seeds, then mix into the limes. Cover and leave to stand for 1 week before serving.

Green Chilli Pickle

Spicy pickles are a perennial favourite with all types of curry. Leaving the pickles to rest for a week after preparation will greatly enhance the flavours.

MAKES 450–550G/1–1¼LB/2–2½ CUPS

INGREDIENTS
50g/2oz/¼ cup mustard seeds, crushed
50g/2oz/¼ cup freshly ground cumin seeds
25ml/1½ tbsp ground turmeric
50g/2oz/¼ cup crushed garlic
150ml/¼ pint/⅔ cup white wine vinegar
75g/3oz/scant ½ cup granulated sugar
10ml/2 tsp salt
150ml/¼ pint/⅔ cup mustard oil
20 small garlic cloves, peeled
450g/1lb small fresh green chillies, halved

1 Mix the mustard seeds, cumin, turmeric, crushed garlic, vinegar, sugar and salt in a sterilized jar or glass bowl. Cover and allow to rest for 24 hours. This enables the spices to infuse (steep) and the sugar and salt to dissolve.

2 Heat the mustard oil in a pan and gently fry the spice mixture for about 5 minutes. (Keep a window open while cooking with mustard oil as it is pungent and the smoke may irritate the eyes.) Add the whole garlic cloves to the pan and fry for a further 5 minutes.

3 Add the halved fresh chillies and cook gently for about 30 minutes until tender but still green in colour. Leave the mixture to cool thoroughly.

4 Pour the pickle into a sterilized jar, ensuring that the oil is evenly distributed if you are using more than one jar. Leave to rest for 1 week before serving.

Mango & Peanut Chaat

Chaats are spiced relishes of vegetables and nuts. Amchur (dried mango powder) adds a deliciously fruity sourness to this mixture of onions and mango.

SERVES 4

INGREDIENTS
90g/3½oz/scant 1 cup unsalted peanuts
15ml/1 tbsp groundnut (peanut) oil
1 onion, chopped
10cm/4in piece cucumber, seeded and cut into 5mm/¼in dice
1 mango, peeled, stoned and diced
1 green chilli, seeded and chopped
30ml/2 tbsp chopped fresh coriander (cilantro)
15ml/1 tbsp chopped fresh mint
15ml/1 tbsp lime juice
pinch of light muscovado (brown) sugar

FOR THE CHAAT MASALA
10ml/2 tsp ground toasted cumin seeds
2.5ml/½ tsp cayenne pepper
5ml/1 tsp amchur (dried mango powder)
2.5ml/½ tsp garam masala
pinch of asafoetida
salt and ground black pepper

1 To make the chaat masala, grind all the spices together, then season with 2.5ml/½ tsp each of salt and pepper. Fry the peanuts in the oil until lightly browned, then set aside on kitchen paper until cool.

2 In a bowl, combine the onion, cucumber, mango, chilli and chopped fresh coriander and mint. Sprinkle in 5ml/1 tsp of the chaat masala. Stir in the fried peanuts, lime juice and sugar.

3 Set the mixture aside for 20–30 minutes, then turn out into a serving bowl, sprinkle with the rest of the chaat masala and serve.

SPICED YOGURT

The spicing in this cool yogurt accompaniment is subtle, creating a refreshing taste to be enjoyed with hot, spicy curries.

MAKES 450ML/¾ PINT/SCANT 2 CUPS

INGREDIENTS
450ml/¾ pint/scant 2 cups natural (plain) yogurt
2.5ml/½ tsp freshly ground fennel seeds
2.5ml/½ tsp granulated sugar
60ml/4 tbsp vegetable oil
1 dried red chilli
1.5ml/¼ tsp mustard seeds
1.5ml/¼ tsp cumin seeds
4–6 curry leaves
pinch each of asafoetida and ground turmeric
salt

1 In a bowl, combine the yogurt, ground fennel seeds and sugar, and add salt to taste. Put in the refrigerator and leave until chilled.

2 Heat the oil and fry the chilli, mustard and cumin seeds, curry leaves, asafoetida and turmeric. When the chilli turns dark, pour the oil and spices over the yogurt and stir to combine. Cover and chill before serving.

CUCUMBER RAITA

This slightly sour, yogurt-based accompaniment has a cooling effect on the palate when eaten with spicy foods, and helps to balance the flavours of a meal.

MAKES ABOUT 600ML/1 PINT/2½ CUPS

INGREDIENTS
½ cucumber
1 fresh green chilli, seeded and chopped
300ml/½ pint/1¼ cups natural (plain) yogurt
1.5ml/¼ tsp salt
1.5ml/¼ tsp ground cumin

1 Dice the cucumber finely and place in a large mixing bowl. Add the chopped chilli and stir to combine.

2 Beat the yogurt with a fork until smooth, then stir into the cucumber and chilli mixture. Stir in the salt and cumin. Cover the bowl with clear film (plastic wrap) and chill before serving.

VARIATION
Use two skinned, seeded and chopped tomatoes and 15ml/1 tbsp chopped fresh coriander (cilantro) in place of the cucumber.

MINT RAITA

This refreshing raita combines mint with finely chopped raw onion and cucumber to create an interesting yet mildly flavoured accompaniment.

SERVES 4

INGREDIENTS
6 large mint sprigs
1 small onion
½ cucumber
300ml/½ pint/1¼ cups natural (plain) yogurt
2.5ml/½ tsp salt
2.5ml/½ tsp sugar
pinch of chilli powder
mint sprig, to garnish

1 Tear the mint leaves from their stalks and chop finely with a sharp knife. Peel and very thinly slice the onion, separating it into rings. Cut the cucumber into 5mm/¼in dice.

2 Put the mint, onion, cucumber, yogurt, salt and sugar in a bowl and stir to combine. Spoon into a serving bowl and chill.

3 Just before serving sprinkle the raita sparingly with chilli powder and garnish with a small sprig of mint.

RED ONION RAITA

This is an extremely attractive raita, with the pink-tinged onion contrasting with the yogurt. Serve with poppadums or as an accompaniment to a main course.

SERVES 4

INGREDIENTS
5ml/1 tsp cumin seeds
1 small garlic clove
1 small fresh green chilli, seeded
1 large red onion
150ml/¼ pint/⅔ cup natural (plain) yogurt
30ml/2 tbsp chopped fresh coriander, plus extra to garnish
2.5ml/½ tsp sugar
salt

1 Heat a small pan and dry-fry the cumin seeds for 1–2 minutes, until they release their aroma and begin to pop. Allow to cool slightly.

2 Lightly crush the toasted cumin seeds using a mortar and pestle or flatten them with the heel of a heavy knife.

3 Using a sharp knife, finely chop the garlic, green chilli and red onion. Place in a mixing bowl with the natural yogurt, crushed cumin seeds and coriander and stir well to combine.

4 Season the yogurt mixture with the sugar and salt to taste. Spoon the raita into a small bowl, cover with clear film (plastic wrap) and chill until ready to serve. Garnish with extra coriander before serving.

FRUIT RAITA

Refreshing yogurt raitas can be made with almost any fruit. This is a chunky raita
that combines whole grapes, walnuts and sliced banana.

SERVES 4

INGREDIENTS
350ml/12fl oz/1½ cups natural (plain) yogurt
75g/3oz seedless grapes, washed and dried
50g/2oz/½ cup shelled walnuts
2 firm bananas, sliced
5ml/1 tsp granulated sugar
5ml/1 tsp freshly ground cumin seeds
salt
1.5ml/¼ tsp freshly toasted cumin seeds and chilli powder, to garnish

1 Put the yogurt, grapes and walnuts in a bowl. Gently fold in the banana slices until the mixture is well combined.

2 Stir in the sugar, ground cumin and salt to taste. Chill and sprinkle on the toasted cumin seeds and chilli powder before serving.

VARIATION
To make banana and coconut raita, slice 2 bananas
and combine with 350ml/12fl oz/1½ cups yogurt.
Stir in 30ml/2 tbsp desiccated (dry unsweetened
shredded) coconut and add a pinch of chilli powder.
Season with salt and lemon juice to taste.

Tomato & Onion Salad

This raw vegetable salad adds a tangy touch to any meal. The inclusion of lime juice, fresh coriander and green chilli gives it a deliciously sharp edge.

Serves 4–6

Ingredients

2 limes
2.5ml/½ tsp granulated sugar
a few fresh coriander (cilantro) sprigs, chopped, plus extra to garnish
2 onions, finely chopped
4 firm tomatoes, finely chopped
½ cucumber, finely chopped
1 fresh green chilli, finely chopped
salt and ground black pepper
fresh mint sprigs, to garnish

1 Squeeze the limes and pour the juice into a small bowl. Add the sugar, salt and ground black pepper and allow to stand until the sugar and salt have competely dissolved. Mix together well.

2 Add the chopped onions, tomatoes, cucumber and chilli and mix well. Chill, and garnish with fresh coriander and mint sprigs before serving.

Variations
- *For a slightly different flavour use fresh mint in place of the chopped fresh coriander in this dish.*
- *If you prefer a slightly milder flavour, use red onions instead of yellow onions.*

Sweet Potato & Carrot Salad

This salad has a sweet-and-sour taste, and can be served warm as part of a meal or made in larger quantities and served as a main course.

Serves 4

Ingredients
1 sweet potato
2 carrots, cut into thick diagonal slices
3 tomatoes
8–10 iceberg lettuce leaves
75g/3oz/½ cup canned chickpeas, drained
15ml/1 tbsp each walnuts and sultanas (golden raisins), to garnish
1 small onion, cut into rings, to garnish

For the dressing
15ml/1 tbsp clear honey
90ml/6 tbsp natural (plain) yogurt
2.5ml/½ tsp salt
2.5ml/1 tsp coarsely ground black pepper

1 Peel the sweet potato and dice. Boil until soft but not mushy, cover the pan and set aside. Boil the carrots for 2 minutes, add to the sweet potatoes, then drain.

2 Slice the tops off the tomatoes, then scoop out and discard the seeds. Roughly chop the flesh. Line a glass bowl with the lettuce leaves. Mix together the sweet potatoes, carrots, chick-peas and tomatoes and place in the bowl.

3 In a bowl, beat together all the dressing ingredients with a fork. Garnish the salad with the walnuts, sultanas and onion rings. Pour the dressing over the salad or serve it in a separate bowl, if wished.

DESSERTS
& DRINKS

Indian meals are often ended with just simple fresh fruit, depending on what is in season. Fruit provides a good balance to a meal after a spicy main course. However, there are several classic desserts that are easy to make and taste delicious. These are often reserved for special occasions but, if you have had a fairly light meal, there is no reason why they should not be enjoyed at any time. There are also classic drinks such as lassi, which is so refreshing on a hot day and can be either savoury or sweet. The yogurt base is easy to make and you will be able to create your own versions depending on the ingredients you have to hand.

RICH RICE PUDDING

Both the Muslim and Hindu communities of India prepare this wonderful dessert known as kheer, *which is traditionally served at mosques and temples.*

SERVES 4–6

INGREDIENTS
15ml/1 tbsp ghee
1 5cm/2in piece cinnamon stick
175g/6oz/ ¾ cup soft light brown sugar
115g/4oz/1 cup coarsely ground rice
1.2 litres/2 pints/5 cups full-fat (whole) milk
5ml/1 tsp ground cardamom seeds
50g/2oz/⅓ cup sultanas (golden raisins)
25g/1oz/¼ cup flaked (slivered) almonds
½ tsp freshly ground nutmeg, to serve

1 In a heavy pan, melt the ghee and fry the cinnamon and sugar until the sugar begins to caramelize. Reduce the heat immediately when this happens.

2 Add the rice and half the milk to the pan. Bring to the boil, stirring constantly. Reduce the heat and simmer gently until the rice is cooked, stirring frequently.

3 Add the remaining milk, ground cardamom seeds, sultanas and almonds to the pan and simmer, stirring continuously. When the mixture has thickened, serve hot or leave to cool before serving, sprinkled with the nutmeg.

CLASSIC VERMICELLI PUDDING

This delicious dessert is prepared by Muslims very early in the morning of Id-ul-Fitr, the feast that is celebrated after the 30 days Ramadan.

SERVES 4–6

INGREDIENTS
90ml/6 tbsp ghee
115g/4oz/1 cup vermicelli, coarsely broken
25g/1oz/¼ cup flaked (slivered) almonds
50g/2oz/½ cup pistachio nuts, slivered
50g/2oz/⅓ cup sultanas (golden raisins)
50g/2oz dates, stoned (pitted) and slivered
1.2 litres/2 pints/5 cups full-fat (whole) milk
50g/2oz/4 tbsp soft dark brown sugar
1 sachet saffron powder

1 Heat 60ml/4 tbsp of the ghee in a frying pan and fry the vermicelli until golden brown. Remove from the pan and set aside. Heat the remaining ghee in the pan and fry the pistachio nuts, sultanas and dates, stirring, until the sultanas swell. Stir into the vermicelli.

2 Heat the milk in a large heavy pan and add the sugar. Bring to the boil, add the vermicelli mixture and boil, stirring constantly. Reduce the heat and simmer until the vermicelli is soft and you have a fairly thick consistency. Fold in the saffron powder and serve hot or leave to cool before serving.

INDIAN ICE CREAM

Ice cream in India is called kulfi *and* kulfi-wallahs *(ice-cream vendors) have always made it – and still do – without using modern freezers. Kulfi is packed into metal cones sealed with dough and then churned in clay pots until set.*

SERVES 4–6

INGREDIENTS
3 × 400ml//4fl oz cans evaporated milk
3 egg whites, whisked until peaks form
350g/12oz/3 cups icing (confectioners') sugar
5ml/1 tsp ground cardamom seeds
15ml/1 tbsp rose water
175g/6oz/1½ cups pistachio nuts, chopped
75g/3oz/½ cup sultanas (golden raisins)
75g/3oz/¾ cup flaked (slivered) almonds
25g/1oz/3 tbsp glacé (candied) cherries, halved

1 Remove the labels from the cans of evaporated milk and lay the cans down into a pan with a tight-fitting lid. Fill the pan with water to reach three-quarters of the way up the cans. Bring to the boil, cover and simmer for 20 minutes. When cool, remove and chill the cans in the refrigerator for 24 hours.

2 Open the cans and empty the milk into a large, chilled bowl. Whisk until it has doubled in quantity, then gently fold in the whisked egg whites and icing (confectioners') sugar. Carefully fold in the remaining ingredients, seal the bowl with cling film (plastic wrap) and leave in the freezer for 1 hour.

3 Remove the ice cream from the freezer and mix well with a fork. Transfer to a freezerproof serving dish and return to the freezer for a final setting. Remove from the freezer 10 minutes before serving.

KULFI WITH CARDAMOM

This classic ice cream can be delicately spiced in many different ways. Here aromatic cardamom pods are used. Make sure you choose green cardamoms, not the white ones, which have been bleached and therefore have less aroma and flavour.

SERVES 6

INGREDIENTS

2 litres/3½ pints/8 cups full-fat (whole) milk
12 cardamom pods
175g/6oz/¾ cup caster (superfine) sugar
25g/1oz/¼ cup blanched almonds, chopped
toasted flaked (slivered) almonds and cardamom pods, to decorate

1 Place the milk and cardamom pods in a large heavy pan. Bring to the boil, then simmer vigorously until reduced by one-third. Strain the milk into a bowl, discarding the cardamom pods, then stir in the sugar and almonds until the sugar has dissolved. Set aside and leave to cool.

2 Pour the mixture into a freezerproof container, cover and freeze until almost firm, stirring every 30 minutes. When almost solid, pack the ice cream into six clean yogurt pots or dariole moulds. Return to the freezer until required, removing the pots about 10 minutes before serving and turning the individual ices out. Decorate with toasted almonds and cardamoms before serving.

COOK'S TIPS
• *Use a large pan for reducing the milk as there needs to be plenty of room for it to bubble up.*
• *If you prefer, freeze the ice cream in a large container and serve in scoops.*

KULFI WITH PISTACHIO NUTS

This recipe calls for traditional kulfi moulds, which are tall, thin metal cones. The result is an elegant dessert that is a treat for both the eyes and the taste buds. The final dessert has a wonderfully delicate colour and flavour.

SERVES 4

INGREDIENTS
1.5 litres/2½ pints/6¼ cups full-fat (whole) milk
3 cardamom pods
25g/1oz/2 tbsp caster (superfine) sugar
50g/2oz/½ cup pistachio nuts, skinned, plus a few to decorate
a few pink rose petals, to decorate

> COOK'S TIPS
> • Stay in the kitchen while the milk is simmering, as it can easily boil over if it gets too hot.
> • If the ices won't turn out, dip a cloth in very hot water, wring it out and place it on the tops of the moulds for a few seconds. Alternatively, briefly plunge the moulds back into hot water.

1 Pour the milk into a large, heavy pan. Bring to the boil, lower the heat and simmer gently for 1 hour, stirring occasionally.

2 Crush the cardamom pods using a mortar and pestle. Add the pods and the seeds to the milk and continue to simmer for 1–1½ hours, or until the milk has reduced to about 475ml/16fl oz/2 cups or by two-thirds.

3 Strain the milk into a jug (pitcher) or large bowl and stir in the caster sugar. Set aside and leave until cooled completely.

4 Place half the pistachio nuts in a blender, nut grinder or cleaned coffee grinder and grind to a smooth powder. Cut the remaining nuts into thin slivers and set aside for decoration. Stir the ground nuts into the cooled milk mixture.

5 Pour the milk and pistachio mixture into four kulfi moulds or small disposable plastic cups and freeze overnight until firm.

6 To unmould the kulfi, half fill a plastic container or bowl with very hot water, stand the moulds in the water and count to ten. Immediately lift out the moulds and invert them on to baking sheet.

7 Transfer the ice creams to a platter or individual plates. Scatter the sliced pistachios over the ice creams, then decorate with the rose petals. Serve at once.

Mango Sorbet with Sauce

After a heavy meal, this makes a very refreshing, tangy dessert. Mango is said to be one of the oldest fruits cultivated in India, having been brought by Lord Shiva for his beautiful young wife, Parvathi.

SERVES 4–6

INGREDIENTS
900g/2lb mango pulp
2.5ml/½ tsp lemon juice
grated rind of 1 orange and 1 lemon
4 egg whites, whisked until peaks form
50g/2oz/¼ cup caster (superfine) sugar
120ml/4fl oz/2 cups double (heavy) cream
50g/2oz/½ cup icing (confectioners') sugar

1 In a large, chilled bowl, mix half of the mango pulp, with the lemon juice and the grated orange and lemon rind.

2 Gently fold the whisked egg whites and caster sugar into the fruit mixture. Cover with cling film (plastic wrap) and place in the freezer for at least 1 hour.

3 Remove the sorbet from the freezer and beat with a fork to break up any ice crystals. Transfer to an ice cream container and freeze until fully set.

4 Whip the double cream with the icing sugar and remaining mango pulp. Chill the sauce for 24 hours. Remove the sorbet from the freezer 10 minutes before serving. Scoop out individual servings and cover with a generous helping of mango sauce. Serve immediately.

Tea & Fruit Punch

This delicious punch is based on Earl Grey tea, with its subtle flavouring of bergamot. It is suitable for many occasions and may be served hot or cold. White wine or brandy may be added to taste.

Makes 875ml/1¾ pints/3½ cups

INGREDIENTS
1 cinnamon stick
4 cloves
12.5ml/2½ tsp Earl Grey tea leaves
175g/6oz/¾ cup sugar
450ml/¾ pint/1½ cups tropical drink concentrate
1 lemon, sliced
1 small orange, sliced
½ cucumber, sliced

1 Bring 600ml/1 pint/2½ cups water to the boil in a pan with the cinnamon stick and cloves. Remove from the heat and add the tea leaves and allow to brew for 5 minutes. Stir and strain into a large chilled bowl.

2 Add the sugar and the tropical drink concentrate and allow to stand until the sugar has dissolved and the mixture cooled. Place the fruit and cucumber in a chilled punch bowl and pour over the tea mix. Chill for 24 hours before serving.

LASSI

This classic Indian drink is prepared by churning yogurt with water and then removing the fat. To make this refreshing drink without churning, use low-fat yogurt. The ingredients might seem a bit surprising, but the result is delicious and lassi is a real thirst quencher, particularly on a hot summer day.

SERVES 4

INGREDIENTS
450ml/¾ pint/1½ cups natural (plain) yogurt
2.5cm/1in piece fresh root ginger, finely crushed
2 fresh green chillies, finely chopped
2.5ml/½ tsp ground cumin
salt and ground black pepper
a few fresh coriander (cilantro) leaves, chopped, to garnish

1 In a bowl, whisk the yogurt with 300ml/½ pint/1¼ cups water. The consistency should be that of full cream (whole) milk. Add more water if necessary.

2 Add the ginger, chillies and ground cumin to the yogurt mixture, season with the salt and pepper and mix well. Divide among 4 serving glasses and chill. Garnish with chopped coriander leaves before serving.

SWEET LASSI

There is no substitute for a good lassi, especially on a hot day. It is ideal served with hot dishes as it helps the body to digest spicy food. Add some puréed fruit if you wish. Choose any soft fruit, such as bananas, melons, guavas, apricots, peaches and nectarines, or even ripe, juicy pears.

SERVES 4

INGREDIENTS
300ml/½pint/1¼ cups natural (plain) low-fat yogurt
5ml/1 tsp sugar, or to taste
30ml/2 tbsp puréed fruit (optional)
15ml/1 tbsp crushed pistachio nuts, to decorate

1 Put the yogurt in a jug (pitcher) and whisk it for about 2 minutes until frothy. Stir in the sugar to taste.

2 Pour 300ml/½pint/1¼ cups water and the puréed fruit, if using, into the jug and continue to whisk for about 2 minutes.

3 Pour the lassi into 4 serving glasses. Chill well before serving, decorated with crushed pistachio nuts.

ICED MANGO YOGURT ICE

This deliciously refreshing yogurt ice is similar to lassi but is made using the freezer.
Yogurt ice is lighter and fresher than cream-based ices.

SERVES 3–4

INGREDIENTS
175g/6oz/¾ cup caster (superfine) sugar
2 lemons
500ml/17fl oz/generous 2 cups Greek (strained plain) yogurt

FOR EACH DRINK
120ml/4fl oz/½ cup mango juice
2–3 ice cubes (optional)
fresh mint sprigs and wedges of mango, to serve

1 To make the yogurt ice, put the sugar and water in a pan and heat gently, stirring occasionally, until the sugar has dissolved. Pour the syrup into a jug (pitcher). Leave to cool, then chill until very cold.

2 Grate the lemons, then squeeze them. Add the lemon rind and juice to the chilled syrup and stir well to mix.

3 Pour the syrup mixture into a freezerproof container and freeze until thickened. Beat in the yogurt and return to the freezer until thick enough to scoop.

4 To make each drink, briefly blend the mango juice with three small scoops of the yogurt ice in a food processor or blender until just smooth. Pour the mixture into a tall glass or tumbler and add the ice cubes, if using.

5 Top each drink with another scoop of the yogurt ice and decorate with mint sprigs and mango wedges. Serve at once.

ALMOND SHERBET

Traditionally this drink was always made in the month of Ramadan, and used to break the fast. It should be served very well chilled.

SERVES 4

INGREDIENTS
50g/2oz/½ cup ground almonds
600ml/1 pint/2½ cups semi-skimmed (low-fat) milk
10ml/2 tsp sugar, or to taste

1 Put the ground almonds into a jug (pitcher), then pour in the milk and sugar. Stir until the sugar has completely dissolved, then taste for sweetness and add a little more sugar if necessary.

2 Divide the almond sherbet among 4 glasses and chill in the refrigerator for at least 1 hour before serving.

SHOPPING FOR INDIAN FOODS

AUSTRALIA
Aurora Spices
21 Nicholson Street
Brunswick East
Melbourne VIC
Tel: (03) 9387 5541

Hindustan Imports
50 Greens Road
Dandenong South
Melbourne VIC
Tel: (03) 9794 6640

Sydney Fresh Food Market
Building D
   at Sydney Markets
   (off Parramatta Road)
Flemington NSW

The Spice Jar
5–6/389 High Street
   (via Edward Place)
Penrith NSW
Tel: (02) 4732 2528

Truespice
145 Corinish Road
Clayton VIC
Tel: (03) 9544 1634

Arason Imports
23 Koornang Road
Carnegie VIC
Tel: (03) 9877 7071

CANADA
A1 Cash n Carry
80 A Nashdene Road
Unit 11
Scarborough, ON
Tel: (416) 321 2135

Ahmad Grocers Ltd
1616 Gerrard E
Toronto, ON
Tel: (416) 461 3140

Alflah Grocer
973 Albion
Etobicoke, ON
Tel: (416) 742 6824

All India Foods
6517 Main Street
Vancouver, BC
Tel: (604) 582 9494

Baba Sweets and Meat
   Shop
95817 28th Street
Surrey, BC
Tel: (604) 582 9494

Hafiz Halal Meats
4960 Joyce Street
Vancouver, BC
Tel: (604) 432 9796

Noor Food Store
289 Hastings Street E
Vancouver, BC
Tel: (604) 687 1940

Pamir Food Market
3665 Kingsway
Vancouver, BC
Tel: (604) 434 7666

Paravan Grocery
   Market
6462 Victoria Drive
Vancouver, BC
Tel: (604) 322 5858

Randeep Foods
9273 120th Street
Delta, BC
Tel: (604) 581 0666

UNITED KINGDOM
A Sweet
106 The Broadway
London SW13
Tel: 020 574 8814

Ambala
55 Brick Lane
London E1
Tel: 020 7247 8569

Bangla Bazaar
216 Cowley Road
Oxford OX4
Tel: 01865 242266

Clifton Sweetmart
118 Brick Lane
London E1
Tel: 020 7247 5811

Curry Club
PO Box 7
Haslemere
Surrey GU27 1EP

Deepak's Cash and Carry
953–959 Garratt Lane
London SW17
Tel: 020 8767 7810

Dokal and Sons Cash
   and Carry
133 The Broadway
London SW13
Tel: 020 8574 1647

Fudco
184 Ealing Road
Alperton
London W10
Tel: 020 8902 4820

Khalid Grocery
366 Cowley Road
Oxford OX4
Tel: 01865 727690

Majid Halal Meat
446b Stratford Road
Birmingham B11
Tel: 0121 772 6788

Mehta Fruit and Veg
111–113 Upper Tooting
    Road
London SW17
Tel: 020 8767 8214

Patel Bothers
187–191 Upper Tooting
    Road
London SW17
Tel: 020 8672 2793

Rana Brothers
145 The Broadway
London SW13
Tel: 020 8574 4481

Sarzan Spiceland
145–151 Princess
    Road
Manchester M14
Tel: 0161 226 3700

Sharma General Store
99 Bromford Lane
Erdington
Birmingham B24
Tel: 0121 373 2943

Sharwood's Ethnic
Food Bureau
125 Old Brompton Road
London SW7
Tel: 020 7244 7359

Sira Cash and Carry
128 The Broadway
London SW13
Tel: 020 8574 2280

The Spice Shop
115–117 Drummond
    Street
London NW1
Tel: 020 7916 1831

Toto Grocers
44 The Broadway
London SW13
Tel: 020 8574 7669

V B and Sons
218 Ealing Road
Alperton
London W10
Tel: 020 8795 0387

UNITED STATES
A K Grocery
5902 18th Avenue
Brooklyn NY 11204
Tel: (718) 259 0604

Ajanta
215 East Armytrail
    Road
Bloomingdale, IL 60108
Tel: (847) 529 4494

Bharat Bazar
21080 108th Avenue SE
Kent, WA 98131
Tel: (253) 839 0252

Bismillah Meat
  and Grocery
2742 W, Devon Avenue
Chicago, IL 60659
Tel: (773) 761 1700

Bombay Bazaar
24823 Pacific
  Highway South
Suite 103
Kent, WA 98032
Tel: (253) 839 0252

Community Grocery
  Zabia Meat
4742 N. Kedzie
  Avenue
Chicago, IL 60625
Tel: (773) 539 5575

Continental Spice,
  Groceries and
  Halal Meat
7819 Aurora
  Avenue N
Seattle, WA 98103
Tel: (206) 706 0326

Dana Bazar
976 W. Lake Street
Roselle, IL 60172
Tel: (630) 529 6565

Indian Sweets and
  Spices
18002 15th Avenue NE
Suite C
Shoreline, WA 98155
Tel: (206) 367 4568

Surati Farsan Mart
11814 East 168th Street
Artesia, CA 90701
Tel: (562) 809 3085

INDEX